Roads Home

Roads Home

Seven Pathways
to Midlife Wisdom

KATHRYN D. CRAMER, PH.D.

WILLIAM MORROW AND COMPANY, INC.   NEW YORK

In case histories, names and identifying characteristics of individuals have been changed.

Copyright © 1995 by Kathryn D. Cramer, Ph.D.

Permissions, constituting a continuation of the copyright page, appear on page 336.

It is the policy of William Morrow and Company, Inc., and its imprints and affiliates, recognizing the importance of preserving what has been written, to print the books we publish on acid-free paper, and we exert our best efforts to that end.

Library of Congress Cataloging-in-Publication Data
Cramer, Kathryn D.
    Roads home : seven pathways to midlife wisdom / Kathryn D. Cramer. — 1st ed.
        p.   cm.
    Includes bibliographical references and index.
    ISBN 0-688-12352-X
    1. Middle aged persons—Religious life.   2. Middle aged persons—Conduct of life.
I. Title.
    BL625.3.C73   1995
    158'.084'4—dc20   94-46145
                         CIP

Printed in the United States of America

First Edition

1 2 3 4 5 6 7 8 9 10

BOOK DESIGN BY JESSICA SHATAN

With love and admiration for my mother and father . . .
who were my first teachers about the
possibilities and rewards of the midlife journey.

Acknowledgments

I wish to thank my teammates at The Cramer Institute for the support you gave me during the months of writing that turned into years of rewriting. Thanks to Dwana Murphy for your persistence; to Dennis Wissler and Dick Strader for your prodding; to Meg Haycraft for your celebrations; to Beth Page for your detective work; to Stephanie Sachs for your organizing; to Judy Dubin for your brainstorming; and to Jane Seagraves and Donna Porteous for your pitching in when deadlines were short. I count each of you as a blessing in my life and in this work.

Thank you to my writing coach, Stacy Prince, for your editorial talent and heartfelt dedication; to my agent and friend, Denise Marcil, for believing in this project and in me; to my editor, Toni Sciarra, for your gifts of clear writing, warm humor, and unfailing wisdom.

For the encouragement from my family and friends I feel especially grateful. Without your interest and love to sustain me I would have spent more time worrying, less time laughing, and too much time feeling alone.

My days and nights continue to be filled with the spirit of adventure and learning thanks to my husband, Grady. I appreciate you for listening, for guiding, for cheering me on, and for wanting to know the real me. No one could ever have a better partner or feel more loved than I do.

Contents

In this birth you will discover all blessing.
But neglect this birth and you neglect
all blessing. Tend only to this birth
in you and you will find there
all goodness and all consolation,
all delight, all being, and
all truth.

—MEISTER ECKHART

Roads Home

At a Crossroads

Listen! I will be honest with you,
I do not offer the old smooth prizes, but offer rough new prizes,
These are the days that must happen to you:
You shall not heap up what is call'd riches,
You shall scatter with lavish hand all that you earn or achieve,
You but arrive at the city to which you were destin'd, you hardly settle
* yourself to satisfaction before you are call'd by an irresistible call to*
* depart,*
You shall be treated to the ironical smiles and mockings of those who
* remain behind you,*
What beckonings of love you receive you shall only answer with
* passionate kisses of parting,*
You shall not allow the hold of those who spread their reach'd hands
* toward you.*

—WALT WHITMAN

It is no accident that five years ago, when I came up with the idea for this book, I was celebrating my fortieth birthday. Since then, I have made it my professional aim to learn all I can about making midlife a magnificent experience. I have been amazed—and thrilled—to discover a wealth of recent findings in psychology, neuroscience, physiology, and anthropology that support my theory that there are many advantages to life after forty. Furthermore, the wisdom found in literature, art, and ancient mythology holds a vast amount of information that can be of great help to any of us who want to maximize these advantages.

Of course, most of the gifts of midlife are not just handed to us; we have to work for them, and in ways quite different from those with which we gathered the harvest of our twenties and thirties. In these pages you will read about my own midlife discoveries and learn how others have struggled to earn the "rough new prizes" of this rich period of life.

On the Road to Nowhere

Sadly, our generation is unaware of the vast possibility for development in the middle years. Our culture is filled with negative messages about midlife. Birthday cards with humorous insults about being "over the hill" flood in along with bouquets of black balloons.

We see evidence that we fear growing older in the proliferation of cosmetic surgeons, fitness trainers, and weight-loss gurus. Whether it be face implants or face peels, tummy tucks, surgical lifts, trendy hairstyles, new hair growth, collagen creams, stress seminars, or Club Med, each strategy promises to ward off the shame of aging. Ultimately these promises fail.

Although we know instinctively that it takes more than cosmetic cures to be attractive, many of us continue searching outside of ourselves for the fountain of youth because we are not sure where else to look. I'm convinced our desperate attempts to appear young stem from our ignorance about what it takes to remain vital as we age. As I've learned, the true source of beauty after forty is found through inner exploration. In order to glow with life from the inside out, those of us at midlife must learn to release untapped talents, banished longings, and passionate desires; expand our skills in solving complex problems; and attune ourselves to the secrets of our souls. *None of this is possible before middle age, and we can't grow without it.*

Left to our own devices, most of us tap into only a small percentage of what can keep us feeling and looking alive. Even when we glimpse a pathway into our inner world (through flashes of insight, nightmares, episodes of depression or intense joy, spiritual awakenings, or encounters with intimacy), we fail to make the most of it, because no one ever taught us how to cultivate those ghostly parts of ourselves. It is important to understand that unless you are a truly unusual individual, you are likely to be completely clueless about how to tackle the challenges that face you. Let me explain why.

As anthropologists tell us, when a critical number of people in a population experience similar challenges, myth and ritual are born. Myth and ritual validate an experience, and, more important, help anyone going through it to make sense of it, survive it, and get the most from it. Myths are created first, when enough people in a culture begin to share the same concerns. Myths give men and women insight into what they need to do to overcome their challenges and excel.

Full-scale rituals evolve when even more people need and use the myths. Rituals formalize, in words and actions, the meaning and experience of the truth being represented. For example, many religions welcome new members into their ranks by performing a physical cleansing (with water) to symbolize spiritual cleansing. Rituals are powerful only so long as the people practicing them are aware of their underlying meaning.

It takes time for myths and rituals to evolve, and, comparatively speaking, the midlife experience has not existed long enough in human history to have spawned many formal traditions with sufficient material to guide us. In the year A.D. One, average life expectancy was twenty-three; at the turn of this century in America it was forty-seven. As a society, we have only recently reached the point where the average person is likely to confront the issues of midlife that must be addressed over nearly three decades of adulthood.

As it stands, the only important rituals we take part in as adults are those of marriage (and not everyone does that) and retirement (and this ritual is on the wane, thanks to the turbulent economy and changes in the workplace). It is even difficult to find good midlife myths in our culture. Allan B. Chinen, M.D., a psychiatrist on the clinical faculty of the University of California, San Francisco, searched societies worldwide for these stories for his 1992 book *Once Upon a Midlife* and was surprised to learn how few there are: "Middle tales . . . constitute only about 10 percent of some five thousand fairy tales I read."

To make matters worse, few of us have good role models for middle age and beyond. If I challenge clients to name five people they know who have aged successfully (i.e., happily), they're unlikely to be able to name even one or two. So at this point in our society, and in your life in particular, there are very few places to turn for information on facing the challenges of aging.

Up until midlife, your growing process was easier. Your urges to develop were recognized and encouraged by your parents and your peers, and you had plenty of signposts along the way to make sure you were on the right track (birthday parties, graduations, promotions, perhaps parenthood). During the first half of your life, you learned to master the *external world*, and you developed self-esteem as a result. Any failure to mature internally was easily overshadowed by your success in the outside world. Now that you have reached midlife, the time for exploring the *inner world*, you may find yourself without signposts, unsure of your path.

One reason for that is that few of us have been taught even the basics of how to develop our inner selves. We are living in a time when the importance of spirituality, self-awareness, and emotional maturity are undervalued at best and devalued at worst. Going against the grain takes knowledge and courage. I aim to give you both.

On the Road to Advancement

As we grow older, prizes from the outer world often begin to hold less fascination. It becomes clear that "growing up" is a fallacy. We begin to feel in our hearts that we are not now, nor will we ever be, grown-up. Adulthood is not the pinnacle of life's journey; it's not an anxiety-free plateau. Adulthood is a phase of development like any other, fraught with ascents and descents into ever-changing arenas of human potential. Learning to conquer the mountains and rivers of our inner terrain with as much gusto as we mastered the challenges of the world at large is the prime objective of midlife.

You may have reached age forty feeling fragmented, with everyone and everything "out there" claiming a piece of you. Don't be surprised if at times you feel burned out, restless, unsure of who you are, and struck by the emptiness of externally defined success. This is the price of maturity, and a sign that now is the time to get back in touch with your innermost drives, talents, and desires. That sense you have of things "just not being right" is nature's way of telling you it's time to change.

In this book I share a road map for making the journey inward over the two and a half decades that span midlife (forty to sixty-five years). This map guides you along seven distinct yet interrelated pathways. Travel down each of the seven pathways at your own pace and you will avoid sleepwalking through life's most magnificent period.

SEVEN PATHWAYS TO MIDLIFE WISDOM
- Pathway #1: *Mental Mastery*
- Pathway #2: *Physical Vigor*
- Pathway #3: *Emotional Vitality*
- Pathway #4: *Interpersonal Effectiveness*
- Pathway #5: *Exceptional Competence*
- Pathway #6: *Spiritual Serenity*
- Pathway #7: *Personal Integrity*

The wonderful gifts you'll find on each pathway are yours for the taking: once you know they're there, they're yours. Together we will explore the inner resources you already have at your disposal in claiming the rewards nature intended you to have, and I will introduce you to new strategies you can use to bring your extraordinary abilities to the surface.

Before you venture down any path, however, it's important to know where you are. For that reason, Chapter 1 provides an introduction to the sorts of "signpost" exercises you'll be doing in the rest of the book, and Chapter 2 contains a revealing self-assessment exercise that will help you figure out how far you have already gone on each of the seven pathways, along with travel tips to help you get the most out of each.

PART I

The Call to Depart

CHAPTER 1

It's Not Too Late to Embark

. . . Come, my friends,
'Tis not too late to seek a newer world.
Push off, and sitting well in order smite
The sounding furrows; for my purpose holds
To sail beyond the sunset, and the baths
Of all the western stars, until I die.
It may be that the gulfs will wash us down;
It may be we shall touch the Happy Isles,
And see the great Achilles, whom we knew.
Though much is taken, much abides; and though
We are not now that strength which in old days
Moved earth and heaven, that which we are, we are;
One equal temper of heroic hearts,
Made weak by time and fate, but strong in will
To strive, to seek, to find, and not to yield.

—ALFRED LORD TENNYSON

When I was forty-one years old, I discovered I was going to have my first baby. The day I called my physician's office for the final pregnancy test results, I heard a nurse in the background say to my doctor, "Do you want to tell her or should I? I don't want to deal with her if she is going to get upset."

Upset? Why on earth would I be upset? The moment I suspected I might be pregnant, I was ecstatic. What a gift to be having a baby at my age! I felt blessed, healthy, eager, and ready as never before to be a mother. For me this pregnancy was the realization of a life-long dream.

I couldn't wait to tell my husband the good news. I knew he would be happy. Grady and I had been married for only two months, but he was the love of my life and I of his. We both had suffered for years in painful, dead relationships before finding each other. I was so grateful to be in a loving marriage. I thought nothing else could ever match such happiness. But when I heard the doctor say, "Kathy, your pregnancy test is positive. Come in and see me next week," I felt a deeper joy. I smiled even in my sleep. I couldn't stop thinking about how wonderful life can be. First the universe had given me Grady, and now a baby!

For the first three months of my pregnancy, I read everything I could find on prenatal development. I treasured the look of excitement on the faces of family and friends as I told them about my impending midlife motherhood. I slowed my exercise routine from running to a gentle jog. I traded my evening cocktail for a glass of club soda. Each day I pondered the practical sides of parenting. Where would the baby sleep? How could I travel on business with an infant? Who would come in to baby-sit and do laundry? I imagined myself reading stories and singing lullabies to the little person who would soon be in my arms.

My first sonogram gave me visual confirmation that indeed life was growing within my womb. I checked my profile in the mirror each morning nonetheless, searching for reassurance that a person was growing inside of me. Someone I could not yet see or hold had completely captivated me. Already a bond was forming.

On the morning of my uncle's funeral, March 2, I began bleeding. One week later, my pregnancy was over. No more life inside of me, no baby to be born. I was stunned. As quickly as my dream of motherhood had come true, it had become a nightmare. Flat on my back on an emergency-room operating cart, I stared up at the ceiling made of row after row of white tiles filled with black dots. Through a stream of tears I prayed I would wake up from this cruel betrayal. I felt abandoned and profoundly alone.

The night I spent in the hospital dragged on, long hour after long hour. Separated from Grady and everyone else I loved, I had no escape from my heartache. The last time I looked at the white clock on the dull gray hospital-room wall, it was 4:10 in the morning. A combination of my exhaustion and a mild tranquilizer finally released me into sleep in the quiet dawn hours.

When Grady came for me at 8:00 a.m., we wasted no time escaping the hospital. Despite the ordeal of the day before, I felt physically energetic and healthy. Mentally, I was on fast forward, trying to occupy my mind so that I wouldn't think about the baby we had lost. I was determined not to let the miscarriage set me back.

After several days, I realized there was no running away from my feelings of abandonment and loneliness, or from the waves of guilt that were dissolving my spirit. I feared that something I had done had caused me to lose the baby.

Each day I fought my depression, yet my sense of failure grew. Not only had I ruined my own chances at parenthood but whatever had failed inside of me had robbed my husband of his opportunity, too. No matter how hard I tried to console myself, I simply couldn't shake my sadness and feelings of remorse. I was trapped.

Finally, since nothing seemed able to rescue me from my downward emotional spiral, I decided to dive right into the eye of the inner storm. I knew that by descending to the center of my turmoil I would eventually find peace. This type of tragedy had blindsided me once before.

When I was not quite thirty years old, my youngest brother, Jim, died from a bout with mononucleosis. He was only twenty-two. His death turned my world upside down, and it took me a long time to grieve and get on with my life afterward. Through trial and error I learned that the only way to survive the tragedy was to allow myself to experience the true extent of my rage and anxiety. Avoiding the pain was not part of the solution then, so I assumed that it wouldn't work this time, either.

In the long run, coming to terms with Jim's death actually helped me to grow. It forced me to examine my own existence. Taking stock made me aware that my life, especially my professional life, seemed stale. With Jim's death as my teacher, I promised myself that I would revive my career by searching for reliable ways of overcoming adversity and finding value in crisis. My approach was to study people who had been successful in making sense of their suffering and putting what they had learned to good use.

Surviving that earlier crisis was the genesis of my first book, *Staying on Top When Your World Turns Upside Down*. The book spawned training programs adopted by hundreds of corporations and hospitals. The methods I developed out of my own need to get beyond my grief helped thousands of individuals in crisis learn how to cope with adversity. My new work breathed a new sense of passion and purpose into my career. Although the price was too high, I am forever grateful for the gifts it brought me.

Armed with the knowledge that grave loss had once renewed my life, I turned inward. Each day I spent time alone, in quiet surroundings. In solitude I closed my eyes and relived, moment by moment, the entire course of my pregnancy.

I dreaded those periods of introspection. Still, painful as it was, I forced myself to experience again the sequence of events: hearing the doctor tell me I was going to have a baby; sharing the good news with our family and friends; feeling my excitement growing. I pushed myself to dwell on each milestone that forecast the miscarriage: the morning I discovered I was spotting; the call from my nurse ordering me to bed; day after day spent on the living-room couch, motionless and frightened. Mentally I rode the roller coaster up the track of fleeting hope, down the track of despair. My tears flowed like a monsoon. But I persisted in the reflection process. I knew that unless I found the courage to confront my pain, it would haunt me forever.

Slowly, I could feel the process beginning to work. Several weeks of silent soul-searching and reconstructing my loss unburdened me and renewed my energy. I found myself feeling more optimistic. The worst phase of my grief and self-recrimination was over the day I gave up looking at the past and began to focus on the future.

I looked forward with a different sense of myself—tougher, more self-confident. My thoughts wandered to my career and where it was going. At first, I assumed these flights of fancy were just nature's attempt to protect me from further strain. Yet no matter how hard I tried to eliminate them, certain images persisted.

One day, I gave in to the intrusions. I stepped into the daydream and participated in the fantasy:

I am in business attire working in a plush suite of offices. Other professionals are gathered in the hallways, drinking coffee and conversing. A man and woman stand at the chalkboard in a large, glassed-in conference room. They are teaching a seminar and mention that I will be in later to address the conferees.

This daydream puzzled me, because at the time of my miscarriage I was in solo practice as a psychologist. I had one office and one assistant.

Mental flashes of myself as an executive leading a team of professionals interrupted my daily work more and more frequently. Clearly my subconscious was sending me a message. As I delved deeper into these flights of fancy, I began to realize that the feelings I experienced in my daydreams—of being a mentor—were very similar to those I had experienced in my daydreams of becoming a mother. Hidden in my grief was the discovery that mentoring could be similar to mothering in the way that running an organization is similar to raising a family.

It's been four years now since my miscarriage, and my dream of becoming a mentor has come true. I founded a training and consulting firm called The Cramer Institute (TCI). TCI is organized as a diverse family of professionals including psychologists, social workers, researchers, instructional designers, and counselors. Each person on my staff is a valued member of the team, dedicated to the mission of the firm and the continuing development of each member.

I have not fooled myself into thinking that mentoring can replace mothering. But losing out at motherhood spurred me to consider other ways of channeling my desire to nurture people and watch them grow. I am grateful for my chance at motherhood, and in a strange way I am thankful for my grief. Had I not had that pain to learn from, I would not have had the satisfaction of running a business.

My personal story reveals how the many challenges, tragedies, and dilemmas of midlife give us opportunities to shift direction and renew ourselves. Thanks to our level of maturity, those of us over forty are better equipped to detect and take advantage of these opportunities than we were in our younger days.

Playing the Odds

As a midlife pioneer, odds are you have undergone or are in store for certain predictable and profound losses—such as mine—that are capable of triggering what we call a midlife crisis:

- Your company betrays you by eliminating your job.
- Your marriage fails, despite years of effort to make it work.
- Your career plateaus and thirty-year-olds pass you in their climb to the top.
- Your parents turn to you for financial and emotional support.
- Your health falters.
- Your teenager becomes addicted to drugs or alcohol.
- Someone you love dies.

While I certainly don't mean to suggest that the setbacks listed above (or any others, for that matter) will happen to you, it's been my experience as a psychologist and as a midlife journeyer that those who do suffer a significant loss or trauma can be devastated if they haven't yet learned—or are unwilling to try—to use their pain as a stepping-stone to new horizons of personal fulfillment.

Chances are you are reading this book because you feel a powerful force telling you that "something must give" (and you don't want it to be you)! Whether you have faced a traumatic loss, feel the vague emptiness discussed in the Introduction, or simply aren't sure what you intend to do with the rest of your life, the first step in charting a safe course through midlife is to follow your instinct and listen to that little voice that's prodding you toward change.

Surprisingly, most people ignore the signs that it's time to make a change. Research shows that of the three possible responses to the pressures of midlife—crisis, thriving, or denial—denial is the most common coping method. Study after study reveals that most people do not fall apart from the pressures of midlife. We don't quit our jobs or leave our families as conventional folklore might have us to believe. Neither do most people mine their disruptive episodes for all they are worth. A landmark study by sociologist Michael Farrell of the State University of New York at Buffalo and social psychologist Stanley Rosenberg of Dartmouth Medical School confirms that in response to the pressures of midlife, most of us bury our heads in the sand, hoping the storm will soon pass.

In my practice, I have seen people go to extreme lengths to avoid dealing with this natural urge to change and grow. Well-intentioned but confused clients resort to everything from overwork to serious depression rather than take a close look at themselves. Denial is much more painful in the long run.

One man who came to me described his family as a hotbed of heartache. The way he saw it, he was a kind, easygoing guy whose family was always bickering. He pointed out to them how futile all this arguing was, but they wouldn't stop. After the bickering went on for too long, he would get angry and yell, which made them all unhappy. He knew something had to change when the frequency and intensity of the battles increased, but he persisted in thinking of himself as the peacemaker, the victim in the situation.

After he explained to me at length how awful the rest of his family was—always in conflict—it became clear to both of us that my client's *fear* of conflict was at the root of the family's troubles. This man realized that the role of family peacemaker (which he had played as a child, when his parents argued) had kept him so busy that he had had no time to think about, much less articulate, his own desires. Over the years he had naturally become resentful, and had started to play his peacemaker role with a vengeance.

Slowly but surely, my client learned to speak up during conflict, not as a peacemaker, but as himself. Not only did his relationship with his wife and children improve, but he was amazed to discover that in the process of learning to assert his own desires, his ability to negotiate with his business partners improved significantly, too.

Like my client, you already have many of the tools you need to begin to make positive changes in your life. When I lost my baby, I called upon memories and experiences I *already had* in order to put my problem into perspective. What came out of that perspective was not a solution (none was possible; I couldn't bring the baby back into my womb), but an *idea for growth* that eased, if not erased, my sadness. Before long, it helped me find great joy.

The Fundamentals of Self-Renewal

The process I recommend for unleashing your inner potential and thriving in the face of midlife challenges is called *Self-Renewal Practice*. "Self-Renewal Practice" is simply a more expressive term for what most people would call an exercise. But the word "exercise" has a burdensome connotation for many of us who feel we can't fit one more task into our busy lives. These Self-Renewal Practices are anything but exercises: they are, like sleep, an important tool for self-restoration, even self-preservation.

The capacity for self-renewal is deeply rooted in each of us on the biological level. One year from today, 98 percent of the atoms in our body will have been exchanged for different ones. Once a month, our skin replaces itself (90 percent of household dust is dead skin cells). Our stomach linings are made brand new every five days. Within a six-week cycle, the liver re-creates itself, and over the course of a three-month period the bones do the same. *Six trillion* reactions are taking place in each cell of the body every second, without our conscious intention or effort, until the day we die. The body thrives on self-renewal.

With Self-Renewal Practice, your mind, heart, and spirit mimic the wisdom of the body, exchanging aspects of your self that are no longer useful for newer, more helpful ones. Self-renewal is as endlessly possible in your personality, your capacity for creativity, your powers of reason, your expression of feeling, your productivity, and your relationships as it is in cell life. The main difference between Self-Renewal Practice and biological self-renewal is the degree of conscious awareness involved in the process. The success of Self-Renewal Practice depends almost entirely upon your willingness to *intentionally penetrate your life.*

Self-Renewal Practice enhances midlife development by activating two basic modes of learning: *conceptual learning* and *operational learning*. Both these modes are in use at every stage of life. Operational learning is the way in which you learn *how* to do things. You learn how to drive a car or how to say a word. Operational learning comes through senses or *from the outside in*. To learn to drive a car, for example, you read the instructions, examine the controls, feel the way the car moves when you turn the wheel. To learn how to say a word, your tongue and facial muscles must form the right vowel and consonant sounds so that the words sound recognizable.

Conceptual learning occurs as you make sense out of what you learned in the operational mode. To use our example of car driving, let's say you're at a four-way stop: it is through conceptual learning that you figure out when it's your turn to go. Conceptual learning takes place *from the inside out*; it is your brain trying to make sense of things. We use conceptual learning to distinguish one person from another, to categorize items as "fruit" and not "vegetables," or to number them one, two, three, and four.

One of the best ways to understand the difference between the two types of learning is to picture a one-year-old learning to talk. When she pronounces the word "Mommy" she's using her operational learning skills. But when she realizes that only one woman—and not every woman between the ages of eighteen and forty-five—*is* "Mommy," then she's using conceptual learning. She's learned the *concept* of Mommy, not just the word.

Both types of learning are necessary for growth in midlife. As we enter the second half of life, most of us have plenty of basic *know-how* (operational learning) to function well in our families, with our friends, and in school or work settings. This level of mastery allows us to turn our operational learning skills to more complex—and often more rewarding—information and skills. We can learn to fly a plane, for example, or how to do exercises that will help us get to know ourselves better. Improving operational knowledge is essential for anyone who wants to advance along any of the seven pathways of midlife reward. For those of us who tend to rely too much on our intellect, it is especially important to reactivate the primal and, frankly, fun mode of operational learning.

Conceptual learning, or the *know-why*, is never more important than in midlife. At this point in life people are asking themselves why. Why me? Why not me? Why love? Why death? Why am I here? While you have probably had some kinds of answers for questions such as these all along, you may now find yourself wanting more satisfactory ones. For that, you'll need to hone your conceptual learning skills through directed thought. It is through conceptual learning that we receive many of the most impressive rewards at midlife and beyond.

I encourage you to approach all tasks and challenges in your life with an eye toward both the know-how *and* the know-why. When you do the Self-Renewal Practices in this book, try to be aware of both modes of learning.

Be forewarned that Self-Renewal Practice is not linear. It is not formulaic; it is full of contrasts. Some practices will focus on the know-how, asking you to talk, paint, juggle, eat, lose control, or play. These practices force you to experience the world and to try new skills, rather than rely on your intellect. Through these practices you will learn once again to act on the urgings of your heart and soul without interference from your sense of what "should be." Other practices will ask you to be quiet, alone, and pensive. That's to help overcome the know-why problem of overstimulation and distraction from the outer world. To assist you in your work, I've often provided examples of how others completed the Self-Renewal Practices.

Some Self-Renewal Practices should be done every day for one week; others need to be performed only once. Some will become as necessary for you as breathing. Every practice will help you in a different way. Try them all and use those that work for you.

People who regularly do these exercises report a deep sense of mental alertness, a new vibrancy in their emotional lives, expanded powers of concentration and creativity, and a more complete fulfillment of their potential. They also feel more confident that they are influencing others positively and making lasting contributions to the world.

The Four Stages of Self-Renewal
Self-Renewal Practice leads you through a four-stage process, taking you from where you are now to where you want to be. This process can happen relatively quickly (in minutes), or it can proceed slowly, over the course of months or even years. Some people go back and forth between stages before a final integration takes place.

Four Stages of Self-Renewal Practice

Stage I, Introspection: the active, conscious search for your own hidden, untapped talents, gifts, and desires. In this stage, rid yourself of anxiety and allow your mind to become a blank slate. Abandon preconceptions, flow with your thoughts and experiences, and absorb whatever happens.

Stage II, Incubation: a time to reflect on your self-discoveries and to give form to what you have found. In Stage II, you will become acquainted with your revelations and digest each and every nuance. Through trial and error, you will learn new ways of thinking, feeling, and acting.

Stage III, Illumination: provides flashes of insight into who you are, who you are not, and who you can become. Illumination cannot be programmed; it happens spontaneously as the result of Stages I and II. This is the stage of enlightenment, of exciting breakthroughs in self-understanding, and of gaining a deeper sense of self-worth.

Stage IV, Integration: ongoing periods of transforming your insights into vision, committed action, and positive self-identity. This is the step in which you take your new self-discoveries and try them on, live them out, and share them with your community.

The best way to master the stages of self-renewal is to practice them in a specific context. Take twenty minutes right now to complete your first excursion through these stages. You will need a piece of paper (a personal journal is best) and a pen or pencil for this exercise (and for those that follow throughout this book).

INTRODUCTORY
SELF-RENEWAL PRACTICE

The Life Map

Focus on the milestone events and significant people who have shaped your life by completing a quick Life Map.* Life mapping gives you a strong sense of who you are in the world, who you have been, and who you will be as you continue to develop. Follow these guidelines:

Stage I, Introspection: Examine the columns on the Introductory Life Map chart on page 21. Make sure you understand the meaning of each of the categories listed across the top of the chart:

- **Peak Experiences:** high points in your life, periods of great joy or accomplishment

- **Episodes of Misfortune:** low points in your life, periods of great disappointment or bad luck

- **Turning Points:** significant changes in your life's course or in your self-image, periods of transition

- **Significant Role Models:** people whom you greatly admire or who take special care to nurture and promote your welfare

- **Significant Critics:** people who undermine your confidence and competence by criticizing you, or who hinder your welfare in any way

* While writing this book I discovered the work of developmental psychologist Dan P. McAdams, researcher at Loyola University, who has devoted his career to the study of how people form their sense of personal identity. McAdams concludes that human beings construct a sense of their own uniqueness by creating what he terms a "heroic story of the self." McAdams's methods of exploring an individual's personal myth are similar to the questions that I recommend you answer in constructing your Life Map. Readers who want more extensive support in expressing their life story should see McAdams's popular text, *The Stories We Live By* (New York: William Morrow, 1993).

Spend about ten minutes contemplating key events and people who have shaped your life. Then reproduce the Introductory Life Map chart in your journal and note under each category the responses that occur to you during this brief survey of your life's course. I'm certain you could spend hours filling in this chart, but that would be counterproductive now. Just note the major highlights. We will delve further into your memory bank in chapters to come: in traveling down each of the seven pathways, you can make additions to your Life Map. Some people actually create separate Life Maps for each pathway. Others create Life Maps for personal areas of interest—career, parenting, sports prowess. There is virtually no area of your life that can't be explored in this way.

INTRODUCTORY LIFE MAP

Peak Experiences	Episodes of Misfortune	Turning Points	Significant Role Models	Significant Critics

Stage II, Incubation: After you have made a spontaneous yet thoughtful search for the events and people that have played a major role in your life, dwell on your notations to determine if any themes or patterns appear. Spend only five minutes on this step. Later in the course of your journey you will have plenty of time to decipher the meaning of these milestone situations and key relationships.

Stage III, Illumination: Ask yourself how each entry on your chart may have contributed to your uniqueness and personal growth. Al-

low only enough time for the most spontaneous insights to emerge
(about five minutes).

Stage IV, Integration: Commit yourself to revisiting your Life Map
notes on a regular basis throughout your midlife adventure. I recommend that you make additions to your Life Map notes as you
proceed down each of the seven pathways. Doing so will sharpen
your memory and help you develop a kind of filter through which
you can view your life, deepening your understanding of current
dilemmas, conflicts, or triumphs.

While Stages I to III are exciting—many clients report amazing
discoveries—do not be tempted to end there. Be sure to integrate
what you have learned into your life. One client of mine, who was
a particularly gifted musician as a teenager, learned to recall the
inspiring words of his music teacher every time he needed to encourage himself to stick with difficult, demanding projects he encountered as a research chemist.

Life-mapping is a good way to extend your know-how *and* your
know-why learning. In terms of *know-how*, completing a Life Map
sharpens your powers of recall and concentration. Dwelling on the
lessons of your Life Map teaches you the *know-whys* of your life
and can bring meaning to your journey.

Now that you have completed this initial Self-Renewal Practice,
it is time to set your sights on specific benefits you seek as you travel
each of the seven pathways to midlife wisdom.

CHAPTER 2

Promises to Keep

. . . to live the heroic life is to live the individual adventure, really. One of the problems today is that with the enormous transformation in the forms of our lives, the models for life don't exist for us. In a traditional society—the agriculturally based city—there were relatively few life roles, and the models were there; there was a hero for each life role. But look at the past twenty years and what has come along in the way of new life possibilities and requirements. The hero-as-model is one thing we lack, so each one has to be his own hero and follow the path that's no path.

—JOSEPH CAMPBELL

Think about the word "promise." When did you make your first promise? What promises do you find hardest to keep? Do you promise frequently? What are your expectations when someone makes you a promise?

Promises are sacred: "I promise to love, honor, and cherish you all the days of my life." Promises arise from deep loyalty: "I pledge allegiance . . ." "Promise" is another word for "mission." It signifies what you intend to make happen.

Midlife holds out the promise of personal growth. But you have to fulfill a promise before you can reap the rewards of midlife's promise: you must take your journey seriously. That is not to say with a heavy heart, or without humor, but thoughtfully, carefully, as you would take any important step.

Keeping the gifts of midlife in mind will help you stay the long and often arduous course along each of the seven pathways I presented in the Introduction. Give yourself a vivid impression of the promises of midlife by pondering a more detailed description of the prizes each route offers:

1. **Mental Mastery:** the ability to capitalize on your accumulated knowledge and experience, to unify your analytical and intuitive powers of reasoning, to use your seasoned judgment to create innovative solutions to complex problems, and to actually become wise

2. **Physical Vigor:** the ability to savor sensory experience without distractions, to maintain sound physical health, to sustain high energy levels, to enjoy a new sense of sexuality, and to foster total well-being

3. **Emotional Vitality:** the ability to bounce back quickly from disturbing events, to connect vibrantly with the pleasures of existence, to free yourself from the bondage of painful episodes of the past, and to enrich your connections to people and events

4. **Interpersonal Effectiveness:** the ability to establish caring relationships with others on the basis of their full range of strengths and weaknesses, and to unify the masculine and feminine aspects of your own personality

5. **Exceptional Competence:** the ability to perform complex tasks with unconscious competence, to assume leadership and mentor roles in the areas where you have particular strengths, and to make significant contributions to the wider world based upon your unique talents and desires

6. **Spiritual Serenity:** the ability to contemplate in ever greater depth the mysteries of the universe, and to achieve a newfound sense of awe, reverence, and continuity with God and nature

7. **Personal Integrity:** the ability to realize your unique personal destiny, to appreciate your own wholeness and worth, and to love yourself, your life, and your fate

Understanding the promises of each pathway is only the beginning. You'll grow farther and faster if you calculate specific objectives within each territory, new capabilities and goals that hold the most interest for you. Which prizes along specific pathways capture your imagination?

One way for you to decide which prizes you value most is to complete the questionnaire that I call Self-Renewal Inventory (SRI). The SRI is a systematic approach to defining the unique set of personal objectives that you will pursue diligently in your midlife quest.

SELF-RENEWAL INVENTORY
SRI

© *The Cramer Institute, 1992*

Directions:

Please respond to each statement using the scale below. Your answer should be the one that best describes you and how often you feel that way. Answer each statement honestly and as spontaneously as possible. There are no right or wrong answers. If none of the available responses appears to fit perfectly, pick the one closest to the way you feel. Do not consult the scoring key until you have finished completing your responses.

Response Code: Almost Never   = 1
Rarely   = 2
Sometimes   = 3
Often   = 4
Almost Always   = 5

I. MENTAL MASTERY

1. I have excellent powers of concentration. _____
2. It is easy for me to see both sides of an issue. _____
3. I am open-minded. _____
4. I rely on my intuition and it serves me well. _____
5. I am decisive. _____
6. I rely on my logic and reason and they serve me well. _____
7. My memory is excellent for important matters. _____
8. I am mentally challenged by complex problems and enjoy seeking solutions to them. _____

9. I have a vivid imagination. _____

10. I am wise. _____

Mental Mastery Subtotal _____

II. PHYSICAL VIGOR

1. I enjoy my sexuality and sensuality. _____

2. I feel healthy. _____

3. My appetite is good and I have a vibrant sense of taste. _____

4. I recover quickly from illness. _____

5. I have a high energy level. _____

6. I have physical stamina. _____

7. I enjoy the rhythmic movement of dance or exercise and engage in these activities regularly. _____

8. My sleep is restful and renews me. _____

9. I seek out and enjoy the visual beauty of nature and works of art. _____

10. I seek out and enjoy listening to the pleasurable sounds in music and nature. _____

Physical Vigor Subtotal _____

III. EMOTIONAL VITALITY

1. I can tell the difference between a present conflict and a restimulation of past, unfinished distress. _____

2. When I am angry, the episode is brief and I let go of it with a sense of closure. _____

3. I express my anger, but choose not to be vindictive, malicious, or retaliatory. _____

4. My mood is not disturbed by the moods of others. _____

5. I have an abiding sense of humor. _____

6. I have an abiding sense of joy. _____

7. I am emotionally resilient. _____

8. I take risks even when I am fearful. _____

9. It is easy for me to identify my feelings. _____

10. I am my own best friend. _____

Emotional Vitality Subtotal _____

IV. INTERPERSONAL EFFECTIVENESS

1. I do not expect anyone to bail me out or to take care of me. _____
2. I appreciate feedback and can distinguish it from attempts to manipulate me. _____
3. I tolerate and value differences in other people. _____
4. I cooperate more than I compete with others. _____
5. I sacrifice and compromise in relationships. _____
6. I freely express caring in words and actions. _____
7. I am well loved. _____
8. I confide in people. _____
9. I communicate well with men and women. _____
10. I am compassionate and take risks to advance the welfare of others. _____

Interpersonal Effectiveness Subtotal _____

V. EXCEPTIONAL COMPETENCE

1. I am productive. _____
2. I am proud of what I accomplish. _____
3. I am able to tap into my creativity. _____
4. I actively develop my own talents. _____
5. I seek to provide for the next generation. _____
6. I am involved in making the world a better place to live. _____
7. I work to my full potential. _____
8. I have a variety of absorbing interests. _____
9. I mentor and teach others. _____
10. My achievements provide me with a sense of fulfillment. _____

Exceptional Competence Subtotal _____

VI. SPIRITUAL SERENITY

1. I trust that periods of darkness and upheaval offer opportunities for personal growth. _____
2. My spiritual beliefs support and guide me. _____
3. I revere the mysteries of life. _____
4. I have abiding inner serenity. _____

5. I have confidence in the forces that operate for good in the world.   _____

6. I recognize and accept that destructive forces are at work in the world.   _____

7. I ponder the mysteries of life.   _____

8. I feel connected to all of nature.   _____

9. I am ready to accept my own death.   _____

10. My life is meaningful.   _____

Spiritual Serenity Subtotal   _____

VII. PERSONAL INTEGRITY

1. I take full responsibility for the shape my life has taken.   _____

2. I accept that I may never receive all the attention I seek or deserve.   _____

3. Each aspect of my life works together in harmony.   _____

4. I accept that it is normal to feel that I don't always measure up.   _____

5. I am not easily pushed around.   _____

6. I feel whole and complete as a person.   _____

7. I trust that my own internal sense of authority is my best source of judgment and guidance.   _____

8. I am satisfied with my life.   _____

9. I look back on my life with pleasure.   _____

10. My life has a clear purpose.   _____

Personal Integrity Subtotal   _____

Summary of Scores

Please review each subtotal score in each category and enter it below:

    I.   Mental Mastery   _____

   II.   Physical Vigor   _____

 III.   Emotional Vitality   _____

 IV.   Interpersonal Effectiveness   _____

  V.   Exceptional Competence   _____

VI. Spiritual Serenity   _____
VII. Personal Integrity   _____

Interpretation and Recommendations

Working from the outer rim inward, shade in the Self-Renewal Chart on page 30 by filling the number of rows in each segment that corresponds to your score for each of the seven dimensions of midlife growth. The shading key shows you how to calculate the number of rows to be shaded for each score. For example, if you scored 23–26 on the Mental Mastery dimension, you would shade the first four rows of the Mental Mastery segment on the chart.

Review your completed Self-Renewal Chart. You may notice that your scores vary by section. Those segments with the most levels shaded represent the inner pathways you have explored and capitalized on most. You have already earned multiple rewards for having traveled those particular paths. You may, however, desire more of a balance in your life, and may hope to add significant layers of shading in each of the categories. Of course, you will always have more shading in some areas and slightly less in others, but the idea is to be well developed and focused in all.

Put an asterisk next to those areas showing the fewest shaded levels. These pathways are the ones you have probably spent the least amount of your time focusing on; therefore they are not as developed as other aspects of your wholeness as a person.

Take time now to formulate some personal growth goals in each of the areas where you rated a 3, 2, or 1. I have provided a sample chart for you to read. The entries on the sample chart correspond to typical objectives generated by participants in my workshops. Feel free to reproduce this chart in your journal and create your own set of objectives to help guide you down each of the seven pathways.

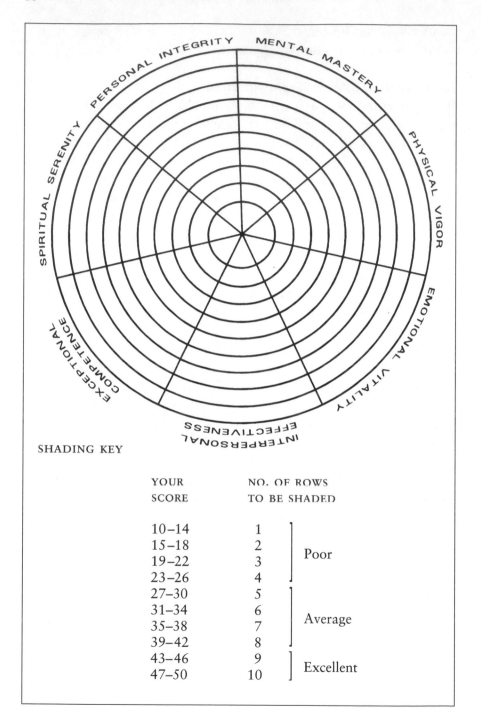

SHADING KEY

YOUR SCORE	NO. OF ROWS TO BE SHADED	
10–14	1	
15–18	2	Poor
19–22	3	
23–26	4	
27–30	5	
31–34	6	Average
35–38	7	
39–42	8	
43–46	9	Excellent
47–50	10	

Personal Growth Objectives

Items from **Mental Mastery,** I rated 3, 2, or 1:	My Personal Growth Objectives:
4. I rely on my intuition. 7. My memory is excellent. 10. I am wise.	• *To trust my intuition in my business dealings* • *To learn ways of memorizing and recalling historical and functional data* • *To rid myself of distracting thoughts and disturbing memories*
Items from **Physical Vigor,** I rated 3, 2, or 1:	My Personal Growth Objectives:
5. I have a high energy level. 8. My sleep is restful. 9. I seek visual beauty. 10. I seek music and nature.	• *To lose weight; increase energy and stamina* • *To reduce nightmares and learn how to fall asleep easily* • *To spend more time developing my interest in art and talent as a musician*
Items from **Emotional Vitality,** I rated 3, 2, or 1:	My Personal Growth Objectives:
1. I can distinguish present conflict from past distress. 2. I can let go of my anger. 7. I am emotionally resilient. 10. I am my own best friend.	• *To learn to forgive those who have let me down and hurt me* • *To conquer my anger* • *To get rid of my depression* • *To love myself more*

Items from **Interpersonal Effectiveness,** I rated 3, 2, or 1:	My Personal Growth Objectives:
2. I appreciate feedback. 4. I cooperate more than I compete. 8. I confide in people.	• *To reduce my defensiveness* • *To reduce my competitive drive* • *To learn to trust others and confide my feelings to them*
Items from **Exceptional Competence,** I rated 3, 2, or 1:	My Personal Growth Objectives:
4. I actively develop my own talents. 5. I seek to provide for the next generation. 9. I mentor and teach others.	• *To expand my talents in music and gardening* • *To take on community development projects* • *To share my executive skills with younger managers*
Items from **Spiritual Serenity,** I rated 3, 2, or 1:	My Personal Growth Objectives:
1. I trust upheaval as opportunity. 4. I have a sense of inner serenity. 9. I am ready to accept my own death. 10. My life is meaningful.	• *To learn how to cope with stressful crises* • *To become more spiritual* • *To find more meaning in my life*
Items from **Personal Integrity,** I rated 3, 2, or 1:	My Personal Growth Objectives:
1. I take full responsibility for my life. 5. I am not easily pushed around. 6. I feel whole and complete. 7. I trust my internal authority. 9. I look back on my life with pleasure.	• *To be at peace with my past mistakes and transgressions* • *To stand up for myself in my family* • *To stop second-guessing myself* • *To develop my full potential*

Charting Your Course

I can't tell you which roads you will travel on your journey, or what you will find on each, but I can tell you that most travelers on the road to self-renewal experience the journey in three phases. To help you give shape to your own quest, I've organized the book around these three phases:

The Call to Depart: You have almost completed the first phase of your journey already—a journey you began when you felt the first stirrings of change in your heart and mind. In Part I you have taken stock of your desires and aptitudes and have set some exciting goals for your journey.

The Rewarding Adventure: Part II of this book consists of seven chapters, each devoted to one of the seven pathways that are at the core of mature selfhood. Each pathway is in itself a mini-journey, and in each you will find signs that you are ready to take advantage of the unique gifts of that pathway, an introduction to the rewards you can earn on that pathway, and ideas for integrating these rewards into your life. The Self-Renewal Practices in each chapter will be of great help to you as you begin to make the rewards of midlife your own. The more you practice self-renewal, the more you will release your inborn potential to grow deeper, wiser, and more resilient.

The Return Home: Part III of the book suggests ways to keep growing after you have followed the guidelines offered in Part II. This section emphasizes the importance of celebrating and continuing your accomplishments, as well as sharing your success with others and encouraging them in their own journeys.

Your three-phase journey mirrors the three-phase motif of the epic hero's quest, as depicted in great literature and art. More than any other kind of story, epic tales symbolize for us what it means to fulfill our greatest potential. Epic heroes face immense challenges that are metaphors for the challenges we must face in our day-to-day lives, as well as metaphors for coming to terms with the biggest challenge of all: death. If we live long enough to have time to *think* about our lives, and by extension our death, we need some help coping with it, and tales from Homer's *Odyssey* to Dante's *Inferno* hold deep truths about facing the demons our minds allow us to see. The midlife adventure is your heroic quest.

As is true of the hero's quest, you can advance from phase to phase of your midlife quest only after you complete the work of the preceding phase. I encourage you to take heart: although the *departures* in Part I can be disturbing at times, the *explorations* of Part II are sometimes painful but always exciting and uplifting, and the *discoveries* of Part III are nothing short of remarkable!

When discomfort strikes you along your journey, remember that episodes of anxiety and confusion are perfectly normal, just as they would be during any journey. Regain your sense of progress by following these recommendations:

- **Be gentle and patient with yourself.** Each person grows at a different pace during every stage of life. Use your newly acquired knowledge from Self-Renewal Practice as a carrot, not a stick. Hold the promise of specific gifts in your mind and heart to encourage yourself. Never berate yourself for not advancing rapidly enough.

- **Surrender to the process.** Get used to chaos in your head. This particular period of personal growth is a journey through multiple levels of the psyche. Expect that whatever you discover will most likely confuse you at first and delight you later.

- **Read directions thoroughly before embarking.** I have found that it works better if people read an entire chapter before practicing individual exercises. Review the whole message first, then go back to reread the sections that hold the most appeal for you.

- **Keep a journal nearby and save all your work.** Whatever you do, don't ever discard your work. Ten years from now it can be illuminating, entertaining, and, most of all, inspiring.

- **Turn to someone else for help.** Recruit someone to accompany you on your journey, and be sure to meet with this person regularly. There is no quicker way to advance past anxious moments than through conversation with a committed listener. Furthermore, talking through your stuck spots and your breakthroughs will help make them more real, just as it is more effective to go on a diet after you've gone public with your intention.

Choose your companion with care. You will reveal many of your inner truths to this person. He or she must be a good listener and must be secure enough not to be affected by jealousy of your progress, anger at your pace, or worry over how your growth might change your relationship.

- **Persevere.** The world belongs to those who show up!

So let's be on our way. Know that as you step forward into your first pathway, Mental Mastery, you can never retreat. From the first word on, you become an official midlife explorer, a person on a mission, a pathfinder on the road to the prime years of your life. There is no better time than the present. I wish you good fortune and Godspeed in creating the most magnificent midlife possible.

PART II

The Rewarding Adventure

CHAPTER 3

Pathway #1: Mental Mastery

*The world we've made as a result of the level
of thinking we have done thus far
creates problems that we cannot solve
at the same level at which we created them.*

—ALBERT EINSTEIN

In a high-backed red leather swivel chair, his elbows resting on the desktop and his head propped on his hands, sat the most bewildered executive I have ever seen.

Walter was dressed in the best executive garb: starched white shirt, red silk tie, expensive suit. But beneath his in-charge exterior was a man adrift. I saw his jaws clench and his eyes tear with embarrassment as he spoke to me about his failing organization. Morale was at an all-time low, teams were performing below industry standards, and Walter himself was receiving criticism from the highest levels of the company for his failure to manage the people side of his business.

Walter had always prided himself on his ability to set objectives, track performance, and solve difficult problems as they arose. He described himself as a strong analytical thinker and considered himself to be brighter than average (maybe even gifted) when it came to applying logic and reason to straighten out tough situations. But this time the intellectual approach he typically found so effective was not working. Day by day, Walter felt his organization disintegrating as his own effectiveness waned.

Although Walter was feeling discouraged, anxious, and clearly confused about how to correct his troubles, he also was facing a golden opportunity to travel down the path of Mental Mastery. The fact that Walter's current *know-how* was not remedy enough to solve his problems gave him the chance to learn new, more creative approaches, and to deepen his understanding of how organizations and people pull themselves out of dilemmas.

Once Walter learned how to use his mind in the new ways particularly accessible to him in midlife, he worked through his problem masterfully. He decided to share with his subordinates the responsibility for improving morale and meeting deadlines. At my suggestion, he made an effort not to control his employees' ideas, but simply to expect them to make positive changes. Using the rewards of Mental Mastery—working smarter instead of harder—Walter realized that his job was to guide others toward success, not solve the problem for them. The result was a more productive, cohesive, and relaxed workforce.

THE CALL TO MENTAL MASTERY

It was a business crisis that called Walter to travel the pathway of Mental Mastery. Other people know that it is time to embark on this road because they find themselves mindlessly moving through daily demands and routines. Tasks that used to require careful thought are now much easier and often lead to boredom. This is a sign that you did a good job in achieving the mental milestones of younger years, but also that you are eligible to develop the powers of your intellect even further.

Look over the following list of signals that indicate you are ready to journey down the pathway of Mental Mastery in search of new prizes of the intellect. Even if you only recognize one or two of these signals, it is a good time to embark.

Midlife Readiness Signals for Mental Mastery
You may find yourself:

- feeling confused when facing complex problems
- searching for novel ideas

- yearning to learn something new
- experiencing routines as boring
- becoming worried over forgetfulness
- clinging to narrow-minded ideas
- lacking creativity
- longing for mental challenges

One woman came in to see me complaining she was sick of housework and feeling guilty over her lack of interest in caring for her family. A computer salesman sought help because he felt overwhelmed by the amount of information coming at him. These common concerns can be dealt with most effectively by turning them into objectives for Mental Mastery.

Before you embark on your journey down the path of Mental Mastery, go back to your journal and review the set of Personal Growth Objectives you formulated after taking the Self-Renewal Inventory in Chapter 2. Feel free to delete, expand, narrow, add . . . as the spirit moves you. Then rank them in priority order—*your* priority order, no one else's.

Read this chapter on Mental Mastery *with your personal growth priorities in mind*. Use the Self-Renewal Practices offered in this chapter as a guide in developing your own set of Self-Renewal Practices. For example, the woman who came to me bored with housework enrolled in college courses as a means of staying open-minded and developing better powers of concentration. The computer salesman bought a book on mnemonics, or memory cues, to help him devise a system for remembering new product lines.

ADVENTURES IN MENTAL MASTERY

As you journey down the pathway of Mental Mastery, be on the lookout for the fruits of your labor in everyday life. For example, some people notice that their conscious attention to the details of their lives leads to better judgment in problem-solving. Others observe that activating their memory for past events expands their ability to understand their deeply rooted intellectual talents and creative gifts. When you achieve your objectives or find an unanticipated positive benefit, stop for a moment to enjoy it. Taking time to relish those wins will help more of them to come your way.

The Self-Renewal exercises you practice along this pathway will help you win the prizes available along each of the other paths as well. It is through inward mental search that you will make the majority of your midlife strides. So take your time on this important pathway before launching expeditions down other roads to discovery.

Mindfulness

When cardiologist Robert Eliot was at the University of Nebraska studying the relationship between stress and heart attacks, he concluded that we are bombarded with information at one thousand times the rate that our grandparents were. Our senses register many thousands of stimuli each day, from the way a colleague's cologne smells to an ad for the circus to the fact that dinner will be at 6:00 at John's. Most people know that it is up to us to decide which of these bits of information to retain. (It would be nice to remember what time to show up at John's, for example.) What most of us don't realize is that *we decide which of these bits to notice or ignore in the first place.*

If you are watching TV and start to read a magazine when the commercials come on, you have decided not to notice the TV for a while. When you drive, you generally decide not to notice too much of the scenery so that you can keep your eyes on the road. Selective "not noticing" is an important adaptive skill and is actually essential to survival. None of us could function in daily life without the ability to filter out unwanted stimuli and focus on what is important.

Like many skills, however, this skill is usually overdeveloped by the time most of us reach midlife. What was essential to our ability to become productive in society is now so automatic that we miss out on a lot that life has to offer. Yes, this is the old "take time to smell the roses" admonition. But it is also a note about what it takes to live your life in the best way possible. Now that you know how to screen *out* the junk, you probably need to go back and reevaluate exactly what it is you *want* to screen out. Let me give you an example.

One of my most popular workshops is one we offer to managers who want to learn how to better empower their employees. And one of the most surprising facts participants learn is that they're only noticing half of what is going on in the office. A workshop dialogue might go something like this:

"I just don't understand why my people won't take risks. I tell them all the time that it's the only way to break new ground in the business."

"What happens when your subordinates do take risks?"

"Usually we see a great improvement in the area involved."

"Is the risk-taker rewarded for risk-taking?"

"What do you mean? The company always does better after something like that. That's the way it's supposed to be; that's why we're in business."

"And what if someone takes a risk and it doesn't pan out?"

"Well, in that case I'd try to help the employee figure out what went wrong."

"So if the results aren't what you'd hoped, you speak to the employee."

"Yes. To help him or her learn."

"And if the employee doesn't take risks at all?"

"Of course then I try to encourage him or her to do so."

"So you're saying that you notice and act on situations in which people are not behaving as you think they should, but don't notice situations in which things are going well."

Manager after manager is shocked to learn that he or she has actually been trained to *ignore* success and "punish" failure, all in the interest of the company. Almost to a person, they understand immediately that noticing, rewarding, and learning from success is more helpful to *everyone* in the company than hunting out weakness.

When we think about it, we all make a habit of selective noticing. We notice the one day our children spill their milk instead of the forty-five days when they do not. We notice that the house needs painting, not that the roof is good for ten more years. And much of what happens in our lives we forget to notice altogether (not smelling the roses). Instead of carefully choosing what we let into our minds, we allow ourselves to be mind*less*.

The Self-Renewal Practice that follows is intended to help you gauge your own level of mindlessness.

SELF-RENEWAL PRACTICE

Time Out

1. Remove your wristwatch and turn it face down.

2. In your journal, write the number of months or years you have owned your watch.

3. Multiply the number of months you have owned your watch by 4 or the number of years by 52.

4. Multiply the number you got in Step 3 by 7.

5. Estimate how many times per day you look at your watch.

6. Multiply the number you entered in Step 4 by the number you entered in Step 5. (This number represents the approximate number of times you have looked at your watch.)

7. In your journal, draw the face of your watch. Do not look at your watch. Include as many details as you can remember. Give yourself sixty seconds to complete this step.

8. Turn over your watch and compare the details in your drawing to the actual face of your watch.

If you are like me, your rendering of the face of your watch does not closely resemble its actual appearance. When I first tried this experiment I drew my watch as if it showed numbers, when in reality there are no numbers on my watch at all! How could I have failed to notice the details of my watch after looking at its face more than 43,680 times?

The answer, of course, is that I looked at my watch mindlessly, not mindfully. If I fail to notice something I observe this often, what other more meaningful or enjoyable details might I be missing simply because I have not consciously zeroed in on them?

Fortunately, mindlessness is fairly easy to conquer. Almost twenty years ago, in a groundbreaking experiment designed to discover how decision-making and assuming responsibility would affect nursing-home residents, psychologists Ellen Langer of Harvard and Judith Rodin of Yale found that over the course of eighteen months, caring for houseplants and making minor decisions about daily nursing-home routines increased the alertness, cheerfulness, and overall activity level of the elderly participants. Nursing-home residents who were not given the same degree of choice and responsibility were more likely to die during the course of this experiment than those in the "experimental" group: 30 percent of those who did not participate in the study died versus only 15 percent in the participant group.

Langer and her colleagues were so intrigued by these results that they embarked on a decade of experiments to investigate the effects of this mental state (which they eventually named *mindfulness*) on such variables as physical and mental well-being, the quality of relationships, and the capacity to have an impact on the world. It turns out that the ability to be *mindful* has a powerful, positive influence on each of these aspects of our middle adult and elderly lives.

Think of mindfulness as focused concentration, as acting on purpose or with keen awareness. When you are mindful you take no situation for granted, not even routines. Mindfulness means being vigilant, looking at what's happening from multiple angles, being open to new information and willing to revise your understanding of the way the world works. Paying attention to the big picture and to the details of your experience is the essence of mindfulness.

The investigations of Langer and other researchers prove that being mindful in our daily life choices can increase self-knowledge while decreasing the likelihood of depression. With these two benefits in mind, practice this simple yet powerful means of Self-Renewal.

SELF-RENEWAL PRACTICE

Mindful Choices

1. At the end of each day, over the course of one week, list three or four choices that you made. Next to each of your entries indicate the alternatives you could have chosen.

2. Reflect on the reason behind each of your choices. Did the choice you made serve your own purpose? Were you accommodating the needs of someone else? Were you acting out of habit?

3. Reflect on the consequences of each option. What impact did your choices have on you? Your health? Your happiness? Your relationships? Your productivity?

4. Based upon this brief but insightful analysis, which choices do you intend to repeat when appropriate and which ones will you replace with more useful, fulfilling alternatives?

Here's an example of notes taken from this type of Self-Renewal Practice to guide your own approach to *mindful choices*:

1. My Choice: To get up at 6:00 a.m. (rather than rising later or earlier).

2. Reason: So that I could get a head start on the busy day, but have enough rest to move at a steady clip rather than a frantic one.

3. Consequences: Relaxed, productive day.

4. Future Choice: Repeat as necessary. Rising early on an occasional busy day is useful for me; I start the day "ahead of the game" and am more confident that I'll accomplish that day's goals. Getting up early is easier on me than staying up late.

You will find that as you become comfortable with making *all* your life choices conscious ones, you acquire a surprising mental sharpness. Clients of mine who practice mindfulness—running their lives instead of letting their lives run them—report that they feel smarter, less forgetful, and more creative. In what might seem a paradox, many say they are more intuitive because they are actively observing what is within them as well as the world around them.

From Self-Consciousness to Self-Awareness

Think about the wonderful things your intellect has done for you recently. Maybe your mind has discovered a new road to work, patted you on the back when you needed encouragement, reminded you of an important appointment, or solved a problem that's been nagging you for weeks. I love my mind. It's a constant companion, helper, and source of entertainment.

Your mind can also protect you. All of us are familiar with the stories of abused children whose minds actually block out pain too terrible for them to feel. Some of these children even develop two or more "personalities" as a way of coping with the abuse. Adults who have survived great pain or danger often report going "outside" themselves at crucial moments.

The mind also functions as protector in situations that are not so dire. When I was a child, my mind helped me get through a devastating accident of birth: I was born with a cleft lip and palate—a gaping hole in the roof of my mouth, left nostril, and upper lip. The plastic surgeons who pieced together my flesh and bones left the crisscross mark of stitches on my tiny face that I knew marked me as damaged goods forever.

I was on shaky ground interpersonally because of my ugly face. Like any child, I wanted to be accepted and loved, but people, especially children, don't like ugly faces. So I entered the world one-down, searching for ways to make up for my fault. And abracadabra! My mind moved in to save me. I became exceptionally good at reading people—what they thought, what they wanted. I figured out that if I could outthink or outsmart people, or, better yet, read their minds, I could give them what they wanted before they even knew they wanted it. Then they would like me! What a plan! Day after day, year after year, I honed in on people's reactions and desires like a laser beam penetrating steel girders.

As an overly self-conscious teenager, I found this skill to be both a blessing and a burden. True, it helped me forecast what others wanted or needed from me, but it also opened me up to every critical comment aimed in my direction. I spent my childhood, adolescence, and early adulthood in the foxhole of my mind, mentally on guard for any chance to advance my mission: to win approval and be accepted. I arrived at midlife battle-fatigued.

But after I hit forty, something wonderful happened. I began to notice that, for some reason, I felt ready to relinquish my mental outpost. And one day I simply declared victory and announced to myself, "I am worthwhile." I stopped worrying about how others reacted to me. I was still aware of others' opinions of me, but I just didn't care so very much.

At first it felt odd not to be vigilant in every social situation. Since I no longer had to analyze every interaction for its inherent danger or opportunity, I found myself building up a huge storehouse of intellectual reserves. I didn't know what to do with all this extra mental energy. Once I realized the gift life had given me, I became very excited. It was as if school had been let out and I was finally free to do what I wanted!

I asked myself, Why not channel all of your keen mental abilities in some new, more productive, less stressful directions? How about getting to know the real you? How about learning more psychology, more art, more names of flowers and trees and birds? Maybe you could grow your business or help get rid of poverty. Ultimately I decided to do all of the above, and I continue to enjoy terrific mental reserves to this day.

What happened to me is not unusual. Study after study shows that most people, at around age forty, experience a dramatic change in the way they view the opinions of the "outside world": these opinions suddenly lose impact.

None of this is to say, of course, that the opinions of others are unimportant. The fact that we care about what other people think is a basic foundation of society, and it helps us "do the right thing" at times when it would be easier, or more fun, to follow our own selfish interests. In his book *The Passionate Life*, psychologist and author Sam Keen defines this caring as *self-consciousness*, or "me watching me through the eyes of outside authorities." Although it was painful at times, seeing ourselves through the eyes of others who were in charge helped us, as children, learn to adhere to the norms of our families and communities. Self-conscious observation spurred us to climb the ladders of success in educational and professional pursuits. By the time we reach midlife, however, self-conscious observation has outlived its usefulness. In order to keep growing, we need a new approach.

According to Keen, adults who experience that magical time when they are ready to give up self-consciousness move on to *self-awareness*, or "me watching through the eyes of my own inner authority." The voice within you that used to say "They think I'm fat" can now say "How do *I* feel about my weight?" or "I need to take care of myself, and part of that is getting my weight down," or "I know I'm in the best shape I can be, and that little blip on my stomach is their problem, not mine."

As you begin to listen to yourself, you find that your mental life takes on two important aspects. First, you begin to approach the external world more deliberately, with your own best interests at heart. Second, you discover aspects of yourself—your preferences, blind spots, quirks, talents, and habits—that you've neglected or pushed away. As you negotiate a new balance between your internal world and the external one, both changes help you face the world with confidence. I believe that getting this balance right is the key to wisdom.

Becoming wise is one of the major objectives of midlife. How wise you become depends in large part on your ability to watch your "public self" with the curiosity of a detective and the compassion of a saint. What you observe yourself doing in the course of your midlife adventure may at times startle you, discourage you, confuse you, and overwhelm you. Be gentle with yourself. Understanding that you will renegotiate this balance over and over in the years to come may help you be patient.

Many people never make the transition from self-consciousness to self-awareness. They get stuck in what I call *self-sabotage*: they stop caring altogether. The man who just "lets himself go" or the woman who says "Oh, I'm just no good at math" is engaging in self-limiting behavior. A self-aware person makes conscious choices about what to do about simple facts: "I weigh 240 pounds, and because I want to live a long, energetic life (fulfilling a personal imperative), I will start exercising." A self-sabotaging person will see the facts, may even see what needs to be done, but will go no further.

Midlife presents you with a gift: the virtual end of self-consciousness. Any of us can use this gift to pursue wisdom. All we have to do to become wiser is to listen to our own internal rhythms and use them in our daily lives. Sounds simple, right? But anyone who has tried it knows that it is constant work. Wisdom is not a goal but a process. Here's a Self-Renewal Practice designed to help you become self-aware. If you do this practice every day for a week, you should make surprising discoveries that can improve your life on several levels.

SELF-RENEWAL PRACTICE

Learn How You Learn

1. *Ask yourself: What have I learned today?*
   Be specific. Think about your day with an eye toward what you accomplished, what you thought, and what you said. Recall any new skill, knowledge, or understanding you acquired. Did you learn a new recipe? Discover something you never knew about a friend? Say something particularly interesting?

   Don't focus on the mundane; zero in on events that fascinate, intrigue, or delight you.

2. *Reflect on: How did I learn what I learned?*

This is not a trick question. You learn in different ways and on multiple levels, often simultaneously. For example:

- Did you learn by listening or reading?
- Did you learn by comparing and categorizing?
- Did you learn by feeling or imagining?
- Did you learn by expressing yourself in writing, conversation, painting, music?
- Did you learn by imitating someone else?

The main point here is to find out how you tend to learn best and most naturally.

3. *Imagine: How can I increase the use of this type of learning in my everyday life?*

If you found that you enjoyed learning through expression, what other ways can you imagine expressing yourself? Could you keep a journal? Write a song? Make sure you have a heart-to-heart with a friend on a more regular basis? If you like to learn through listening or reading, consider expanding your reading to other areas. Perhaps you learn a lot about life through poetry, or could benefit from reading work-related books and magazines.

4. *Commit to actions that will help you capitalize on the ways you learn best.*

Take steps to put yourself in situations where you tend to learn best. If you learn best by categorizing, make a conscious effort to categorize more often, even in areas that wouldn't seem to call for it. Let your mind go; categorize people, places, and things. See if this helps you make new connections, new discoveries. If you learn well when you allow yourself to feel, let your emotions be your teacher. Listen to your fear, anxiety, joy, or love feelings.

———————————

You might find it helpful to see how I used this Self-Renewal Practice to understand more about myself:

1. Today, while working on my book, I learned a brand-new way to relate anecdotes. This new skill brings freshness to my writing. I feel a strong sense of accomplishment, especially since I know I will be able to use this skill in many aspects of my work.

2. I found that imitating my writing coach dramatically improved my description of case examples. The way my coach did it seemed so simple, and I found that doing it "her way" was actually faster than trying to do it "my way."

3. I can:
   - make more of an effort to notice how experts do what they do.
   - ask for more coaching in areas where I want to make improvement, and not be embarrassed about it.
   - stop thinking of imitation as an illegitimate form of learning; I know from my research that it is one of the most valuable and effective ways to learn.
   - remind myself that anyone can be my coach or teacher. I've learned a lot already from watching Grady make keynote presentations and Dad make stock buys.

4. I will read more. I know that reading the work of good writers can help my own writing. I will look for coaches in all situations (watching TV, talking to children) and not just the ones I'm used to (fitness training, art class). I will sign up for a course in selling to large accounts.

You'll have new insights into your most effective learning styles each time you do this exercise. Many of my clients laugh with recognition when I tell them that the other name for this practice is "Learning All Day Long."

Aging Intelligence
What happens to intellectual performance as we age? Depict your version of aging intelligence by reproducing the graph on page 53 in your journal and drawing a line that shows your estimate of intelligence level over time. If you can't relate to lines on a graph,

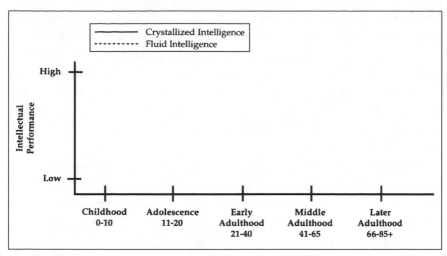

Intellectual performance as we age

write several sentences in your journal describing your view of how intelligence changes with age.

Most people expect intellectual performance to be on a steady *incline* until the stage of middle adulthood; they presume some degree of *decline* after that. They are surprised to learn that intellectual performance after early adolescence is virtually impossible to predict, because it depends more on how the mind is used than anything else. The fact is, those of us over forty *can actually expand our intellect as we age*.

Many of the improvements in intellectual performance during midlife are made possible by advances that take place in our brain physiology as we mature beyond age forty. As it turns out, our ability to learn new information, solve problems, and remember things depends on the *connection between* our brain cells, not the number of brain cells we have. Although we do lose some brain cells over time, the cells that remain amply compensate for this by growing more interconnections, or neurons. *We actually grow more brain tissue and increase the number of neural connections as we age.* Research shows that active individuals over the age of eighty have many more neural interconnections than fifty-year-olds.

As you may remember from high school biology class, brain cells are independent of one another; no two ever touch physically. Instead, they form integrated networks by reaching toward each other across a gap, or synapse, via branching filaments called dendrites (the word "dendrite" derives from the Greek word for tree). Current estimates indicate that the average person grows three million millimeters of dendrites per year during middle and later life. Only after age ninety does our capacity to multiply our neural connections begin to diminish.

To put this information in perspective, the average adult is blessed with a hundred billion neurons that produce more interconnections than the number of stars in the universe. A typical neuron can make ten thousand interconnections with other cells, yielding over ten trillion synapses (the gap between one nerve fiber and another). From birth to old age, we are biologically equipped to take in one thousand independent units of information per second, but most people use only a minuscule percentage of their capacity. So you see, it is not our brainpower that fails us as we age, it is our *expectation* of declining intellectual performance that lets us down. Even people who know better persist in the belief that mental performance declines with age. I still operate out of this mode myself sometimes. Just yesterday, I was riding down a department-store escalator when a woman in her late seventies spoke to me.

"Pardon me, young lady"—I was thrilled at the adjective— "which way do I go to get out of the store?"

I smiled and motioned to the level above us.

"Oh no, I'm going the wrong way!" she exclaimed. "It's terrible to be old. I thought that since everybody was getting on this escalator, it must be the way out."

Feeling compassion for her frustration, I thought to myself, she's right. Getting older must be disheartening sometimes. In that instant, however, it dawned on me that I, too, had found it difficult to navigate my way through the store's maze of aisles, entrances, and exits. I turned to the woman and blurted out my confession. "It's not your age that's confusing you, it's the layout of this store."

Once the truth was out, both of us were relieved. With the gratitude of a lost child found, she looked at me and said, "Thank goodness I asked you for help. You have been so kind."

I walked away feeling somewhat guilty for having presumed at the start of the conversation that I was dealing with a mentally limited older adult. If I had been more mindful, I would have realized sooner that this seventy-plus adult was actually quite mentally alert. She had attempted to solve the riddle of how to exit the store by following a large group of moving people. Not a bad strategy. Then, to further resolve her uncertainty, she had queried me.

Both of these thoughtful problem-solving approaches indicate sound performance in what psychologists term *crystallized* or *pragmatic intelligence*. *Crystallized intelligence* refers to how well we solve practical problems in everyday life and how well we reason through interpersonal dilemmas involving strong emotional content. To use crystallized intelligence, we depend on our storehouse of facts, as well as our verbal comprehension, word fluency, and numerical abilities.

This practical yet complex aspect of human intelligence either remains stable through life or continues to grow as we age. Making it grow involves nothing more than staying mentally challenged. I find it helpful to compare crystallized intelligence to computer software. A person acquires pragmatic intelligence by living; thus, your crystallized intelligence is programmed by your experience.

The other major type of intellectual performance—the one that scientists try to measure through traditional IQ tests—has been called *fluid intelligence*. If crystallized intelligence is like computer software, think of fluid intelligence as computer hardware. Fluid intelligence is responsible for the mechanics of how your mind works. Memory capacity, the speed with which we process new information and recall facts and experiences, and the rate at which we acquire skills and form new concepts are measures of fluid intelligence. In my escalator encounter, fluid intelligence would have helped the woman *remember* how to get out of the department store, crystallized intelligence is what she actually drew upon to *solve* her dilemma.

In Chapter 1, I asked you to consider both the *know-how* and the *know-why* when doing Self-Renewal Practices. It might be helpful for you to think of fluid intelligence as the basis for know-how (operational learning) and crystallized intelligence as the basis for

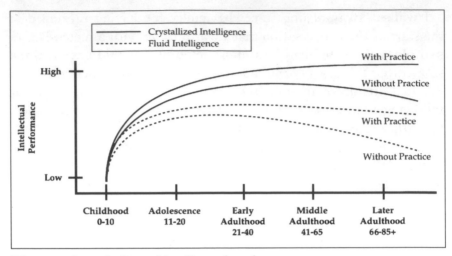

The growth or decline of intellectual performance as we age

know-why (conceptual learning). Like the two types of learning, fluid and crystallized intelligence work in tandem, one building off the other.

Nearly fifteen years of cognitive research investigating the effects of aging on intelligence shows that without specialized training, the mechanical operations of fluid intelligence do begin to decline at about age thirty. Nonetheless, we now have substantial evidence that if you are willing to put forth the effort, you can improve the functioning of your intellectual "hardware" by engaging in relatively brief training. The gains you reap in fluid intelligence after training are roughly equal to what you would lose between the age of sixty and eighty if you did not practice.

The results of recent studies demonstrating the benefits of being mentally challenged are mapped out on the graph above.

Without mental challenges, crystallized intelligence plateaus before midlife and remains relatively unchanged thereafter. Fluid intelligence declines progressively after midlife without the right kind of practice. But, as the graph also shows, there is a good chance of preventing losses in fluid intelligence and actually improving your crystallized intelligence if you properly stimulate those two types of mental operations.

The way to stimulate crystallized intelligence and sustain fluid intelligence is through learning. You can raise your crystallized intelligence quotient by tackling ever more complex problems in your profession, or by becoming an avid bridge or chess player. Challenges such as these require you to reconcile contradictory evidence, deal with uncertainty, revise earlier decisions, and simplify complexity without becoming too rigid. Continuous improvement in this aspect of your intelligence typically results in strong emotional and interpersonal mastery.

If you wish to prevent declines in fluid intelligence, you need different tactics. Your fluid intelligence stays in shape when you practice memory-enhancement techniques and information-processing strategies. For example, memorizing lines of poetry or the names of flora and fauna give your powers of inputting and recalling information a good workout. Learning more about subjects that interest you, with an emphasis on absorbing greater quantities of information at a growing pace, is a sure way to strengthen your fluid intelligence. (We'll talk more about exercising your memory in the next section.)

When you make strides in crystallized intelligence, you automatically offset declines in fluid intelligence. This happens because pragmatic knowledge is such a powerful modulator of the mind. The facts and procedures that you know (crystallized intelligence) determine what can be accomplished with a given set of mechanics (fluid intelligence). Thus, if your mechanics are a bit rusty, but you know a great deal, you will outperform someone who may have newer cognitive "hardware" but is lacking the sophisticated "software" to get the job done.

A good example of how crystallized intelligence can compensate for the leveling-off of fluid intelligence was demonstrated in a psychology experiment that compared performance of good typists, younger and older. When people type, their "tapping speed" is governed by the operations of fluid intelligence: tapping speed is, in general, significantly slower in older typists than in younger ones. Surprisingly, however, this study revealed no difference at all in *overall* typing performance between the younger and older typists. How could this be?

Researchers concluded that the older typists made up for what they had lost in tapping speed by reading farther ahead in the text to be typed than did younger typists. This improved the older typists' performances because they were able to maintain a more consistent speed, pause fewer times, and make fewer mistakes than their younger counterparts.

Reading farther ahead in the text is a prime example of how having more advanced strategies for task completion (a function of crystallized intelligence) can help us overcome any age-related deficit in cognitive mechanics (which depends on fluid intelligence).

Crystallized intelligence helps level the playing field in practically any endeavor. Imagine that you are a novice tennis player, nineteen years old, a quick learner, and in excellent shape. Your opponent is a slightly overweight forty-nine-year-old. She has been practicing tennis almost daily for the last ten years and is a self-confident but slow-moving player. You lose the match, shocked that a person more than twice your age could have beaten you. It seems you could outrun her, outlast her, but not outsmart her. Your more experienced opponent's game strategies helped her compensate for whatever she might have lacked in terms of agility, speed, or endurance.

Playing chess, working puzzles, and solving complex "brain teasers" are especially good ways to activate and expand your crystallized intelligence. Try the Self-Renewal Practice that follows and give your mind a healthy workout as it attempts to crystallize the elements of the puzzle and solve the problem.

SELF-RENEWAL PRACTICE

Polishing Your Crystal

Polish those brilliant crystals of your intelligence by solving these conceptual puzzles. You may find these brain teasers familiar or brand new. One thing is for sure: puzzles have been helping us enhance our brilliance since humans first acquired a reasoning mind. Scientists believe that the first puzzles are at least four thousand years old. Solutions to the puzzles are given at the end of this practice.

Puzzle #1
Write an English word (spelled correctly) that allows you to move from the first to last word by changing only one letter at a time.

Example:	**BOOK**		**BOOK**
	_ _ _ _		<u>C</u>OOK
	_ _ _ _		CO<u>R</u>K
	_ _ _ _		COR<u>E</u>
	CARE		**<u>C</u>ARE**

Test:	**FAIL**
	_ _ _ _
	_ _ _ _
	_ _ _ _
	PASS

Puzzle #2
Rearrange these six matches to make "nothing." No matches may be bent, broken, or placed over one another.

Puzzle #3

Each snowflake shape in the boxes has a numerical value. The sum of each line and column has been given for all but one line. Fill in the missing sum.

❋	❋	❋	❋	?
❋	✳	❋	✳	85
❋	❋	❋	❋	87
✳	❋	❋	❋	82
87	86	93	79	

SOLUTIONS

These puzzles are excerpted with permission from *The Mensa Genius Quiz-a-Day Book* (Reading, Mass.: Addison-Wesley, 1989). Author Dr. Abbie Salny provides us with solutions and the percentage of Mensa readers who were able to solve the puzzles accurately.

Puzzle #1

FAIL, PAIL, PALL, PALS, PASS
(There are several alternatives. 100 percent of Mensa members found one that worked.)

Puzzle #2

Two answers:

(20 percent of Mensa respondents chose one of these answers.)

Puzzle #3
The total for the top row of snowflakes is 91. (Only 48 percent of the Mensa respondents were able to solve this puzzle.)

Most people experience a rush of pleasure the moment a puzzle solution comes to them. Maybe that's why puzzles have been a part of our lives for so long: they intrigue us and simultaneously give our weary brains a rest from solving far more serious riddles. In the course of his research, author and puzzle archaeologist Dominic Olivastro has come to believe we invent and solve puzzles for the sheer joy of it, just as we ride a roller coaster at breakneck speed for the thrill of the experience. Not only is working out the answer to a difficult puzzle emotionally rewarding but it also keeps our mental muscles in tone for tackling more practical challenges.

Any endeavor that requires you to see patterns, make connections, organize or eliminate material, and make judgments will help you increase your crystallized intelligence. If you enjoyed this Self-Renewal Practice, you might decide to subscribe to a games magazine or buy books of brain teasers. Learning a new language, reading in practically any area, and participating in team sports—anything that involves synthesis or strategy—are other good ways to develop your brain synapses. More practical crystal polishers such as these may have the added advantage of saving your sanity in the process!

Memories Are Made of This

The Greeks personified memory as Mnemosyne, the mother of the nine muses, and exalted her for giving birth to all of the arts and sciences. In fact, memory is humankind's oldest, most fundamental mental skill. Without memory, crucial survival skills—how to find food, how to stay warm, how to avoid predators—would have to be developed anew each time the need arose. Scientists know that animals possess a kind of "instinctual" or species memory that takes the place of speech; baby birds call upon their species memory to "remember" how to fly, though they have never flown before. Memory is also the basis of conceptual breakthroughs. It is responsible for logging the crucial experiences during infancy that allow human babies to separate the world into the categories of "me" and "not me," which in turn allows them to form their initial concepts of objects and their relationships to them. As the memory expands, so does intellectual capacity.

Ancient sages encouraged memorizing to help people increase their mental capacity. Though they probably lacked a model similar to our fluid and crystallized intelligence paradigm, they understood that exercising one part of the brain helped the entire organ. Furthermore, before the invention of written notation systems, *all* knowledge had to be memorized, then handed down from person to person. In most cultures, storytellers had the primary responsibility for remembering and relating all the group's history, myths, and rituals; many were charged with storing immense amounts of material. For that reason, the ancients not only revered memory but came up with powerful memory aids that allowed for prodigious memory storage.

According to psychologist and author Jean Houston, the famous rhetorician Cicero recommended one particularly effective memory technique. In her book *The Possible Human*, Houston reports that Cicero encouraged speechmakers to create visual associations for each part of a speech by walking through the rooms of a building as they memorized. The memorizer would practice the first section of his speech in one room, then move on to other rooms for subsequent sections. Furthermore, he would focus on specific objects within each room—art, furniture, ornamentation—and assign each a smaller part of the narrative. In this way, the speechmaker could then recall the details of his talk simply by walking from room to room in his mind's eye and recalling the cues he had previously "planted" there. Houston explains that the phrases "in the first place," "in the second place," and so on are holdovers from this technique of classical speechmaking.

Interestingly, these feats of memory were as accessible to the older members of a community as to the younger ones. Houston tells the story of the rhetorician Seneca, who "could repeat two thousand names in the order they were given. Upon listening to a class of over two hundred students, each in turn speaking a line of poetry, he could recite all the lines in reverse order. . . ."

Of course, the creation and wide dispersal of paper and books decreased the need for such prodigious memories. With our Filofaxes, computers, libraries, postal systems, and telephone lines, we have less need to memorize than any past generation.

When you complain that you can't find your keys, you are, in part, mourning the loss of an important cultural skill. And because memory is a function of fluid intelligence (which we know can decline with age), it needs more attention at midlife than during your teens. Scientific research confirms that our ability to remember can become and remain exceptional as we grow older, provided we are healthy and continue using our memories. This thinking flatly contradicts our cultural insistence that memory is the first thing to go and that there is nothing we can do about it.

To understand how well memory can function at midlife, you have to change the way you view memory. We usually think of memories as fragments of information and experience stored away in boxes and trunks in a kind of neurological attic. Some boxes are right up front, easy to find and rummage through. Other memories were packed away long ago in trunks that have rusted over the years and are now difficult to open.

This metaphor for memory seems logical, but it is far from accurate. Memory scientists today are revolutionizing our beliefs about the way we make, store, and retrieve memories. In his book *Neural Darwinism*, Gerald Edelman, who won the Nobel Prize for his discovery of the antibody molecule in 1972, offers us a new way of understanding the mechanism for memory. He proposes that at the most basic, physiological level, memory is a creative process, not a static accumulation of remembrances. His work reveals that as we experience what happens to us, individual neurons interact with one another in a particular pattern. Thus, memory-making and memory retrieval depend on teams of neurons acquiring new habits of communicating with one another.

Other research extends the notion of the cell as the transmitter of memory signals. In his recent book *Ageless Body, Timeless Mind*, Deepak Chopra reports that transplant patients who have received a donated kidney, liver, or heart often begin to "participate" in the donor's memories.

In one instance, a woman woke up after a heart transplant craving beer and Chicken McNuggets; she was very surprised, because she had never before wanted either. After she began to have mysterious dreams in which a young man Timmy came to her, she tracked down the donor of her new heart, which had come from the victim of a fatal traffic accident; when she contacted his family, it turned out that the victim was a young man named Timmy. The woman was stunned to discover that he'd had a particular fondness for drinking beer and had been killed on his way home from McDonald's.

Rather than seeking a supernatural explanation for such incidents, one could see them as confirmation that our bodies are made of experiences transformed into physical expression. Because experience is something we incorporate (literally, "make into a body"), our cells have been instilled with our memories; thus, to receive someone else's cells is to receive their memories at the same time.

Although the exact mechanisms of memory remain a mystery, the experience of the ancients and the exciting new research in the field suggest that memory is anything but static. And if it is true, as I now believe, that memory is a process, it follows that humans should be able to enjoy storing and recalling memories *throughout* their lives. So don't make the mistake of thinking that a few years' worth of misplaced car keys and forgotten names at cocktail parties condemn you to some sort of inevitable post-forty dementia.

In order to keep our memories functioning at peak levels in midlife and beyond, we need first to acknowledge that recalling our memories may occur more slowly than in youth. Scientists tell us that after the age of about thirty, it takes longer for our brains to complete the neural dance required to bring memories into the forefront of our minds. This decline in retrieval speed applies even to well-memorized subjects, and is due to the fact that overall thought speed (a function of fluid intelligence) slows somewhat as we age. Fortunately, this reduction is barely noticeable in the course of everyday living; thought speed diminishes on the order of a few milliseconds to a few seconds, depending on how old we are. All this means is that your memory will be a tad slower in certain situations, not that it isn't in top working order. In other words, memory *retrieval* isn't the problem.

What is the problem, scientists tell us, is the way we *store* our memories. According to recent research, what appear to be memory deficits during midlife are really input problems in disguise.

Input problems occur during midlife due to several factors. Some people face fewer requirements for memorizing after formal schooling or job training demands slow down, so they are simply out of practice. Too, almost everyone complains about information overload during midlife: there is so much to remember, and so little time. Moving through your schedule on fast forward causes mindlessness (discussed earlier in this chapter), which interferes with your ability to store memories.

So how do we learn to store memories effectively? To put it simply, you have to care about what you want to remember. I recently met a woman who drove this point home to me in the most wonderful way. I was attending a benefit dinner, which included a lecture on Tolstoy's novella *The Kreutzer Sonata*. I was seated across the table from a woman in her early fifties who turned out to be a memory master. After the lecture, as everyone at our table was discussing Tolstoy and his work, I listened with awe and envy as my dinner partner recited fact after fact about Tolstoy's wife, Sophie.

"If you don't know Sophie, my dear, you don't know Tolstoy," she whispered to me. Then she went on to say out loud, "Sophie bore Tolstoy thirteen children, managed his aristocratic social affairs, and spent five hours every night transcribing his writings. She was his word processor! Without her, we would not have Tolstoy."

Our table was mesmerized as this scholar continued. "But Sophie was no doormat. She tolerated Tolstoy's indignities, his insatiable demands and cruelties, because she *chose* to be married to a genius. Many women do that, you know. I personally would never tolerate such abuses simply so I could be married to a genius."

Stunned by this woman's intimate knowledge of Tolstoy's wife, I asked, "What prompted you to learn so much about Sophie? Is literature a big part of your career? Are you a professor?"

"Oh, no," she answered. "I am just a perpetual student, and I love Tolstoy. I've read everything he's published, even his diaries. I read and memorize all I can get my hands on that is written about him; I take every course, talk to every expert I can find. My search to know Sophie began during college after I read *War and Peace*. You should go back and reread *War and Peace* if you haven't done so recently. Read it every two years or so. It will speak to you more profoundly every time."

People who delve into the details of whatever ignites their passion will always impress others with their mental vitality, just as my dinner partner did. Whether your mental passion be sports or art, music or the Civil War, poetry, fiction, or Greek mythology, this would be a good time for you to decide what subjects will make up your menu of memorable mental delights.

Unfortunately, we also have to remember all sorts of things we just don't give a fig about. For example, you may be highly motivated to learn how to program the VCR, but the 1-2-3 of figuring it out puts you to sleep. The good news is that researchers have come up with all sorts of ways you can trick your mind into caring. Try the following Self-Renewal Practice, a variation on a popular party game, and see if you can't teach your brain to care about something completely mundane!

SELF-RENEWAL PRACTICE

The Magic of Memory

Memory Challenge #1
Read *all* of the directions before you begin.

Pages 67 and 68 contain pictures of two trays of several common objects. Scan the objects on Tray #1 for sixty seconds with the goal of committing to memory as many objects as possible. (Set a digital watch or kitchen timer to ring when the allotted time has lapsed.) I'm not going to give you any tips for improving your memory this round. Just flow with the strategies that come most naturally.

Immediately after the time is up, turn to a blank page in your journal and give yourself sixty seconds to list the items you can recall, either in words or pictures. When you have finished testing

Tray #1

your recall, look back at Tray #1 and note how many objects you remembered correctly.

Memory Challenge #2

Turn to the next page of your journal. Read all of the instructions before beginning this exercise.

This time, follow the same process as in Challenge #1, but examine Tray #2 and use the following memory improvement technique. In your imagination, group the objects so they relate to each other in some way and create a story—the more outlandish the better. For example, if you see a bee, apple, airplane, screen door, paint can, shovel, top hat, napkin, and trumpet, you could imagine that the bee in the picture is wearing a top hat while flying an airplane that contains an apple as its cargo! Then you could picture the plane dive-bombing its way through a screen door and crashing into a can of paint that is leaning against a shovel. In the final scene, you might

Tray #2

imagine the bee jumping out of the plane, wiping the paint off his face with the napkin, and blowing the trumpet in victory.

As soon as you have invented your outrageous mental movie (within the sixty-second time limit), turn back to your blank page and list the items you are able to recall from Tray #2. Give yourself sixty seconds to complete your recall. Then look back at Tray #2 and count the number of objects you remembered correctly. How many did you recall this time?

If you are like most people, your recall improved in the second memory challenge.

The memorizing technique I gave you in your second game combines several of the enhancement techniques memory experts recommend: association (linking something new to something familiar), establishing patterns (the story line), visualizing (creating a mental picture and retracing the steps), and emotional content (the humorous aspect of the scenario). Other valid ways to aid memorization include using acronyms or mnemonics to help you remember lists of information or items; students memorizing a string of facts, dates, or parts of the body find these methods effective. Equally effective is using rhythm. The next time you call information for a phone number, improve your odds of recalling the right sequence of numbers by singing the numbers back to yourself to the tune of "Mary Had a Little Lamb."

Memory storage exercises can easily be applied to everyday living. The Self-Renewal Practice that follows can help you stop forgetting things by helping improve your input.

SELF-RENEWAL PRACTICE

Preventing Forgetting

1. Select one memory problem that is most bothersome (name, keys, procedures, whatever) and zero in on improving your memory track record for that target subject for a period of one week.

2. Carve out extra time when encountering the target problem. In the case of learning how to remember names, repeat the name of the person as often as you can in your conversation with him or her. If you are formally introduced, pay close attention to the *sound* of the voice of the person who introduces you. Finally, look at one single feature of the person's face as you say his or her name. (The facial feature you select and the sound of the introducer's voice become *auditory and visual cues* to help you trigger the name when you want to recall it later.)

   In the case of objects such as car keys, pay close attention to the color, size, shape, and other features of the location in which you place them. Another crucial detail to register is your emotional state at the time. (Are you feeling worried, excited, sad, joyful, timid, embarrassed?) The more *details of the context* you note at the moment of inputting a memory, the more easily you will recall the name or location of an object. Some people try to notice other sensory characteristics of the setting, such as pleasant or unpleasant odors (scientists tell us that olfactory memories are the most evocative) or physical movements made by anyone or anything present.

When you must remember a sequence of items such as instructions or a grocery list, give each item or step an alphabetical tag (A for "apple," R for "Remove widget") and make up an acronym for the list: Apple, Pear, Banana would be APB. If you can, give these letters a further meaning: All-Points Bulletin? Ate Poor Buttons? The more meaning you give the letters, the more likely you are to remember them. This memory device is called mnemonics.

3. Test your input before you actually need the information. A few minutes after you input the information, see if you can recall it. Visualize the scene, relive your mood, and repeat the name of the person or location. Use your mnemonics.

4. When it is time to recall the name or object, be sure to relax. Closing your eyes and taking a deep breath first helps set the stage. Once relaxed, mentally put yourself in the place and time of the memory "storage." Visualize the details of the surroundings. Recapture the sounds of the voices of anyone speaking. Recall the emotions you experienced while meeting the person or while finding a place for your keys or other objects.

The more vividly you reconstruct the context within which the subject of your recall took place, the faster you will be able to remember what it is you stored.

Most people find the effort of committing names and location of objects to memory worthwhile, especially if recalling certain information—such as a person's name—is vital to their success. *Slowing your mind down long enough* to link the subject to your emotions and the sensory details of the context is the main ingredient of effective recall.

Of course, there are other ways to ensure that you are able to locate your keys when you need them. Memory experts suggest relying on *organizational* skills to head off forgetfulness stemming from overload. Regularly place keys, purses, and other household items in one location so that you get in the habit of finding them there. Memory joggers such as timers, Post-it reminders, appointment calendars, and the like can free you to concentrate on more important matters.

Because memory loss is one of the biggest worries of those of us at a "certain age," I'd like to share one more Self-Renewal Practice. This one will help you retrieve personal memories. Beyond the fact that it is beneficial to our emotional well-being to keep these memories in our conscious minds, retrieving memories that are difficult to recall has been shown to sharpen overall memory skills.

SELF-RENEWAL PRACTICE

Personal Remembering

1. Each day for the next ten days, set aside ten minutes for practicing the art of personal remembering. You can write your remembrances in your journal or speak them into a tape recorder.

   Begin each practice session by writing or saying the phrase "I remember . . ." Create a sentence out of that stem, using anything that comes to mind. When you have finished relating a particular memory, repeat the phrase "I remember . . ." and begin again.

2. Keeping to a ten-minute limit provides a sense of energy and focus. Some people like to set a gentle-sounding timer for ten minutes; others check their watches periodically.

   Do not censor your thoughts. Allow your mind to travel many years back in time, or only a few moments into the past. If you come upon painful memories, don't worry. You will only recall what you are capable of handling. If by some small chance you do trigger frightening flashbacks of memories that haunt you and disrupt your sleep or daily activities, be sure to seek professional help. This is your mind's way of telling you it is time to heal some long-forgotten wound.

   If you are writing your responses, keep your pen moving at all times. The pen-on-page contact will help your thoughts run more smoothly. If you are speaking, try to keep talking even if you feel you have "nothing to say." Just keep going for the entire ten-minute period. It doesn't matter if the memories seem disjointed.

3. When your ten minutes are up, read the memories aloud or play the audio tape. See if there are patterns to your memories. Have you recalled events, people, places, feelings that are related to one another? How do these remembrances expand the entries on your Life Map? (See Chapter 1.)

Is there a way for you to benefit from these memories in the present moment? For example, can you use what you recalled to appreciate your good fortune, deepen your love for someone, or forgive yourself or someone else? Remembered experiences can enrich our daily lives by putting us more in touch with what really matters to us and what makes us tick. Remembering hurtful moments makes us more compassionate toward ourselves, less likely to be controlled by the sadness, fear, and anger that might surround the memories. We can use memory as an active, constructive process, one that can take the remains of yesterday and with a more mature approach turn it into fertilizer for a better adult life.

After you are comfortable with this Self-Renewal Practice, you may want to try it with a partner. The memories of one person can prod the memories of another. The exercise will not work, however, unless both participants listen well and allow the dialogue to flow naturally. Here is an example of my doing this exercise with my husband, Grady:

Kathy: "I remember roller skating on the hard concrete slabs behind our school building for hours. I never wanted those afternoons to end."

Grady: "I remember riding my bike downhill into town without holding on to the handlebars. Sometimes I ate a Milky Way at the same time."

Kathy: "I remember playing dolls and arranging everything in my room for a tea party and my brother Dan throwing all of my carefully placed dishes and cups on the floor. With a snide smile, he would taunt me, take hold of the table legs, and flip over the entire setting."

Grady: "I remember the Christmas I was seven when David got a brand-new bicycle and there wasn't any money left to buy me one. My mother told me I could have David's bike once he outgrew it."

Kathy: "I remember sailing on the Intracoastal Waterway in Florida with a man I was dating. He built the boat and taught me how to sail, but I've never felt so alone in my life as I did on that occasion."

Grady: "I remember being married to my first wife and feeling alone for nineteen years."

You can see how Grady's and my memories built on one another. What started out as innocent childhood recollections grew into memories of more emotionally charged events and ended up with remembering times of painful loneliness. This pattern of moving from rather neutral memories to more intense memories, stored at a deeper lever of consciousness, frequently occurs when you do this Self-Renewal Practice.

I hope you will invent some of your own ways to extend your powers of remembering. Developing your memory sustains the capacity of your fluid intelligence in much the same way that cardio-vascular exercise sustains your heart. When practicing ways of improving memory input and retrieval, you set off a kind of Fourth of July explosion of electrically charged chemicals in your brain, helping to stimulate neural pathways to grow more branches. Why not be among those in midlife who choose to use rather than lose the most basic mental gift of all?

Sculpted Creativity

I can hear what you're thinking right now: "I'll buy the idea that I can improve my memory skills and that I can become more mindful.

I'll even admit that you make a convincing case for increasing my intelligence. But *creativity*? No way. I'm just not very creative. Now my sister, *she's* creative. You should see what she does with a blob of clay!"

If you're thinking thoughts like these, turn them off for a second. You *are* creative and can be more so; it may simply be that you don't know it yet. It may also be that you don't quite understand what creativity is.

Creating is not the same thing as making (though the two words are often used synonymously). A painting that I execute from ideas in my own head is indeed a creation; a paint-by-number landscape that I complete is not. Both may be considered art, but only the former is creative. The same thing goes for cooking. Any good cook can follow a recipe, but only a creative cook can find imaginative ways to combine tastes and textures.

Or perhaps you have fallen into the trap of viewing creativity as synonymous with art. The same mental processes that support a painter's creative efforts also allow the creative salesperson to come up with new sales stategies and the creative doctor to try new remedies. There is no endeavor that can't benefit from a creative approach.

Remember Walter, the executive I told you about in the beginning of the chapter? He came to me for help because he was "out of ideas." He felt that his brain was empty. What stymied Walter turns out to be a common mental mistake in midlife: he relied too much on his powers of analytical thinking and relied too little on his creative imagination to achieve his business goals.

When we problem-solve using analytical thought, we size up a situation, take it apart, and try to fix whatever is broken. Creativity, unlike logic, thrives when we approach a problem with no preconceived ideas about what will or will not work. We become creative by temporarily letting go of logic, suspending judgment, discarding any assumptions we may have about the problem or its solution. If we can open our minds to new or unusual ideas, we can experience synchronicity: the seemingly coincidental coming together of meaningful events. (According to psychologist Carl Jung, it would be synchronistic for you to walk into the library, pick a book at random, and find that it contains a poem you have been trying to locate since high school.) It is only when we step out of the realm of 2 + 2 = 4 and step into the land of uncertainty and surprise that creativity can flourish.

In a classic experiment on creativity, children were given a conventional IQ test and another test to measure creativity. The children who scored best on the IQ component tended to be from families with higher educational status and greater degrees of class consciousness. They were also more motivated by financial concerns. In contrast, the children who scored best on the measures of creativity tended to live in families that were less class-conscious and less concerned with finances. Thus, even in school-age children, intelligence (the capacity to learn) is linked to conformity, while creativity (the capacity to conjure up something new or unique) is linked to nonconformity.

By the time we reach midlife, most of us have adopted the concerns of conformity: we have well-developed powers of reason and timid, undernourished powers of imagination. We make it even more difficult on ourselves when we believe that creativity is a gift reserved for a chosen few.

The fact is, anytime you express yourself in a unique way, you are being creative. Take a moment right now to learn what I mean. Find a sheet of paper and a ball-point pen. Write your name as you would if you were signing a letter to a friend. Now write your name so that it fills up the entire page. Though you had no "intent" to "create," you have just done something no one else in the world can do—express you. The visual effect of what you have done can be copied (forged), but a forgery will never be the true expression of who you are. Handwriting experts—graphologists—can actually tell from handwriting if someone is sick or well, happy or sad, lying or telling the truth. Signatures, and handwriting in general, reveal an immense amount about the "artist."

Now turn your large signature upside down, and look at the figure before you as you would a piece of art. Do you see loops? peaks? daggers? What would you say about this piece of art if you saw it hanging in a museum? What feelings does it evoke?

When you sign your name, you are being creative. After you've mastered cursive and have practiced for a few years, it is something you perform without much thought. The fact that you don't think about it much may be one of the reasons it is such a powerful expression of you: you don't censor it or think to yourself that you can't do it. In most other areas of your life, however, you will probably have to work at getting the conditions right if you want to enjoy a similar degree of self-expression. For example, I have been painting since I was five years old. Born with good hand-eye coordination and manual dexterity, as well as a visually oriented mind, I have always found it relatively easy to draw pictures of houses, trees, and people. Visual beauty drew my attention, and I attempted to honor it by reproducing it in crayons, paint, and pencil.

Until recently, my artistic endeavors were largely exercises in improving my skills at blending colors, drawing lines and shapes, and reproducing images. There's nothing wrong with honing my craft, of course, but the craft of painting is only one dimension of being an artist. In order for me to achieve creative moments while painting, I must digest whatever I see and transform it through my own being *before* applying the paint to the canvas.

There is no getting around the fact that creativity is an "inside-out" phenomenon. The earlier works of Pablo Picasso show him to have been a wonderfully skilled representational artist; it is only when he began to convey his feelings about his subjects—his own vision—that he became a ground-breaking artist. As he himself put it, "Art is a lie that helps us know the truth."

Another interesting lesson we can learn from Picasso is that, like any good artist, he didn't sit around and wait for inspiration to strike. He honed his craft, did everything he could to create an environment in which creativity could flourish. That's exciting because it proves that one can "nudge" creativity along.

Compare Picasso to someone like Mozart who, it would seem, sprang from the womb quill in hand, writing some of the most inspired music ever heard. The youthful Mozart apparently heard complete compositions in his head before ever writing them down. Mozart described his early creative episodes this way:

All this fires my soul, and, provided I am not disturbed, my subject enlarges itself, becomes methodized and defined, and the whole, though it be long, stands almost complete and finished in my mind, so that I can survey it, like a fine picture or a beautiful statue, at a glance. Nor do I hear in my imagination the parts successively, but I hear them, as it were, all at once. What a delight this is I cannot tell! All this inventing, this producing, takes place in a pleasing, lively dream.

If historians are correct, Mozart's creative genius continued to flow despite his ill health and concerns about money; he was able to create even in the absence of the conditions most of us would consider basic for survival.

If you have never done much to encourage creativity and find yourself blessed with it anyway, you have had an experience of what French psychologist Elliot Jacques terms *hot-from-the-fire creativity*. Hot-from-the-fire creative acts are more common in young adulthood (ages eighteen to thirty-five) than they are in midlife, and few individuals find this type of explosive genius easy to come by. However, the marvelous inspirations of *sculpted creativity* can be accessible to almost everyone.

Sculpted creativity emerges through attention and practice, even in people who have never had flashes of hot-from-the-fire creativity. And because sculpted creativity requires you to set up the right conditions—to "do your homework" before you invite it in, so to speak—it is yet another mental skill that is more readily available to us at midlife than at any time in our lives up until then.

Consider the cases of two individuals whose creativity began to bloom after age forty:

Author Isaac Asimov wrote an astonishing number of books during his career—over three hundred. What is truly encouraging to us in this context is the fact that he published the vast majority of his work after his fortieth birthday.

Jane Addams, well-known and much-admired woman of her time (1860–1935), distinguished herself as a midlife mental master by publishing her most notable work, *Democracy and Social Ethics*, at age forty-one. She published her classic treatise on poverty at forty-nine, ran for president when she was fifty-one, and was awarded the Nobel Peace Prize a few years before she died.

And then there's the old saw about Thomas Edison trying a thousand different times to get the light bulb to light up before he finally found what worked, and his "1 percent inspiration, 99 percent perspiration" maxim for success. Most of us do have to perspire before we experience a breakthrough.

Fortunately, you don't have to sweat aimlessly. I've noticed in my work (and studies support my contention) that there are several specific ways you can encourage sculpted creativity:

1. Bone up on the basics.
2. Find a vision.
3. Change your mind-set.
4. Have confidence in the process.

Boning up on the basics is the easiest of the four. Learn the facts, practice the technique, use your analytical mind as much as you can to get you ready for your breakthrough. Use the strengths of your fluid and crystallized intelligence to advantage. This work sets the stage for creativity, helps you recognize it when it comes, and prepares you for perfecting your creative discoveries.

Finding a vision is a bit more challenging. It requires you to imagine that your goal has already been achieved. A vision works as a kind of magnet, drawing you closer and closer to realizing your aims.

The way your unconscious mind works, you are actually attracted to—moved psychologically toward—what you think about. If you think about being fat, for example, your mind moves you toward fat. It doesn't matter if you were thinking "I don't want to be fat": the mind hears "fat." There is an immense amount of clinical evidence supporting the idea that *what you think is what you get*. The most concrete examples of how visualization works are found in studies of athletes. In one experiment, a group of basketball players was divided up into two groups, and both groups were given tests to determine their skill at free throw. The first group then spent a set amount of time practicing free throws. The second group practiced free throws as well, but they practiced only in their heads; they were told to picture themselves executing flawless free throws. When the groups were tested afterward, researchers found that, as expected, the first group had improved. What was amazing, however, is that the second group had improved as well, and *their gains were greater than those of the players who had physically practiced.*

Visualization works best when you associate yourself with the positive expression of what you want (making a free throw, for example) rather than the negative aspect (not missing the basket). Think of visualization as the "power of positive thinking" gone one better: you're not only anticipating the best, you're allying yourself with it. For that reason, when you encounter the inevitable barriers on your way to your goal, you'll tend to look at the problem from the winner's side.

You can use visualization to lose weight, learn to play the piano, sell more product, or find a new job. Before you select a long-term goal, try this fast demonstration of how visualization can improve performance.

SELF-RENEWAL PRACTICE

Your Balancing Act

Read all of the instructions first, then practice.

1. Test your current ability to balance:

   A. Position yourself in front of a digital clock or a clock with a sweep second hand.
   B. Fold your arms comfortably in front of you.
   C. Check the time.
   D. Close your eyes and raise one foot about six inches off the ground.
   E. When you lose your balance, note the time.
   F. Calculate the number of seconds you stayed in balance.

2. Test the power of a vision to improve your balance:

- Follow Steps A through C.
- In Step D, add this new component: visualize someone you trust standing behind you with his or her hands gently supporting you at the elbows, helping you stay in balance. See this person as clearly as you can.
- Proceed with steps E and F.

Most people improve their balance significantly when they envision someone helping them. This is a simple yet powerful demonstration of how maintaining a vision of what we desire will support us in accomplishing our goals.

Even with your vision firmly in place, you will not achieve the results you desire unless you put yourself in a creative frame of mind. Most research on activating the creative process suggests that changing the *way* you think is more important than any other factor in determining your ability to be creative. Researchers have identified three key ingredients of a creative mind-set:

- **Fluency**—generating a continuous flow of novel ideas. You can get your brain into this mode by taking a pair of scissors and thinking of ten nontraditional uses for them. Do not pause between ideas; keep them going. Stop the analytical or judgmental side of your brain from scaring off ideas that may at first seem odd. Try this often, with many different objects.

- **Flexibility**—coming up with novel ideas that represent different levels of thinking. In our "nontraditional uses" exercises, you may have come up with several similar ideas. Using the scissors as a stake for shaping plant growth and using them as a tent stake are two similar concepts (scissors as upright support). Using scissors as adornment for a birthday present and using scissors as a pointer in teaching would be two distinct levels of novel thought and would therefore demonstrate flexibility. Make an effort to let your thoughts be as wide-ranging as possible. Flexibility is an especially good mind-set to adopt when you find yourself in a rut.

• **Elaboration**—building upon ideas by adding details and nuances that embellish them. Take one of the novel ideas you generated in your fluency mode—using scissors as an ornament atop a gift —and elaborate on the details of the plan. How big are the scissors? What color are they? What brand? How are they designed? Will the scissors be used to open the gift? The more detail you bring to your ideas, the more vivid and "real" they seem to you.

You've probably discovered that this three-stage process requires a playful attitude. Unfortunately, the demands of adult living rarely provide the opportunity for play. Educational psychologist Carl Rogers observed that most adults, fearful of ridicule, hide their ingenuity behind layers of fear. Many people suppress the unique ideas that somehow manage to break through. To encourage *sculpted creativity*, let yourself play, using fluency, flexibility, and elaboration as your toys.

The proof of any creative endeavor is its outcome. At some point you must decide which combination of ideas will yield the best results. Too often we dismiss ripe ideas too quickly; sometimes a good but seemingly unworkable idea needs nothing more than to have the creative process applied to its implementation. This is especially true when two attractive ideas seem impossible to pursue at the same time. Many ideas that seem mutually exclusive at first can yield superior results if you bring to idea selection and implementation the same open-mindedness you brought to idea generation.

For example, let's say you want to go to a movie and your friends want to go to dinner. You can't agree, so you don't see one another. In this case, you have *polarized* your actions unnecessarily. Perhaps you can eat a quick bite before the film. Perhaps you can agree to take turns—next time you'll see a movie. Or maybe you'll buy takeout and rent a movie.

One of my clients complained to me the other day that she was stumped by a vexing paradox. She was beginning to think her boss had been embezzling from their company, but she was not sure enough about the facts to confront her boss or go over the boss's head and tell *her* boss. Neither was she comfortable simply putting the situation out of her mind. "If I confront the boss, I risk losing my job, or at the very least the goodwill of this woman, who has always treated me well. But I can't in good conscience tell myself that nothing has happened. I can't work with someone I can't trust. I think I have to quit."

After we talked through the problem, my client came to see that she didn't have to make a choice at all.

"You're looking at confrontation as 'black,' and forcing yourself to trust your boss as 'white,' " I told her. "There may be a middle ground here. Perhaps this is just a 'gray' situation. Can you give your boss a little 'provisional trust' until it becomes clear whether she has been embezzling?"

"What do you mean 'provisional'?"

"Proceed as usual. Protect any of your flanks that need protecting—you don't want to be accused of any dishonest activities—but go on the assumption that she's straight. At the same time, keep an eye out for anything that might suggest further action is needed. You may want to prepare your résumé in case you need it."

"You mean wait until I have a real reason to act."

As my client realized, it was only her polar thinking that created a problem situation. It turns out that the boss was not embezzling at all, but was following her own boss's directions to collect evidence against another worker in the department who *was* embezzling. My client was relieved that she had not taken action on the basis of her suspicions and quit a job she loved.

Paradoxes seduce us into thinking the only resolution to a problem is win-lose. It takes practice to break out of this mental trap and see that there are unlimited shades of gray that blend the strength of the two opposites.

This brief Self-Renewal Practice is designed to entice you to pause whenever you feel trapped into pursuing one idea at the expense of another.

SELF-RENEWAL PRACTICE

Reconciling

Come up with as many solutions as you can to each of the following black/white dilemmas:

1. Your mother wants to come into town the same weekend as your father, from whom she is divorced. You have one guest room.

2. The $750 you wanted to spend on vacation will have to be put into a new hot-water heater.

3. Your child desperately wants to watch a TV show of which you do not approve.

Possible solutions:

1. Tell them of the dilemma and let them work out the scheduling. Put one of them up in a hotel. Find an excuse for one of them to come another time. ("Why don't you come on the 21st, Mother; there's a flower show at the Pier.")

2. Take a few days and install the heater yourself (saving $500); spend the rest of your week vacationing. Ask the plumber to swap her skills for some of yours; you'll mow her lawn all summer or work on her car. Take your vacation at home, catching up on your reading or going on day trips.

3. Watch the show with your child and discuss the objectionable parts. Offer your child an inducement not to watch the show (a trip to the zoo) or accept an inducement to let him (he'll do the dishes for a week). Ask your child to censor *your* TV-watching for a few days while you censor his.

Once you see the gray area in a given situation, you can apply fluency-flexibility-elaboration skills to come up with the best strategies for taking advantage of this powerful middle ground.

———————

Confidence in the creative process is, for many of us, the most difficult aspect of inviting creativity. Far too many people grow up receiving recurring messages that they lack creative ability. Recall some of the negative messages you may have received from others or yourself in the past: "You can't even draw a straight line!" "You've never had an original idea." "You don't have a creative bone in your body." "When they were passing out artistic talent you must have been absent." If you want to supplant those messages, you must learn to coach and encourage your creative potential.

SELF-RENEWAL PRACTICE

The Inside Story

1. Select a time in your recent past when you had a *eureka* experience. This eureka may have come from solving a complex problem especially quickly or cleverly. It might have been an unexpected insight into a relationship dilemma, a business challenge, or even a golf match or bridge game.

2. Next, compose a newspaper headline that describes your mental victory. Be bold. Give yourself credit. Write a headline that will grab a reader's attention.

3. Write a short article that describes the steps you went through to deal with the situation. Write your column in three parts:

   • Report on your state of mind just *before* you solved the problem. How did you feel? What factors kept you engaged in trying to solve the problems? Were you using logic? Your imagination?

- Review the actual moment you had your insight. What conditions supported your mental breakthrough?
- Close the article with a rousing description of how your solution spawned benefits for you and others.

Look at these sample headlines from the inside stories of some of my workshop participants:

Coal Executive Prevents Future Layoffs
New Hire Revolutionizes Approach to Selling
Family Spends More Time Together, Thanks to . . .
New Voice-Mail System Puts Manager in Touch
Teenage Son Gains New Respect for His Father

The last headline on the list was written by a man whose article, below, inspired a whole group of his peers to view a job search as more than just a career challenge.

John Smith, 43, was laid off from his job as an aerospace engineer last year. Smith faced all the usual concerns of a man out of work: How will I pay my bills if I don't get a job right away? I do good work; why did I get fired? But Smith had another worry: How would he keep the respect of his teenage son?

Smith, like many parents, wanted to be a role model for young Jason. Smith said in a recent interview that "too many kids don't have heroes. I had Superman and Batman, then Stevenson and Kennedy. These guys have nobody. And so many parents aren't even on the scene." Smith was determined to show his son what a man was made of.

His breakthrough came when he realized that adversity was a fact of life. "It came to me that how a man coped with adversity was the measure of that man," relates Smith. "I might have lost my job, but I am still a good role model. A good father. I asked my son to come in for a heart-to-heart talk and told him just how I felt. That one of my goals while I looked for a new job was to make him proud of how I coped."

Smith's son took the role of student with gusto. He would ask his father questions about how he felt. "I wanted to be sure he kept his energy and spirits up," said Jason. Before long Smith admitted to himself that his family's love and support would be the most important factor in his getting a new job.

"I'll never forget the day I finally found a new position," smiled Smith. "Jason came into the den and shook my hand. Man to man. And he said thanks. I felt like a million bucks—and it had nothing to do with the new job!"

Another way to improve your confidence in your creativity is to do a Life Map, like the one you did in Chapter 1, for creativity. Do whatever it takes to give you the confidence that you can and will be creative.

VICTORIES OF MENTAL MASTERY

I have not guided you down the path of Mental Mastery with the hope of getting you into Mensa, though you may find that working toward membership in Mensa will keep your mind functioning at its peak. What I hope you take away from this discussion of the mind is the many different levels on which your mind can work, and the many different ways in which you can explore and expand this mind, using it to help you decide what you want in life and how to get it.

In order to make the very best use of your mind, pay special attention to the integration phase of learning, which we discussed in Chapter 1. Without it, none of the other phases matters. If you engage in Self-Renewal Practices on a regular basis, you will develop concrete mental skills that have an obvious application to daily life. More important, your work will actually promote neurological change, which can increase the rate and depth of your growth.

For example, training yourself to become more mindful will help you in your day-to-day decision-making and remembering. It also will shorten your learning curve and make learning more satisfying. Solving mental games can actually raise measurable IQ (you'll notice that you get better at these supposed "capacity-to-learn" puzzles if you practice them), but this crystallized intelligence workout also facilitates your understanding of complex issues in your personal life. Finally, in pursuing the rewards of Mental Mastery, you are laying the groundwork for other areas of growth. If your mind is sharp, you'll have an easier time understanding the paradoxes of spirituality, or the fundamentals of interpersonal effectiveness.

Becoming a midlife mental master is quite an accomplishment. Once you have reached a place where you continually challenge and enjoy your mind, you deserve to celebrate. Nice as it would be to be given a mental black belt ceremony, you're probably going to have to come up with a rite of passage yourself. Express your gratitude to the universe. Allow yourself to be proud. Or make a real statement and perform a more concrete rite of passage. In his commentary to the book *The Circle of Life*, Arthur Davidson discusses ways in which women are trying to consecrate their coming into wisdom:

> American women are creating new rites drawn from goddesses of antiquity, specifically Persephone, who represented the crone's mature feminine wisdom. . . . Persephone also provides a model for connecting with deeper levels of consciousness.
>
> Other women are finding ways to honor the wisdom of age within the context of their own faith. When she carries the Torah, traditionally a male function, [a] Jewish woman in California is carrying the wisdom of her people. In the company of female friends, she receives a new name that recognizes her new status in life and empowers her future. Her croning rite begins when she says, "A vibrant beauty from within marks not only an elder's accomplishments in life, but the inner enlightenment we call wisdom."

Rituals of this kind (and you can create any number of them) can help you appropriately revere the rewards you are sure to reap along the pathway of Mental Mastery.

CHAPTER 4

Pathway #2: Physical Vigor

*How old would you be if you
didn't know how old you was?*

—Satchel Paige

I am on a ski slope in Colorado, braving the below-zero windchill for my seventh run of the day. I am forty-one years old, and I feel younger physically than I did at twenty-five. I can breathe more easily at this altitude; my thigh muscles are stronger and more toned; my stamina is better than it was back in my graduate student days, when I skied on spring break.

I am proud that my body has actually improved over time, especially when someone my age complains about the physical burdens of getting older. You know the comments:

"My knees just aren't what they used to be."

"I don't have any energy anymore."

"Once I hit forty, I gained fifteen pounds."

When I started the research for this book, I wondered if I was some sort of physical oddity. My body had bloomed later than average in many respects. But my research suggested that my after-forty spurt in physical fitness was probably due more to my lifestyle than anything else.

At twenty-five, the most exercise I got was from lifting a fork to my mouth, lugging my book bag across campus, and chasing trains I was about to miss. At that stage of young adulthood, I focused only on exercising my mind. I smoked cigarettes, drank too much coffee, and turned to scotch when matters became too intense for sleep. I also starved myself to stay thin. I operated my body as if it were an indestructible container for my powerful intellect.

Then my brother Jim died. I was twenty-nine; he was twenty-two. Bodies, I learned, do not last forever—even twenty-something bodies can fail. At the funeral, no one but me knew that I was in such terrible physical condition. Never have I felt as physically fragile as I did the year my brother died.

In reverence for the body Jim lost in dying, I promised to reclaim my own health and physical well-being. At thirty, I began the slow, painful process of rebuilding my strength and stamina. One at a time, I tackled each facet of my sloppy existence. Quitting smoking was by far my toughest task. It took me five tries to give up the addiction that sapped my energy and yellowed my skin. Rationing —three cigarettes a day—finally broke me of the habit. After a while I came to hate selecting which moments I would allow myself for my addiction. Eventually I had to stop smoking to restore my self-esteem. I began to exercise and to eat more nutritious meals.

For fifteen years, I have been faithful to my healthier lifestyle. I don't feel like myself unless I have huge reserves of energy, strength, and physical resilience at my disposal. For me, physical vigor is a hard-won way of life, one that I treasure.

THE CALL TO PHYSICAL VIGOR

If you're like most of us at midlife, you're not terribly happy with your body. Perhaps you are heavier than you'd like to be. Maybe you find it distressing that your hair is grayer, or that you've had to buy reading glasses. There is a good chance that you find climbing stairs, lifting heavy objects, or even playing the piano more difficult than you did when you were younger. For many midlifers, worry over the physical aspects of getting older far overshadows other concerns, and it is tempting, in the face of so many seemingly immense obstacles, to throw in the proverbial towel and focus instead on mental or emotional skills that can compensate for physical decline.

There are two reasons to listen very closely to your feelings about your body. The first is that much of what upsets you can be fixed or improved upon; current research on biological aging is very encouraging. The second is this: the physical component of your journey is intricately tied to all the other components. Your mind, emotions, and relationships cannot be at their peak if your body is not functioning near its best.

Read the list below to see if you are experiencing any of the signs that the path of physical vigor is one you should travel.

Midlife Readiness Signals for Physical Vigor
You may find yourself:

- worrying about changes in your physical appearance
- lacking regular exercise
- longing for sensual experiences
- trying to lose or gain some weight
- desiring a less stressful lifestyle
- searching for ways to maintain health, energy, and attractiveness as you age

Over the years, I've heard clients describe every type of physical concern—from horror at a minute amount of cellulite to rage at recurring impotence. Return briefly to your own goals in this area, which you outlined in your journal after you completed the Self-Renewal Inventory in Chapter 2. As you did with Mental Mastery, decide which of the practices will best help you achieve your goals. In this chapter, however, it is more important than ever for you to be honest with yourself. Recognize that certain physical concerns, such as impotence or aching joints, require the attention of a health care professional. Go to the doctor if you need to. Go to the doctor if you're not sure whether or not you need to. Go to the doctor if you haven't had a checkup in the last two years. And realize that no advice anyone can give you will stop those gray hairs from coming in. This chapter is about making the best of what you have, not making you sixteen again.

ADVENTURES IN PHYSICAL VIGOR

If you're like most people, you see your body as a part of you that has to be controlled. It is demanding, unruly, and disappointing. It says, "I like sitting on the couch with a pile of chocolate chip cookies." If you have come to view your body as an enemy you haven't been able to conquer, the truce you've made with it is probably more than a little unsatisfactory.

Your body may like hanging out on the couch, but it also wants and needs regular exercise, nutritious food, and understanding. It was *designed* to want these things. But somewhere along the line you forgot how to listen to your body's signals. So the body that nature intended to crave a carrot now wants carrot cake.

Many people in my workshops dread disappointing themselves yet one more time when it comes to managing the physical aspects of who they are. If you doubt your body's ability to respond well to your well-intentioned efforts, take heart. The *know-whys* in these rewards are comforting, and the *know-hows* are not as insurmountable as you might fear.

The midlife rewards along the pathway of Physical Vigor are available to novices as well as experts in the physical arena. Tailor your travels to suit *your* pace and needs. The measure of your success is how happy you are with the way you feel, look, and perform physically. Most important, is your body willing and able to take you where you want to go?

If you're already in terrific shape, don't make the mistake of assuming you have nothing to gain by going down the path of Physical Vigor. There is more to the physical side of you than simply "being in great shape." Midlife offers all of us the opportunity to enrich our physical experience by becoming more attuned to the unique ways our bodies express their needs. Furthermore, by giving yourself more peak physical experiences, you put yourself on the road to greater mental, emotional, and spiritual rewards.

If you are reading these words with a certain amount of apprehension, I hope that you will give yourself and your body one more chance to establish a good rapport. It may help to think of all the amazing things your body has *already* done for you. Does it walk you around the office all day? Survive the onslaught of Vanilla Fudge Ripple? Create beautiful children? Remind yourself that even the smallest change in how you treat your body can make a difference in the way you look and feel.

Longevity Lifestyles

Whenever I find myself in the health and fitness section of my favorite bookstore, I have to laugh. There are hundreds of books in this category, and the author of each feels he or she has something important to tell us about how to take care of our bodies. Yet even these experts don't agree: Absolutely don't eat meat; a little meat is okay. Dairy foods are the best way to get calcium; dairy food is indigestible in most humans. Exercise thirty minutes, three times a week; exercise twenty minutes every day. It's enough to make any sane person want to *run*—out of the store.

In the interest of simplifying the issues a bit, let me tell you about a landmark study that outlines seven "short cuts" to health in aging. In their 1965 study of aging patterns among seven thousand subjects in Alameda County, California, UCLA public health researchers Nadia Belloc and Lester Breslow reported that seven lifestyle behaviors distinguished people who survived the five-year course of the study from those of similar age who died. Look at the seven behaviors listed below. Some are primarily health-promoting; others are more focused on disease prevention.

SEVEN LIFESTYLE FACTORS RELATED TO LONGEVITY

1. Eating breakfast daily
2. Avoiding snacks
3. Maintaining ideal weight (if you are not certain if your weight is on target, check with your health care professional)
4. Exercising regularly (taking part in any physical activity that builds endurance, strength, and flexibility)
5. Sleeping seven to eight hours per night
6. Not smoking
7. Moderate drinking (on the order of two alcoholic drinks per day)

The results of this study suggest that practicing these simple habits has a more powerful impact on well-being than does a person's income, physical condition, or genetic endowment. For example, in this research sample, forty-five-year-old men who observed *three or fewer* of these habits could expect to live another 21.6 years, while men of the same age who engaged in six or seven could expect to live an additional 33 years! A person in later midlife (age fifty-five to sixty-four) who practiced all seven good habits was found to be as healthy as a younger adult (age twenty-five to thirty-four) who practiced only one or two. The results of this research have been replicated many times over, so you can be confident that living a balanced, healthy lifestyle can add decades of well-being and vigor to your adult life.

Think of these seven habits as life preservers that will allow you to be more resilient during turbulent times and more buoyant on ordinary days, too.

SELF-RENEWAL PRACTICE

Long Life Preservers

This is a self-renewal practice you can begin today, but one you will work on for a long time. *Do not attempt to "fix" everything al once.*

1. Review the chart of factors that promote longevity.
2. Evaluate your physical status. How many of these life preservers do you have in your boat? Count up the number of habits you already practice.

    Even if you only practice a few, do not be demoralized. In this endeavor it is very important to know where you are, because the knowledge will help you to be gentle and patient with yourself as you go. You might also want to make a separate list of other healthy habits you subscribe to that don't appear on this list. Are you a vegetarian? Do you meditate? Remind yourself or your strengths, and of any ways in which you are already in concert with your body's needs.
3. List the longevity factors that you do not currently practice in the

order that would be *easiest* for you to accomplish. (That is, your first priority would be the habit that you view as easiest to acquire.)

4. Work to acquire each habit you desire, *one at a time*, beginning with the easiest. Then tackle the next easiest, and so on. Many people sabotage their effots at lifestyle change by taking on too much at once. Only after one habit becomes almost automatic (and this may take days, months, or years) should you proceed to the next one.

Don't be surprised, however, if in accomplishing one positive life-style change you spontaneously acquire another. Our bodies have a tendency to shift in many ways with only one intervention. Look for these physical epiphanies and welcome your newfound capacity to bring balance and harmony to your body's internal dance.

Some people find that they simply cannot integrate one or two of the lifestyle habits listed above into their lives without some kind of professional assistance. Smoking, for instance, can be very difficult to give up without professional help (it can also prevent the gains in other areas from being as substantial as they could be). You may also discover that your inability to meet goals (such as weight control) has more to do with emotional than physical issues. If that is the case, consider joining a support group or consulting a psychologist.

If, in the end, you can't reach that magical number 7, be kind to yourself. You may get there next year. Even if you never get there, *any* gains you have made will help offset the deficit.

Let me tell you about a friend of mine named Judy, who is one of the most well-read people I know. By the time Judy reached mid-life, a tough travel schedule and the stress of parenting teenagers had conspired to make her lose some of her physical equlibrium. She knew from her reading that eating breakfast was important, but because she'd never been much of a breakfast lover, she had let breakfast slide from her busy schedule. With the demise of her morning meal came a decline in her energy and a slight weight gain.

As Judy made plans to once more make breakfast a part of her day, she decided that she'd have a better chance of sticking to her plan if she chose breakfast foods she enjoyed. So instead of eating toast or eggs, she started to eat "lunch" food, specifically soup, which she had always loved. She stocked her freezer with individual servings of soup and now makes breakfast a satisfying part of her morning routine.

A bit of diligence with this relatively easy shift in Judy's lifestyle habits helped her revive her stamina and shed those few extra pounds (nutritionists tell us that the earlier in the day we start eating, the earlier we begin to increase our metabolism and burn calories). Judy's creative approach to improving her lifestyle is a terrific example of the ways in which individual tastes can be the heart of individual success.

The Fountain of Youth

Several years ago, while serving as director of the stress center at St. Louis University Medical Center, I interviewed scholar and anthropologist Ashley Montagu for a film about how to thrive in response to life's biggest challenges. With the cameras rolling, I asked my first question: "Dr. Montagu, what advice do you have for elderly people who are faced with the challenges of aging?"

With a gleam in his eye and a broad smile, Montagu, a man in his seventies, looked squarely into our cameras and said: *"You must die young, as late as possible!"*

Montagu went on to explain his belief that men and women can revolutionize their lives by incorporating "juvenile" traits into their behavior. This process, which he called *neoteny*, involves making a conscious effort to make use in adulthood of certain characteristics—such as curiosity, playfulness, a sense of wonder, and high energy—usually associated with children. Montagu argued that many characteristics we believed to be intrinsic to success in childhood, from the need to organize to a willingness to experiment, were in fact the building blocks of all human success.

Montagu's thesis rings true for most of us, and is certainly supported anecdotally; many biographies of successful men and women show them to possess the childlike qualities Montagu describes. Studies have shown that people who make an effort to reactivate childlike traits in themselves do indeed become more creative, happier, and even physically stronger and more resilient. We made these points in our film by using Montagu's commentary as the voice-over for footage of an East Coast ski team of senior citizens barreling down the slopes.

It's not difficult to understand how Montagu's concept of neoteny can be useful to adults trying to make the most of their lives. What is surprising is that there may be a way for us to achieve a kind of *biological* neoteny as well. Researchers William Evans and Brian Rosenberg of Tufts University's Center for the Study of Human Aging, in their studies of the effects of exercise on older Americans, found that adults could actually grow younger! Their book *Biomarkers* gives a full report of the major symptoms of biological aging. I have summarized their findings, which fall into ten categories, for you here:

- **Lean body mass.** The average American loses 6.6 pounds of muscle each decade after young adulthood. Without regular exercise to increase muscle-to-fat ratio, the rate of loss accelerates after age forty-five.

- **Strength.** Between the ages of thirty and seventy, the average person loses 20 percent of his or her muscle. Most of this loss is in the large muscle groups, such as the thighs, but it also takes place in some smaller muscle groups. Loss of strength is related to *five* other adverse changes in biomarkers: slower metabolism, increased body fat, decreased aerobic capacity, lower blood sugar tolerance, and diminished bone density.

- **Basal metabolic rate** (your caloric expenditure at rest). The body's need for calories to sustain itself declines at the rate of 2 percent per decade after age twenty. This means you need one hundred fewer calories per year each decade after age twenty to maintain status quo unless you increase your muscle-to-fat ratio.

- **Body fat.** The average person doubles the ratio of fat to muscle between the ages of twenty and sixty-five. The average sedentary sixty-five-year-old woman is approximately 43 percent adipose (fat) tissue, while men of this age and sedentary status are 38 percent.

- **Aerobic capacity.** Without regular exercise, the body's ability to use oxygen efficiently after age sixty-five will decline an average of 30 to 40 percent.

- **Blood sugar tolerance.** The risk of Type 2 diabetes increases with age, because the body's ability to use glucose in the bloodstream declines as we get older. By age seventy, 20 percent of men and 30 percent of women have abnormal glucose tolerance curves. Low-fat diets and muscle-building exercise work to regulate glucose metabolism and help individuals avoid adult-onset diabetes.

- **Cholesterol (LDL/HDL ratio).** "Good" cholesterol (HDL) tends to decline and "bad" cholesterol (LDL) tends to increase in men and women after age fifty. Low-fat diets can lower LDL, but only exercise can raise HDL.

- **Blood pressure.** Blood pressure increases steadily with age for most Americans, primarily because of consumption of fat, salt, and alcohol; smoking; and insufficient exercise.

- **Body density.** The skeletal system loses calcium with age, making bones less dense, weaker, and more brittle. A brisk daily walk can prevent development of osteoporosis.

- **Body temperature.** As the body ages, its ability to maintain a steady temperature declines. Regular exercise corrects this decline by increasing water retention in the blood. Exercise promotes sweating, which is the body's primary method of cooling itself. Because fit people have "more diluted" sweat, they can sweat more without losing crucial potassium, sodium, and chloride.

Where's the good news in these findings? There is conclusive evidence that *all ten of these biomarkers can be reversed in people over age sixty!* The Tufts University team proved that by concentrating on *only two biomarkers*—building muscle tissue and increasing muscle strength—people between the ages of sixty and seventy-two can rejuvenate their entire physiology.

Participants in this study engaged in weight training three times per week for three months. Under supervision, these adults trained at 80 percent of their repetition capacity. By the end of the experiment, the participants had tripled the size of their hamstring muscles and doubled the size of their quadriceps. Anecdotal reports by researchers noted that at the completion of this study, the sixty-plus subjects could lift heavier boxes than could the twenty-five-year-old laboratory assistants!

Scientists do not fully understand how reversing the first two biomarkers of aging improves the other eight. But we do know that without weight training, the body's tendency is to double its fat and lose half of its muscle mass by age sixty-five. This tendency creates problems, because fat tissue is metabolically inactive, useful only as reserve during periods of starvation. Muscle tissue is metabolically active and therefore requires caloric food to maintain itself. Hence, if you maintain a higher ratio of muscle to fat tissue as you age, you eliminate the decline in basal metabolic rate that typically occurs.

Improving muscle-to-fat ratio and muscle strength also spurs the body to improve blood sugar tolerance, regulate and stabilize its internal temperature, maintain healthier blood pressure levels, and increase its aerobic capacity, because you have more working muscles consuming oxygen. Even more amazing is the finding that adults who exercise their muscles on a regular basis report psychological benefits, such as an increased sense of well-being, youthful vigor, and self-esteem. So do not hesitate. Go directly to the gym.

While writing this chapter, I found myself frustrated not to be able to give you lots of Self-Renewal Practices to help you along the road to physical vigor. But when it comes to building muscle tissue and increasing muscle strength, there's simply no substitute for the words of that famous Nike ad: "Just do it." Join a gym, get a personal trainer, figure out a way to use common household objects as weight-training devices. If you're interested in reversing the effects the years have had on your body, you're going to have to all but literally *lift* the weight of those years off yourself.

One thing I *can* tell you is that incorporating playfulness, from Montagu's prescription for staying young (the neoteny model), will make anything you do more enjoyable. Remember times as a child when you were completely absorbed in physical play? Activities such as building forts in the snow, swinging, playing kick the can, playing cowboys and Indians, and riding bikes are all playful challenges children enjoy without any sense that they are benefiting their bodies in the process. Try to adopt this attitude when tackling your muscles.

One way to reengage in the joy and challenge of physical play is to play team sports. Another is to track your progress so that you become your own competitor. The other is simply to try new physical challenges (such as lifting heavier and heavier weights as you increase your condition). The Self-Renewal Practice that follows will not increase your lean body mass, but it will put you back in touch with the *joys* of physical vigor. I have experimented with teaching this practice to many attendees at my workshops who in the main *laugh* and squeal with delight as they master the new physical challenge.

SELF-RENEWAL PRACTICE

Your Juggling Act

Isn't it satisfying when you juggle work, family, friends—and all the demands of your life—successfully? Juggling is the perfect metaphor for all we have to do. Well, literal, physical juggling is just as challenging and rewarding. And it can help you regain the sense of physical vigor you may have lost over the years (not to mention preventing age-related declines due to slower thought speed).

So put your own juggling ability to the test and remember that such complex bodily movements (those that engage the right and left side of the body simultaneously) provide rhythms that have the power to elevate your mood, spur your creativity, and put you in touch with the physical side of your nature that is often forgotten in the mad dash to meet the demands of the day.

1. Hold one marshmallow in your dominant throwing hand. Toss it from hand to hand with high underhand throws—like tennis lobs. The pinnacle of the trajectory should be slightly above your head. Say "throw" when you toss the marshmallow, to distract yourself from worrying about catching it. Trust yourself to catch, and focus instead

on the throwing. Keep your eyes focused at the top of your toss and your hands at waist level.

2. Next you will begin with one marshmallow in each hand. Focus on throwing one marshmallow at a time, allowing it to drop to the ground. Begin tossing with the dominant throwing hand, and say "One." When the first marshmallow reaches its peak, say "Two," and throw the second marshmallow. Do not try to catch them.

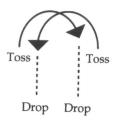

3. Now repeat the second step, but this time you will catch the marsh-mallows. Keep your focus on the pinnacle and concentrate on throw-ing. Allow your hands, at waist level, to catch the marshmallows without trying.

4. Now begin with two marshmallows in your dominant throwing hand and a third in your other hand. Once again, this is an exercise in *throwing*. Do not try to catch the marshmallows; let them fall to the ground. Start tossing with your dominant hand and say "One." When the first marshmallow reaches its peak, say "Two" and toss the second marshmallow, which is held in your nondominant hand. When the second marshmallow reaches its peak, say "Three" and toss the third marshmallow, held in your dominant hand. Keep your eyes at the pinnacle, and try to get the throws at equal heights, keeping your hands at waist level.

5. Now try to catch the marshmallows. Start with two marshmallows in your dominant throwing hand and a third in your other hand. Start tossing with your dominant hand and say "One." As the first marsh-mallow reaches its peak, say "Two" and throw the second marsh-mallow, held in your nondominant hand. When that marshmallow reaches its peak, say "Three" and toss the third marshmallow, held

in your dominant hand. When that marshmallow reaches its peak, say "Four" and keep going. If you don't catch the marshmallows, don't worry. Eventually you will begin to catch them.

Follow the spirit of neoteny in any physical activity you undertake, whether it be for fun, a fitness edge, or the remarkable reversal in physical aging that can be achieved through building more muscle.

Jack Benny

Whenever I would ask my grandfather how old he was, he would smile and say, "I'm thirty-nine, just like Jack Benny." I had no clue what he meant—why did "thirty-nine" and "Jack Benny" get a laugh from all adults within earshot? I did realize that Grandpa was trying to avoid giving me a direct answer to my question.

It was not only my grandfather who dodged questions about age. Aunts, uncles, and even my parents guarded the truth about their ages as closely as they did the size of their incomes. The more I probed, the tighter their lips were sealed.

Those of us born between 1945 and 1965 probably find it even more difficult to embrace the physical prospects of aging than did our parents and grandparents. For one thing, we were the first generation to buy into the youth culture so completely. For another, we made a bargain with nature early on to eat nutritiously, exercise regularly, manage stress, and balance our lifestyles, in exchange for looking and feeling young. But eventually, no matter how good our genes or how diligently we pursue healthy habits, nature reneges on its end of the agreement.

Noticing one's own aging can be disconcerting. One of my clients, Becky, told me:

"Last Wednesday I was pasting some photographs from our summer vacation into a scrapbook when I came across a strange-looking snapshot . . . some woman I didn't recognize had her arm around my son's shoulder. They were sitting on the porch swing at our cabin.

"I stared at the picture, moved it back and forth, grabbed my reading glasses. As I got a good look, I realized it was me! The person I couldn't recognize was me.

"How is it possible that I couldn't recognize myself? I sat at the kitchen table stunned, silent, examining every detail of my face. I swear even the shape of my nose seemed different. The tiny grooves around my mouth looked just like my mother's.

"I have been walking around in a state of shock ever since. I can't believe how much older I look. And now I'm worried that I got so upset. I don't mind looking like my mother. She's a beautiful woman. But I'm forty-three and she is seventy-eight."

Becky and I took a deep breath almost simultaneously as her disappointment filled every corner of the office. She broke the silence. "I guess I never realized what a hard life being a lawyer, wife, and mother can be." We both laughed. So often we make the mistake of equating ourselves with our physical shape, size, energy level, or degree of health.

I pointed out to Becky the reason why she had overlooked her body's gradual changes. Each of us possesses a life-giving force within that blinds us to the physical signs of our own aging. I call that inner force of self-preservation the *ageless me*.

It is good to experience the ageless me at forty-five, just as it was at twenty-five, and as it will be at sixty-two or eighty. The ageless me hangs in there with you during good times and bad. In my case, the same ageless me that won the role of Snow White in the kindergarten play started a successful consulting business at age thirty-nine. The ageless me has a best friend named Barbara, loves chocolate chip ice cream and riding my bike. The ageless me doesn't pay attention to details and cringes now and then when waiters feel a need to call me ma'am.

The one who is, has been, and will always be me at one stage weighed seven pounds, eight ounces; at another forty-three pounds; at yet another 125 pounds. Once the ageless me stuttered. Now the ageless me can speak on stage for hours without a glitch. Through all my changing, the ageless me stands ready to support me, lead me, follow me, do whatever I may ask as we travel through experience after experience together.

Not to honor and identify with this unfailing inner core of who we are is to miss the essence of our own spirit. After practicing yoga for some time, a friend told me that in the bold, quiet rhythm of her movements she realized that she is not her body; she only happens to inhabit her body.

SELF-RENEWAL PRACTICE

The Ageless Me

Separate your *ageless self* from your physical body by thinking about yourself as independent of your body. Write your thoughts in your journal.

1. Close your eyes and breathe deeply for a minute or two.

2. Think about the self you are, have been, and will be, the self who is not defined by your body. Feel the pleasure your ageless self brings you.

3. In your journal, write down a few of the characteristics of your ageless self.

   Take a look at the notes my client Becky made about herself after we discussed going beyond surface signs of aging to discover an abiding sense of who she is, was, and always will be—regardless of her age.

THE AGELESS ME
Good at math
Lots of energy (can't sit still for long)
Loves the mountains
A strong leader
When things get tough—a survivor
A caring friend and confidant
Known for hugging people

4. Return to this form of self-renewal whenever you want to reconnect yourself to your true essence. Avoid being tyrannized by wrinkles,

gray hair, loose skin, layers of fat, fatigue, even illness by relating to the part of you that cannot be defined by the physical aspects of your being. Spend a few quiet moments when you wake up in the morning and just before you fall asleep recalling the deepest attributes of who you are—the ones that survive the test of time and thrive in spite of the weight of accumulating years. Do this self-renewal practice especially when you sense your body's vulnerability to aging, illness, or exhaustion.

After doing this self-renewal practice regularly for a few weeks, if you still find yourself thinking about how old you look, you may need to work on your self-esteem. If you invest too much of your self-worth in the way you look, nature's gentle physical changes begin to seem like personal insults. You might want to complete a Life Map (see Chapter 1) for the area of appearance. You might also want to attend to this issue when you look at the pathways of Emotional Vitality and Interpersonal Effectiveness.

Many people who care too much about the way they look resort to cosmetic surgery to keep themselves looking young. According to a plastic surgeon friend of mine, these patients are never satisfied with their surgeries, because no plastic surgeon is capable of "erasing" age. No matter how many wrinkles the doctor eradicates, a patient's face will reveal its chronological age within five years. (Now I know why some people always seem to be having a "little something" done!) My friend said that he has another kind of patient, too, a type he much prefers working with. "These people don't care about looking young; they want to look good. It sounds like a fine distinction, but someone who wants to look her best at forty-five will always be happier with her surgery than someone who wants to look thirty at forty-five."

A woman at one of my seminars brought this point home to me a few months ago. Whenever I discuss the subject of the "ageless me" with a group of men or women, at least 10 to 20 percent of the group will approach me after the talk to discuss the merits of plastic surgery. This woman eagerly explained: "I had a face lift three weeks ago. I'm sure you already know this, but plastic surgery can really be terrific if you have it for the right reasons. I don't mind looking my age—you'll notice I don't even color my hair—but I was getting really tired of looking mean. I inherited deep ridges around my eyes and mouth from my father, and as the years went by I was noticing that people were reacting differently to me. Not my husband or friends, but new colleagues, acquaintances, even people in stores. I'm only forty-six, and I didn't want to live the rest of my life feeling like my face didn't reflect who I am. I had surgery to keep myself *looking* like myself. And I'd do it again in a second."

No one can decide for you how much attention you will give your looks. For most of us at midlife, it is enough to dress well, get a good haircut, and generally make the best of what we have. All of us are in for some of the age shock Becky experienced. But who we are is in fine shape somewhere deep inside. So why worry about the vagaries of the flesh? You are a fierce, energetic, living person. Call up the ageless Jack Benny of your spirit and let him give you some inspiration and a few good laughs.

The Empty Suit Syndrome

How many times do you force your body to do something at its own expense? You may push yourself to run faster, lose more weight, stay up later, get up earlier, work longer, lift one more box, plant one more shrub—at a time when your body is screaming "STOP!" in fatigue or pain. You fight back, maybe pop a couple of pills, and keep on going.

We learn how to mentally dominate our physical needs early in life. That's what potty training is all about. But often, what starts out as a healthy effort to adapt bodily functions to fit social dictates ends up causing strain and damage. I can remember the terrific sense of accomplishment I felt when I made it through an entire day of third grade without going to the bathroom. One evening after school I bragged to my mother about my victorious efforts at self-control. She was horrified and made me promise I would never again abstain from relieving my swollen bladder.

I'm not the only one who conceives ingenious tricks of self-discipline in order to control what appears to be an unruly, disruptive set of physical needs. Even something as simple as the desire to lose weight can turn into a regimen of starvation diets and compulsive exercise.

My term for the collection of symptoms resulting from mental tyranny of the body is the *Empty Suit Syndrome*. We've all survived a round or two of the Empty Suit Syndrome. Your mind tells you to work overtime day after day to achieve your objective. Your mind insists on finishing that novel, even if it means reading into the early hours of the morning, preventing you from getting enough sleep. Your mind circles obsessively around one knotty problem, draining your energy and enthusiasm for other endeavors. Many of my clients feel that the concerns and burdens of midlife make the Empty Suit Syndrome unavoidable.

Occasional self-induced strain on your physical system is not harmful. In fact, it can be responsible for many extraordinary achievements in business and personal life. Michelangelo contorted his body into cramped, elevated spaces for years in order to complete the ceiling of the Sistine Chapel. Enduring physical strain to care for a sick child, close a business deal, or finish a project on time is part of what life is all about. Eastern monks have become so proficient at achieving mental control over their bodily functions that experiments measuring the electrical conductivity of the skin have shown that some monks are able, through intense concentration, to fire a single neuron. Such responsiveness to mental direction is an example of how positive the approach of "mind over matter" can be in matters of healing tumors, lowering blood pressure, or relieving pain. Biofeedback, which makes use of a monitoring device in conjunction with a patient's concentrated efforts, has made these benefits available even to those of us whose level of Mental Mastery is somewhat less than that of the monks.

When a person's body is subjected to relentless, abusive demands of the mind, however, physical mechanisms start to break down. In fact, many physical symptoms that we attribute to "getting older" are actually manifestations of physical strain. For example, high blood pressure, trouble digesting certain foods, and chronic pain, along with more debilitating cancer and heart attacks, are often manifestations of unrelenting strain. Honor the wisdom of the body by slowing down long enough to figure out how to alleviate the stress it is under.

Listening to your body has many rewards. You'll be healthier, of course, and you'll feel better. You'll find it less difficult to say no to demands and requests that would tax your body unduly. Decision-making becomes easier when you take your body's cues seriously; you'll waste less time debating over whether to go for a walk or bother making a salad for dinner. You'll notice that you really do sleep better if you exercise, or that a second helping of dinner makes you uncomfortably full.

The better you become at listening to your body, the better your body will treat you. For example, some nutritionists claim that if you give your body only the healthy foods *it* cries out for, *you* will actually stop craving unhealthy foods. And when your body gets the exercise it needs, it will reward you with more energy, and improved attitude, and increased emotional stability.

Your aches and pains, poor sleep, or lack of stamina may be the early warning signs of unresolved stress on your body. You are probably pushing yourself too hard, perhaps as a result of some internal pressure to perform. Rarely are symptoms such as these related solely to the aging process. If you leave them unresolved, you are opening the door to physical decline.

Your body is designed to communicate with you, to help you achieve mind-body balance. As you might imagine, busy, achievement-oriented people find it difficult to give up control over the body. If this is true for you, begin letting your body be in charge by doing the Self-Renewal Practice that follows.

SELF-RENEWAL PRACTICE

Matter over Mind

Many people find time to do this exercise on a ten-minute break during working hours or in the evening just before mealtime.

1. Focus on any bodily sensations or feelings you may be experiencing at this moment. Scan your entire body, starting at the top of your head and moving slowly down the upper torso and arms to your

waist. Notice any positive and negative sensations along the way. (You can do this scanning with your eyes open or closed; closed is best.)

You may encounter areas of pain or tension in your upper back, neck, head or stomach. You may feel pleasant sensations, such as a sweet taste in your mouth or a sense of calm in your chest. Slowly continue your scanning, down the remaining part of your torso and through your legs and feet. Make a mental note of pleasant and unpleasant sensation in these lower zones. Your lower back may ache or your legs may feel heavy and lethargic, or perhaps they feel energized.

2. Next, return mentally to those portions of your body that signal negative or uncomfortable sensations, one at a time. Ask yourself about your contribution to the discomfort zones. Have you tensed muscles in response to stress? If so, what can you do to relieve the discomfort? Relax? Massage the area? Rest? Change your thoughts? Take a walk? Review your pleasure zones one at a time, too. Ask yourself how you have contributed to your physical well-being in each of these healthy zones. Make a note of the strategies that work best for you. What can you do to maintain or even extend your comfort zones? Assume a more comfortable posture? Stretch your muscles? Drink a glass of water?

There are a vast number of ways to ease bodily discomforts and enhance physical pleasure. Invent your own methods for meeting these goals. Be sure to select actions that have an immediate payoff. It's fine to have some longer-term strategies, such as exercising after work or taking a relaxing bath or shower, but giving yourself an *instant* boost will best help you learn to listen to your body.

3. Activate your pain-relieving and comfort-enhancement approaches as soon as possible. Tuning in to your body on a regular basis (at least once daily) is your way of telling your body that it matters. And as with any relationship, the more you respond to your body's messages, the more likely your body will be to take good care of you.

———————————

Most people who use this technique report positive results in their energy levels after about three weeks. Other benefits may include relief from physical symptoms such as headaches, lower back tension, insomnia, eye strain, upper shoulder (trapezius muscle) pain, and jaw strain. Even if you have no noticeable physical stress symptoms, practicing the matter-over-mind exercise will help you relax and achieve that all-is-well feeling that comes from not taking your body for granted.

Not everybody learns the signals of the body easily, but everyone who heeds the body's wisdom benefits, just as a fifty-two-year-old design engineer did. In the passage that follows, he describes how he learned to let his body be in charge after practicing this Self-Renewal Exercise.

During my late twenties and early thirties, I lived every day with a sense of urgency and drive. Most of the time, I was oblivious to my body except that it felt like it had been shot out of a cannon. I was stuck on fast forward.

When I reached my early forties, I decided to slow down to a saner pace. I remember saying to myself after a particularly grinding road trip, "What is your hurry? You can't go on racing from city to city, from day to day, from person to person. You're moving so fast you can't even enjoy your work!" That was the turning point for me. From then on, I decided to create a better rhythm to my life.

I disciplined myself to schedule an extra half day to reach travel destinations. I made daily exercise something I never missed. I started paying more attention to my body, and once I relaxed, I was shocked to find out how tense and tired I had been for the previous ten years! Now I practice the matter-over-mind exercise at least once a day. It teaches me how to pace myself and stretch out when my body really needs a break. I have more energy than I've ever had. None of the changes I made came easily—but they were definitely worth every ounce of effort.

The next reward will help you extend your ability to take advantage of what your body is telling you.

Twenty-four-Hour Dancing

I once read an account of how Pacific salmon spend their first four years at sea, then set out on a thousand-mile journey back to the freshwater lakes where they were born. They must swim every mile of the return upstream, conquering countless rapids and man-made dams along the way. Once they arrive home, they spawn and die.

On the surface it may appear that the fish's death is a result of the grueling nature of the homeward journey: first near-exhaustion, then an orgasmic burst of energy that ensures the continuation of the species, then death. On closer examination, scientists have learned that it is not the challenging trip upstream that does the salmon in. Rather, it is the lethal dose of cortisol (a potent stress hormone present in all animals) that kills them. Pacific salmon have genetic programming that instructs their adrenal glands to release massive quantities of cortisol immediately after spawning. No amount of care or stress reduction along the arduous journey upstream could alter the course of nature that guides the Pacific salmon: Birth → Adventure → Reproduction → Death. In fact, the salmon who die at home after spawning are living in perfect harmony with their natural rhythms.

Note that the stress hormone cortisol is released in salmon *after* the stress of their journey is completely over; in humans, the adrenal glands are programmed to release cortisol in small doses in response to any threatening situation that comes our way *during* the course of a day. Deadlines are missed, the traffic is congested, your funds are depleted. Whatever the source of the threat may be, once we interpret something as potentially harmful, our brains respond in exactly the same way they did in our primitive ancestors, who were more likely to confront a hungry saber-toothed tiger than a traffic jam.

We become hyperalert, vigilant, ready to move. We calculate ways of dominating, obliterating, escaping. Our hearts pound so hard we can hear them, perspiration beads up on our foreheads, we grimace, clench our teeth, breathe rapidly, tense our muscles. Blood rushes to our extremities, engorging the striate muscles in our legs and arms. We are physically and mentally primed. Our brain has declared a state of emergency and we are geared up to fight or flee.

As the flood of adrenaline, released from the adrenal cortex, races through the body and creates this emergency response, internal balance is disturbed. Every cell in the body converts its operations from a building-and-renewal process (called anabolic metabolism) to a breaking-down-and-dispersement process (called catabolic metabolism). This emergency response ensures that we have the massive resources necessary to fight off an attack. As a reaction to countless, unrelenting pressures of daily existence, however, it causes physical damage and promotes premature aging.

Bombarding our bodies with cortisol and converting our cellular activities from anabolic to catabolic metabolism on a prolonged basis is disastrous. This constant running on fast forward eats holes in our stomach linings, encourages hypertension, depresses our moods, lowers our resistance to disease, and promotes chronic fatigue. Unless we take special measures to interrupt the prolonged stress response, we are, in effect, shortening our lives.

Relaxing the inner workings of the body and regaining the biological equilibrium that allows cells to renew themselves (and build new tissue) is crucial to achieving physical vigor throughout midlife. In a study of the effects of meditation on aging, physiologist R. K. Wallace of UCLA reported that people who restored biological equilibrium by practicing meditation on a regular basis for five years or less showed a biological age as many as five years younger than their chronological age. Those who had been meditating for longer than five years showed a biological age twelve years younger than their chronological age. (Wallace published his findings in 1978, and used measures of blood pressure, hearing acuity, and near-point vision as age markers.)

The work of Wallace, and other researchers on the effects of relaxation techniques such as meditation, biofeedback, and yoga reveals that those of us who practice regular relaxation become sick enough to go to the hospital only half as often as people who endure an uninterrupted stress response. Those who learn how to relax exhibit 80 percent less heart disease and 50 percent less cancer than their overstressed counterparts. These comparisons hold up for all adult age groups, with the most benefit evidenced in people sixty-five and older. Relaxation is as important as exercise to your physical balance and well-being.

There are many ways to encourage your body to relax. Meditation and yoga, mentioned above, are two of the best techniques of reducing stress and achieving mental and physical balance; most people require a formal, disciplined ritual to keep their cortisol levels down. Ask friends what they do to relax; go to the library and look into different relaxation philosophies (some are more spiritually oriented than others) and instruction. If you enjoy learning by reading, Herbert Benson's classic *Relaxation Response* offers practical, well-documented guidance into how to achieve the benefits of relaxing. His approach is a no-nonsense, logical one that demystifies why relaxation works. Perhaps the most comprehensive recent review of mental approaches to stress reduction and healing has been documented by Bill Moyers in his 1993 printed text and videotape series *The Healing Mind*. Through interviews with scientists and healers of the Western and Eastern traditions, Moyers deluges us with far-reaching, long-standing evidence that our minds and our bodies are intimately connected and can influence one another for better or worse whether we realize what's happening or not.

If you learn better through hands-on instruction, find yourself a teacher or take a class. Many times you can find the best teachers through word-of-mouth referrals. The American Society of Clinical Hypnosis certifies its members in meditative techniques. Ask at your YMCA health education center for the name of yoga masters and meditation teachers who have established good reputations in your community. *The additional relaxation ideas that follow are not intended as a substitute for regular relaxation periods.*

One of the most natural but often ignored ways to help your body relax is to learn to come into harmony with the ebb and flow of your body's natural rhythms. You and I know intuitively when we are operating synchronously with our internal cycles. We have a strong sense of well-being; we feel relaxed and energized simultaneously. Our logic is sharp, and we concentrate on whatever interests us. We express a full range of emotions—sadness, grief, frustration, anger, anxiety, elation, joy, surprise, thrill, excitement —and are sensitive to the feelings of others. When we are tired, we

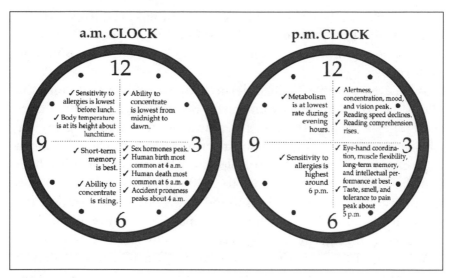

Peak Performance and Circadian Rhythms

rest and are able to sleep. No hurry, no worry; the present moment is all there is, and it is good.

Experiment with how you schedule your work, family, personal, and leisure activities. Even when we are bound to schedules driven by the demands of others, we often have more flexibility than we think. It is possible that you have all the freedom you need to govern the rhythms of your activities satisfactorily.

Almost twenty years ago, research psychologists working for the Navy and the Veterans Administration Hospitals tested many critical body functions at various times of day and found patterns in the way circadian (daily) rhythms of the body arrange themselves within the twenty-four-hour light-and-dark cycle. Read over the charts above and think about how you might better meet the demands of your life if you take your internal body rhythms into account.

Don't take the word of chronobiologists as fact. Chart your own critical rhythms. Notice which activities work best for you at given intervals of the day. I know people who could never be happy or in harmony with their internal clocks if they exercised in the afternoon. They move best in the early hours of the morning. Researchers have found that people who consider themselves to be "morning people" are more physically active and have sharper thinking during morning hours, while people who call themselves "night people" have the opposite pattern. You are the best judge of your own optimum-performance cycle.

Whenever possible I schedule my day into blocks of time that allow me to take full advantage of my biological rhythms. I reserve 7:00 a.m. to 8:00 a.m. for planning and organizing my day (this is when I am in my best short-term memory mode). The morning hours from 9:00 to 12:00 I block off for writing or other high-concentration tasks. From noon to 2:00 p.m. I schedule meetings to take advantage of the elevated mood and sharp concentration that occur in me and in those with whom I meet. Sometimes my husband and I lunch together to gain a fresh perspective on family issues.

Whenever I have an afternoon audience, I plan activities that include physical movement, to take advantage of the natural post-meridian mind-body peak. (When I am alone, my afternoons are for reading and running.) Socializing and family gatherings I plan for early-evening hours. For me, the best time for chores (the mindless, requirement-of-living tasks) is during the mid-evening hours when my brain and body are at their lowest ebb.

Why not plan to exercise, solve a problem, savor a good meal, engage in romance, write a report, darn a sock, take a nap, or inspire others to accomplish difficult tasks at times when your own inner rhythms are most favorably predisposed to the demands of the activity?

Another way to achieve harmony with your inner workings is to take advantage of what scientists call *ultradian rhythms*. These shorter cycles—alternating periods of mental activity and rest—occur about twelve times during the twenty-four-hour (circadian) cycle. Ultradian rhythms provide us with a ninety-to-one-hundred-minute phase of relative alertness, followed by a twenty-to-thirty-minute phase of relative mental relaxation. (You could easily verify the existence of the ultradian pattern by hooking yourself up to the appropriate equipment and watching on an oscilloscope the fluctuations in your physiological correlates of alertness and relaxation.)

During the day, the ultradian fluctuation is not always noticeable to busy people who are not on the lookout for its alternating waves.

You may have detected your body's ultradian rest cycle, however, in the form of midmorning lulls in concentration or midafternoon lapses in attention. At night, the ultradian rest period that occurs while you are sleeping corresponds to the REM cycles (rapid eye-movement periods of dream activity).

Make an effort to notice your own ultradian rhythms and to tailor your activities to your natural highs and lows. Overly active adults generally have no problem making best use of the "alert" phase of their ultradian cycles, but push themselves when they enter the resting phase, which can cause unnecessary stress. The Self-Renewal Practice that follows will help you get the most out of your rest phase.

SELF-RENEWAL PRACTICE

Taking an Ultradian Break

Practice this exercise whenever you detect a slight drop in energy or lapse in concentration. Signs such as these are subtle cues that you are in the rest phase of your ultradian cycle.

1. Sit in a comfortable chair and rest your hands loosely in your lap. Relax your upper body by taking two or three deep breaths and lowering your shoulders. Gently close your eyes.

2. Allow your mind to wander until it remembers a time when you felt happy and energized. Zero in on a specific event that felt good physically, something that gave you a sense of physical excitement or exhilaration, stimulated your taste buds, tickled your nerve endings, or brought you scintillating sounds or smells. Give yourself five minutes or so to relish these moments.

3. Once you have reveled in the pleasures of those moments past, remind yourself how marvelous your body truly is, not in a trite sense, but with genuine appreciation and respect.

I often use this technique at the close of physically and emotionally demanding workshops. Participants given a relaxation exercise at the end of a workshop report more restful sleep than they have at similar workshops that do not incorporate relaxation as a closing exercise.

––––––––––––––

Relaxation practice of any type renews and energizes you at the same time. It is in this paradox of promoting inner calm and outer vigor that we learn to dance with the demands that come our way.

Walking Your Talk

Last weekend I addressed over one hundred people at a conference for health care managers. After talking at length about problem-solving strategies, I asked everyone in the audience to find a partner.

Once the group had paired off, I explained that each team would be asked to work for ten minutes at solving two problems. One partner was to introduce his or her problem first, and the couple was to work for five minutes at solving it. Then the other partner would broach a concern, and the couple would discuss that issue for the second five minutes. Pretty standard fare for workshops. What made this practice different is that I asked the participants to undergo the entire exercise *while walking.*

Two by two, they paraded counterclockwise around the perimeter of the large auditorium. Each pair was deep in conversation, some even arm in arm. After two or three minutes the roar in the room rose; everyone seemed to sense the energy of the crowd. Feet marched, arms waved, heads nodded in a rhythmic cadence.

After ten minutes had passed I said, "Stop. Return to your seats, please." When they were seated I continued. "Let's talk about what happened. How did walking while talking influence your attitude toward your problem?"

"Standing up made me feel more in charge of my situation," said one woman.

"Walking gave me a sense of progress, of moving forward," said another.

"Good. Tell me more about what you experienced."

"I could zero in on what was most important to say. I didn't get bogged down."

"I realized the problem wasn't really very significant."

"I think walking made me in a bigger hurry to solve the problem and then just get on with it."

"Thank you all," I said. "Now, think about this question. What effect did walking while talking have on the quality of your listening and coaching?" Two people stood up to answer at once. One man said, "I found I could concentrate better."

"Oh, really? How could that be the case? The noise and distractions in this crowded room were much worse than they would have been had you been able to go somewhere more private."

"Well, somehow walking around eliminates those distractions for me."

"Exactly," I said. "Walking helps you screen out those distractions because the physical movement competes for your attention and you have to put more effort into listening. Your mental focus is split between concentrating on what your partner is saying and not running into walls or the people in front of you. You *choose* to pay attention. The act of choosing to listen improves your listening."

I turned to the second person, who was still standing waiting to talk. "Did anything else happen in your experience of coaching while on the move?"

"I felt I could be more creative on my feet. I offered a lot of suggestions. I was enthusiastic and upbeat about how things could turn out."

"A psychologist by the name of Robert E. Thayer would not be surprised by what you just observed," I commented. "He conducts research on how complex physical movement, such as walking, affects our minds. In his book *The Biopsychology of Mood and Arousal*, he reports that ten minutes of complex movement—moving so that the right and left sides of your body are working in tandem—increases physical energy, elevates mood, and clarifies thinking for up to two hours!"

In workshop after workshop I hear participants say that walking puts them in a position to be creative, to listen intensely, and to coach others from a relaxed yet energetic perspective. It would appear that brisk, in-charge, directed movements of the body (such as those experienced in walking) set up the mind to operate in similar ways. In essence, walking becomes a metaphor for how your mind approaches your problems.

With this formula in mind, why not let the nature of what you want to accomplish mentally guide your physical activity? When you want to mull over an idea, try thinking about the subject while lying down. When you need to solve a problem, try walking, running, biking. When you're tired of writing the same old reports in the same old way, or of holding meetings that put people to sleep rather than inspire them, *get physical*.

Hold your meetings standing up (watch how little time is wasted!). Pace while you write that report, or write it after playing a wild game of tennis, or jacks. I've known executives who would never give a speech without working out in the two hours before the event. One time I was asked to give a seminar immediately following a bowling contest between the two sales forces who made up my audience. After bowling thirty frames, they were so physically primed they were ready to listen to anybody!

SELF-RENEWAL PRACTICE

Talk Walk

You might want to try my workshop exercise yourself.

1. Pick a partner, someone you know well and trust to be your confidant. Agree to meet each other for a ten-minute exchange of ideas about how to solve problems that are troubling each of you.

2. Start walking. Wear appropriate shoes. Walk briskly. Don't subject yourselves to inclement weather or difficult terrain: being physically comfortable is best.

3. Begin the conversation by describing your current problem. Ask the other person to listen and suggest solutions. Discuss your problem for five minutes.

4. Now, still walking, reverse the roles. Have your partner present his or her problem for discussion. You listen and make suggestions. Focus on solving your partner's problem for another five minutes.

5. When you have finished your ten-minute walk, stop your conversation and review what happened. Ask yourselves questions such as:

   • What effect did walking while talking have on the way we each presented our problems?
   • How did walking while talking affect the content of what we said and how we chose to express ourselves?
   • How did the experience of walking while talking affect our attitudes toward our particular problems? Were these attitudes different because we were standing (not sitting), moving forward (not still)?

   Be daring with your answers. Push yourselves to go beyond the obvious.

6. Next, examine the impact of walking while talking on the quality of your listening and coaching:

   • In what ways did moving forward in your walk together affect the solutions you were able to offer?
   • What impact did walking while talking have on your concentration while you listened?
   • In what ways was your experience as a walking coach and confidant different from what it would have been if you had been sitting down?

When you practice *Talk Walk*, your body's movements stimulate your creativity, logical thinking, and decision-making abilities, as well as providing you with the obvious benefits of moderate exercise. Realize from this practice and others you invent that the way you use your body has a strong impact on the quality of your life.

The Triumphs of Touch

Touch is the first sense we develop and the last sense to fade. Long after sight, hearing, smell, and taste have peaked, our sense of touch can continue to give us great pleasure.

Studies have shown that the amount of physical affection human infants receive has a huge impact on the overall physical health of these children. In the first of several now-famous experiments with young rhesus monkeys, Emory University researchers showed that these small primates instinctively choose touch (the soft, furry dummy mother monkey) *over* food (the sterile dummy mother with a bottle attached). Studies of children raised in orphanages corroborate these findings. Other social scientists provide conclusive evidence that touch is crucial to the healthy *emotional* growth of children as well. If a baby receives enough holding, he or she feels safe and thrives. Parents and others build a child's confidence through squeezes, hugs, pats on the back, and good-night kisses. To a child, the message of positive touch is loud and clear: "You are lovable."

Health care professionals are revolutionizing high-tech medicine by introducing the component of touch. Patients who receive daily massages as part of their nursing care often get well more quickly than patients who do not. Therapeutic massage is known to stimulate circulation, aid in the elimination of toxins, and induce deep states of relaxation. It also seems to help patients develop more compassion for their own bodies, which is thought to aid the healing process. It is interesting to note that the person doing the touching does not have to be someone close to or loved by the patient; just someone sincerely interested in the patient's recovery.

For centuries, healing through touch was a primary function of doctors, midwives, shamans, and medicine men in cultures all around the world. Even when "medicine" (herbs, for example) was prescribed, touch, along with the intense state of concentration of the practitioner, was the pivotal element of the cure. It is unclear exactly how the laying on of hands encourages the healing process. Some scientists believe in the value of increased circulation and relaxation, as mentioned above; others suggest that touching can rebalance disturbed energy fields. There is little doubt that touch reduces levels of anxiety and increases one's sense of security.

Even in old age, touch is vital. My own hunch is that nature left this one sense relatively responsive so that older humans would still have access to the life-saving benefits of pain—without pain you wouldn't know to take your hand away from a burning flame or go to see the doctor when your knees start to go. But the pleasurable side of touch has great benefits for this age group, too. You may be familiar with recent nursing-home studies in which residents who were given small pets and asked to stroke them daily were found to live longer and suffer less depression than their non-pet-owning counterparts.

Critical as touch is to human health and happiness, however, few of us get much of it after childhood. It is no coincidence that the virtual end of nonsexual sensuality comes at puberty: the hormonal drive toward sexuality is so strong that it typically subordinates other kinds of sensuality. As our sexual drives awaken, the medium of touch not only soothes but excites. It is during this period of sexual blossoming that our impulses to touch and be touched are most urgently felt and most stringently curtailed. Parents, teachers, clergy, and all manner of adult caretakers converge on the adolescent, working feverishly to channel teenage sexual desires into almost any intense activity that will prevent premature intimacy and pregnancy, as well as the many life-threatening sexually transmitted diseases to which a sexually active teenager is vulnerable. But while many adults work overtime to ensure the safety of teens, it would seem that an equal number of adults are trying desperately to make adolescents look at the world through sex-colored glasses. Advertisers, television producers, and movie makers, even clothes designers, have found that "sex sells," and teenagers (as well as younger children) are bombarded with sexual and sexualized messages. By the time a teen nears his or her second decade, the social barriers to direct sexual expression recede, while the cultural inducements continue unabated. It is the rare young adult today who is not sexually active.

Concentrating so much on sexuality leaves sensuality in the dust. Everything in our lives has become so highly sexualized that even an affectionate but nonsexual sensual act, such as holding a friend's hand, gains unnecessary sexual overtones. Study after study shows that teenage girls will submit to sex because they simply want "to be held." Sadly, it has become almost impossible to satisfy the human need for touch in any other way than through sexual contact, leaving the partnerless and the sexually unready yearning for this most basic of sensory experiences. In fact, sex therapists have noted that many problems perceived by couples as sexual in nature are actually the result of *sensual* dysfunction.

In midlife, most of us are aware of the fallout resulting from the marriage of sex and touch. A backrub becomes sex. A simple caress is interpreted as an invitation. We think twice before we hug a colleague. Many of the typical behaviors of a midlifer having what is unkindly referred to as a "midlife crisis" have a strong element of sensual yearning. Finding a new sex partner, overeating, and buying new toys (from sleek, cool guns to fast sports cars to luxurious lingerie) are all methods by which we try to reactivate our senses of touch. Most of these efforts fail, not only because they don't solve the psychological problems attendant to them, but also because they do not satisfy that basic and quite simple need for human touch.

Adult primates groom each other throughout their lives. Adult humans need this sort of touch as well. This is not to say that you have to braid your friends' hair or have somebody else bathe you. But to feel complete as a person you will need to invent ways to satisfy your natural and healthy urge to touch.

The hunger to be touched can be fed through simple means, such as patting a friend on the back, giving a hug, or getting a therapeutic massage. You can also find sensual pleasure in touching luxurious fabrics, stroking the soft fur of an animal, or reclining on cool grass or warm sand. But these methods do not hold a candle to the impact of a sensual exchange between two human beings.

Whom you touch is not important; why you touch is. To be effective, touch must come from the heart, from a true desire to give or receive affection, concern, or empathy. Touching to manipulate or control, or to communicate complex feelings, will not have the same result.

We know from studies of communication that nonverbal behavior conveys 93 percent of our message, far surpassing the power of the spoken word. Most of us have no trouble communicating through touch with our children or our significant others, but shy away from connecting in this way with colleagues, friends, or strangers. Or, as mentioned above, we throw a mantle of sexuality over our feelings about touch, and fear that our actions will be misinterpreted. (For that reason, be sure you do not reach out to someone physically without that person's consent; the misuse of touch is at the core of the current concern over sexual harassment.) But don't let the "touching taboo" stop you from enjoying one of the most important means of maintaining physical vigor and connection to others.

Rediscovering the joys of touch may take a while. If it has been a long time since you allowed yourself to make use of this simple and pleasant mode of communicating, it may feel silly at first. It may take courage. Modify the Self-Renewal Practice below in any way you desire. Make it comfortable for you. Be creative, and take small steps. You can do this exercise with anyone which whom you feel comfortable—a friend, a family member, even a fellow class-mate or coworker whom you trust.

SELF-RENEWAL PRACTICE

Back to Back, Face to Face

This Self-Renewal Practice is adapted from an exercise invented by Gay Gaer Luce and published in *Your Second Life*. Read through the entire set of guidelines before you begin the exercise. Many people find it helpful to tape-record the steps of this Self-Renewal Practice so that they can more deeply relax during the experience. If you tape-record the instructions, be sure to pause sufficiently between each step. For this practice you need a partner—someone you know and trust.

1. Sit with your back against your partner's back. (This is easy when you are sitting on the floor or carpet.) Close your eyes and take three very deep breaths. Sigh and relax.

Pay close attention to breathing in relaxation and breathing out tension. Feel your partner's breathing rhythm through your back.

Sense your partner's feelings by his or her breathing. You can do this by imitating your partner's breath.

2. Without speaking, one of you lean on the other very slowly. Relax and let your head come to rest against your partner's head. Let your shoulders relax. Lean on your partner as far as your partner can bear your weight.

You may be able to lean on your partner completely, totally relaxed. Give yourselves time to experience this state of tandem relaxation.

Massage each other, back to back. You may massage your partner by rolling your head against his or her neck and shoulders. Now put your hands behind your head and feel your partner's neck.

Let your partner lean on you.

Repeat the entire procedure.

3. When you have repeated Step 2 again, and your partner has massaged your neck and head, turn and face each other.

Take your glasses off if you wear them.

Without speaking, decide which of you will go first and feel the other person's face. Let the first explorer gently touch his or her partner's face, exploring the features. Both partners should have their eyes closed. Then switch and let the second partner explore.

When you have both gently explored each other's faces, open your eyes and tell each other how it felt.

Luce gives the following example of how effective this type of exercise can be:

Two women who had not known each other well threw their arms around each other. "I didn't know I liked you so much. Then I felt your back rubbing against mine. It was your spine tickling me." People were astounded at the pleasure and relaxation they drew from feeling themselves back to back. They were amazed at the affection conveyed in that simple contact with another person's back. Then when they explored each other's faces, they touched each other with a fond tenderness that they hadn't felt an hour earlier.

With one squeeze of the hand or caress of the face, the welcomed touch of another person can delight you, excite you, soothe you, and fill you with desire, wonder, and appreciation, all at once. Giving another the same gift is equally rewarding. The more you communicate through touch, even in small ways, the easier it will be. And once you rediscover how effective it is, the more you will want to do it.

VICTORIES OF PHYSICAL VIGOR

The rewards of Physical Vigor are mutually enhancing. Most people find that living a healthier lifestyle heightens their enjoyment of all physical activity, because they feel more energetic, alert, and agile. Taking advantage of natural bodily rhythms makes it easier to optimize exercise, good nutrition, and rest periods. Inventing new ways to stimulate the sense of touch brings gains in relaxation and healing.

Now, more than ever, your body can provide you with a way to stay grounded. Smell the earth, caress a puppy, pedal a bike on a summer day, and you know you are alive. As you stay in touch with physical sensations, you can more easily stay in touch with your emotions and pace yourself so you can go the extra mile to meet the demands of your days.

For people who want to contribute to the world during their midlife years, stamina and sound health are indispensable. Consider the contribution Indira Gandhi's body made to her midlife career. Mrs. Gandhi was first elected prime minister of India in 1966, when she was forty-nine. During her comeback election campaign in 1980, when Prime Minister Gandhi was sixty-three years old, she traveled 94,500 miles in sixty-three days. During this physically demanding campaign, Gandhi had the energy to speak to over 240 million of her countrymen in open-air meetings.

Athletes and artists continue to push the midlife envelope of physical prowess. Famed dancer Fred Astaire was called out of retirement when he was forty-eight to star in *Easter Parade*. Astaire then restarted his career, a testament to the physical stamina and grace that is possible during midlife. When he was fifty-five, Fred Astaire starred in *Daddy Long Legs*; at fifty-seven he starred in *Funny Face*; and at sixty-one he starred in *Silk Stockings*. Even at seventy-eight, Astaire was working, this time in a dramatic role in the television drama *A Family Upside-Down*.

Being grounded in the body is not just for professionals. Body wisdom can elevate anyone to a new plane. Any of us who has felt his or her heart beating strongly while panting for breath, or noticed the simple joy of being held, has experienced the wonder of just being. This is a basic foundation for spiritual serenity. It is also the basis for passion. Without a strong connection to your body, you cannot feel the full force of your emotions.

When you do what is necessary to stay healthy on the inside, you become more attractive on the outside—and you lay a great foundation for remaining healthy longer. From now on, do what people with true physical vigor do: welcome any physical activity as a gift, always ready to give you a boost and lift your spirits. May your body pay tribute to the incredible, pivotal point of midlife by feeling better, looking great, and staying healthy.

CHAPTER 5

Pathway #3: Emotional Vitality

*since feeling is first
who pays any attention
to the syntax of things
will never wholly kiss you;
. . . then
laugh, leaning back in my arms
for life's not a paragraph*

And death i think is no parenthesis.

—E. E. CUMMINGS

One evening over a dozen years ago I sat at a small Formica table in my friend Stacy's kitchen, crying my heart out. This was the fourth breakup of the same romance, and the fourth time Stacy was nursing me through the crisis.

After much sobbing and an agonized analysis of my troubled relationship with Henry, I turned to Stacy for her response. Looking as exhausted and bewildered as I felt, Stacy leaned across the table and said, "Kathy, don't you realize that it is your job in life to be joyful?"

I stared back at Stacy in stunned silence. What did she mean? How was joy possible at this moment of profound grief? What on earth does joy have to do with getting over a broken heart? I didn't know what to make of her words, but something about them rang true, and they stayed with me.

Several days later, feeling a bit more calm, I took advantage of some quiet moments after work to wonder about the absence of joy in my life. It dawned on me that not since my childhood had I experienced what I would term true happiness. The realization shocked me and triggered another difficult-to-swallow thought: from the time I was a teenager until my early thirties, many of my most intense emotions had been negative ones. I felt sorry for myself when I lost at romance; I railed against the universe when I failed to move ahead fast enough in my career. The only time I rated my existence as even mildly happy was when my life was going according to my detailed plans. When my wishes were not met, or when I failed at meeting a self-imposed goal, I felt discouraged, and I had to admit that "discouraged" was how I felt far too much of the time. If Stacy was correct about joy being my *job* in life, I was failing pretty miserably.

Confused, yet determined to deal with this business of being joyful, I slowly worked my way out of chronic discontent. I made an effort to enjoy the good things that came my way—from the office party that would previously have just gotten in the way of my work to the kind words of a stranger admiring my outfit. My perspective began to change.

I furthered my emotional quest by studying how feelings are *supposed* to evolve over a person's lifetime. To my surprise, I found that my experience of joy as "happiness when things go my way" is typical during the first half of life. During the second half of life, however, emotionally healthy adults are capable of experiencing true joy despite the bad things that might happen to them. After half a lifetime, most of us catch on to the idea that some days things "work" and some days they don't, regardless of how hard we try. We lose the grandiosity of youth that says we can and must be the force at the center of life. If we can take advantage of this perspective—which is one of the gifts midlife just hands us—we can enjoy our children, laugh at a joke, and sleep just fine despite the fact that our dinner party flopped, our marriage is faltering, or a big contract just blew up in our faces. If we do our emotional homework, our feelings can continue to be a source of great excitement, as they were in our teens, twenties, and thirties, but they can also cease to burden us the way they did when we were young. They may even bring us happiness.

Just the other day I took a break during a seminar and went for a walk through a meadow behind the hotel. The field turned out to be thorny and a bit treacherous for a woman in heels. Ten years ago I would have cursed, ripped my stockings, and told myself I was an idiot for attempting an impromptu nature walk. But at forty-five, with lots of emotional work behind me, I could ignore the frustrating terrain and focus on the fact that something about the field reminded me of the special "alone place" I went to as a child, and I felt a huge surge of spontaneous joy.

THE CALL TO EMOTIONAL VITALITY

Few people come to me at midlife with a "joy" problem, but many complain to me that they feel depressed. Others wonder aloud whether they are turning "soft" in their middle age: all of a sudden a simple act of kindness, or a news story of a tragedy halfway around the world, has the power to bring tears to eyes that never used to cry. Then there are those who tell me that they have felt so many strong emotions for so long that they fear they have become numb. All are relieved to learn that these experiences are nature's signs that they are ready to move to a new level of emotional depth, resilience, and spontaneity.

Check the list below and see if you are ready to journey down the path of emotional growth.

Midlife Readiness Signals for Emotional Vitality
You may find yourself:

- experiencing more frequent or more intense periods of depression.
- feeling the need to improve the way you express your feelings.
- worrying that your emotions are running away with you.
- being unexpectedly flooded with positive or negative emotion.
- wanting to trust your feelings more when making decisions.

- noticing a new ability to see the humorous side of things, even in tough situations.
- reaching deeper levels of joy and sadness than seemed possible before.

The call to Emotional Vitality may be less clear than the call to Mental Mastery or Physical Vigor. Our language contains far more words for talking about ideas than it does for expressing feelings. Furthermore, it is the very nature of emotions to get tangled up. A feeling as basic as "love" can be tied to trust, respect, support, understanding, sex, and more.

But by far the toughest problem we face in our emotional lives is that we have had so little emotional training. Few of us *know how* to respond competently to anger, pain, and fear, or *know why* our current coping mechanisms do not work. The need to deal with our emotions occurs with greater frequency than the need for reading, arithmetic, or knowledge about sex positions, yet we know more about these latter areas than we do about emotion. There seems to be an unspoken assumption that this most basic facet of human existence is just something we have to figure out on our own.

Research on emotion lags far behind research on other areas of social science, in part because emotions are so difficult to quantify and evaluate, but also because the emotional arena has been dominated by religion for so long. It is only in the last hundred years that the average person has been able to conceive of his or her emotions independent of spirituality; the increasing secularization of society has meant that fewer of us turn to religion—with its precepts, rituals, counselors, and promises—when we experience emotional pain. Perhaps most important, the world changes that have taken place in the last century have increased the need for emotional support systems, yet we have not as a culture developed any new ways of keeping up with the pace and intensity of our emotions. Increasing numbers of psychologists and psychiatrists agree that the complexities of modern life, and our culture's devaluation of feelings, may necessitate an emotional revolution as forceful as the sexual revolution of the last quarter century.

Only rare individuals ascend to midlife in full harmony with their innermost feelings. Most of us reach the prime of our lives burdened by unresolved feelings from childhood and unaware of the bounty unadulterated feelings can provide.

So do not be hard on yourself if you discover that some of the gems in your emotional treasure chest are outdated. Go back to your Life Map and objectives for this area, which you outlined in Chapter 1, and pay special attention to problems you would like to resolve. Begin slowly and recognize that you are forging a path through your wilderness.

ADVENTURES IN EMOTIONAL VITALITY

The rewards of emotional vitality are so many and so far-reaching that you may find yourself wishing you had made this journey long ago. But only a midlife traveler can appreciate and take advantage of the rewards along this pathway; you need the confidence and outlook that come after spending a few years on the planet to make the most of the discoveries found here.

In this chapter you can learn to free yourself from the tyranny of depression, rage, and free-floating anxiety—those unwanted visitors that have drained your energy and zest for life. I will show you ways to get back in touch with what you truly feel, and to use your feelings to change your life for the better. Midlifers who are willing to do the work of getting in touch with what matters to the heart report huge gains in mental clarity, physical energy, interpersonal communication, and spiritual readiness. Best of all, they say they have a better sense than ever of who they are and how to present that self to the world.

Cooling Your Hot Buttons

My friend Anabel's mother kept a beautiful multicolored tin full of buttons hidden away in her linen closet when Anabel was a little girl. Anabel's mother didn't sew, which made the cache of pretty buttons that much more special. It had been handed down from *her* mother, and I know Anabel hoped that one day it would be hers. She and her siblings treated each button like a valuable jewel, and she swears that in all their games of Who's Got the Button? not one button was ever lost.

When Anabel first told me this story, I was working with a client who was trying to get her emotions "out of the closet," and the button box struck me as the perfect metaphor—quite dreamlike in its symbolism—for what she was going through. The client, whom I will call Gwen, was a forty-two-year-old woman who had an unusually difficult time handling rejection.

In the course of our discussions it came out that Gwen's mother would punish Gwen for typical childlike misbehavior by refusing to speak to the child or show her any affection *for days at a time*. As a little girl, Gwen was so terrified by her mother's emotional absence that she would dissolve into tears, begging her mother to hold her and talk to her. Not surprisingly, the adult Gwen found herself completely undone when ignored by anyone in authority. In fact, she had come to see me after a demoralizing fallout with her boss, who had unwittingly "pushed her buttons" by withdrawing from her, precipitating an emotional upset entirely out of proportion to the situation. Gwen told me that because of a previous disagreement, "my boss decided to boycott the conference I was in charge of running. As soon as I got the message that I was in disfavor, I began crying and could not stop. No effort on my part to reconcile our differences was successful. I made three direct attempts to contact him by phone the next day and four more attempts through intermediaries. The response was always the same: no discussion was possible at this time. His mistreatment of me felt exactly like the punishment my mother used. I was humiliated to be treated with such scorn."

In this ghastly game of Who's Got the Button? she was coming out the loser every time.

Thanks to research conducted at Harvard University's Department of Human Development and the work of scholars in the departments of psychology at the State University of New York and Denver University, we now have evidence of how our basic emotions develop and how these emotions in turn develop us: by the time we reach adulthood, we have learned to avoid seeing our inner emotional experience as a teacher and instead have suppressed our emotions in order to adapt to the outside world.

Researchers in many areas of psychology have suffered from this error, too, claiming that rational thought is superior to the presumably less complex accomplishments of emotionality. Fortunately, the emerging view is that reason and emotions are two equally valuable modes of learning about oneself and the world. Reason allows us to reduce inner and outer events into manageable bits of information, while emotion gives us a direct experience of whatever happens and feeds our sense of personal significance. As developmental theorist Jerome Bruner concludes, *both* modes of experience are necessary to advance our maturity, and they work best in concert.

By midlife, many of us find that the good work our minds did to protect and socialize us when we were young has outlived its usefulness. In Gwen's case, her healthy psychological *defenses* protected her, in childhood, from recognizing the unbearable truth that her mother, on whom she was completely dependent, could be terribly cruel. Rather than admit the unthinkable, Gwen convinced herself that she deserved the harsh punishment. Her well-founded fear of abandonment caused her to play up to, even idealize, the very person who was hurting her. Unfortunately, Gwen's defenses were still up in adulthood, despite the fact that she was no longer technically dependent on those in authority.

Gwen was determined to relieve herself of this heavy emotional baggage from childhood. The legacy of her mother's rejection was rendering her helpless as an adult. Together, we devised a plan. We agreed that every time Gwen experienced a sense of rejection, no matter how small, she would give herself permission to cry, without holding back, to let out her anger and shame. As soon as the initial burst of emotion had passed, she was to assess what might be causing the other person to act inappropriately. Gwen needed to learn how to be curious about the faults and failings of the rejecter instead of concentrating so much on her own possible failures.

Over time, Gwen learned to stop falling into her old habit of hating herself and glorifying her abuser. Eventually, she came to believe that her childhood trauma was a direct result of her mother's perpetuating the abuse she herself had endured as a child. Once Gwen could admit that her mother's distress was the real reason for her behavior, Gwen was able to see her own innocence in the matter, mourn her mistreatment, and actually find compassion to forgive her mother for punishing her so unjustly. Grieving for her own pain and forgiving these parental transgressions was Gwen's ticket to emotional freedom and maturity.

Gwen's case is a clear example of the ways in which the emotional injuries of our childhood can carry over into adult life. It is important to take a close look at your own past to see if you have any "buttons" that interfere with your ability to make the most of your emotional life.

No matter how good our experiences with our parents or at school might have been, each of us harbors episodes of childhood anger, fear, and shame that are frozen in the past and are carried along with us, as unresolved issues, into adulthood. Can you remember times in your childhood when you sat alone somewhere, feeling small and angry and humiliated? Maybe someone wouldn't let you play outside, or made you go to bed when others were still awake, or couldn't buy you the toy you wanted more than life itself. There were prohibitions against your natural urges to express your true feelings in direct ways such as hitting someone who angered you, screaming in fear, running for joy. Sometimes you even got into trouble for simply *saying* how you felt ("I hate you!").

There were probably occasions when you could not contain your feelings and hit your brother, or took your frustrations out on yourself ("I'm so stupid!"), but rarely would you have the courage to go up against the big guys, for fear of antagonizing them. Unless you grew up in an unusually enlightened household, you never felt safe expressing the full measure of your emotions, and so learned early on to depress, not express, negative emotion toward those who were in charge. And because it was too painful to believe that the people you loved the most could not see (or cope with) your feelings, you yourself began to underrate your emotions.

Alice Miller, psychiatrist and ground-breaking author of the classic *The Drama of the Gifted Child*, explains in her new book, *Break-*

ing Down the Wall of Silence, how important it is for us to come to terms with emotional wounds from childhood. She states:

> . . . We build walls to screen ourselves from painful facts because we have never learned whether or how we can live with this knowledge. . . . Behind the wall we erect to protect ourselves from the history of our childhood still stands the neglected child we once were, the child that was abandoned and betrayed. It waits for us to summon the courage to hear its voice. It wants to be protected and understood, and it wants us to free it from its isolation, loneliness, and speechlessness. But this child who has waited so long for our attention not only has needs to be fulfilled. It also has a gift for us, a gift that we desperately need if we truly want to live, a gift that cannot be purchased and that the child in us alone can bestow. It is the gift of the truth, which can free us from the prison of destructive opinions and conventional lies. Ultimately, it is the gift of security, which our rediscovered integrity will give us. The child only waits for us to be ready to approach it, and then, together, we will tear down the walls.

If you are not sure where your own emotional hot buttons are, look at situations in which you find yourself overreacting. Do you go crazy waiting in line at the supermarket? You may want to think back to times you were kept waiting as a child. Did you have to wait until your father got home to eat dinner? Wait for your parents to finish speaking before you could have your say? Not every childhood event is emotional fodder. What you are looking for is areas in which you have a knee-jerk emotional reaction, and situations where you look back at your adult behavior with a certain amount of dismay.

In my work helping people heal emotional wounds at midlife, I have noticed a distinct pattern. First, the individual experiences several upsetting episodes of emotional button-pushing, and reacts much more intensely than circumstances require. (Family and friends may voice concern over unusual outbursts or withdrawals.) Once the emotional cat is out of the bag, the person begins to question what is going on inside himself or herself that could be causing such powerful feelings of anger or depression or anxiety or guilt or shame. Then comes a crucial crossroads: the midlife journeyer chooses to rationalize his or her behavior (as a biochemical disturbance of menopause, a "midlife crisis," personality quirks, or unusually stressful circumstances), or takes personal responsibility for turning inward to heal the self.

The choice to attend to painful blows from long ago is at the heart of the challenges presented to many of the midlife heroes depicted in great literature. Of this daunting odyssey into the inferno of the inner world, Dante said: "Midway this way of life we're bound upon,/I woke to find myself in a dark wood,/Where the right road was wholly lost and gone." A little-known Sumerian myth, committed to clay tablets in the third millennium B.C., tells of the descent of Inanna, Queen of Heaven and Earth, into the underworld. Jungian scholar Sylvia Brinton Perera describes the ruler of Inanna's inner realm this way: "She is full of fury, greed, the fear of loss, and even self-spite. She symbolizes raw instinctuality split off from consciousness—need and aggression in the underworld." One of our jobs in becoming full-fledged adults is to embrace the pain we could not afford to feel during our younger years. Allowing yourself to "live" the unexperienced pain of the past is the only way to unclog your emotional system and live in the here and now.

Take a few minutes right now to look at a Self-Renewal Practice that you can use whenever you need to release feelings that may be trapped inside you. It is a good idea to isolate yourself in order to try out this Self-Renewal Practice. Be as gentle, patient, and loving with yourself as you would be with an innocent and pained young child. Allow yourself to feel awkward or strange, frightened or sad. Explore ways to feel safe while experiencing and expressing the full range of your emotions.

SELF-RENEWAL PRACTICE

Unfreezing Your Emotions

This practice is designed to help you bring neglected or unexpressed emotional responses from your past to the forefront of your mind so you can recognize them and release their negative energy. Pay attention to any physical sensations that arise as you work on this exercise. Symptoms of stress are a sign that you are hitting close to home; these symptoms should lessen once you work through the issues.

1. Select the type of disturbing situation for which you want to devise a different emotional response. Situations that are painful or that cause you to overreact are good candidates for reprogramming. In your journal, describe as specifically as possible what it is that disturbs you about the experience.

2. Ask yourself what threatens you the most about your disturbing situation. What is at the root of your fears? What could hurt or harm you? What could you lose?

3. Think about what might happen if you acted on your most extreme feelings. Then imagine how you would feel if you did just that. Listen carefully to what you hear.

4. Recall childhood experiences that triggered similar negative feelings. How did you respond to those uncomfortable emotions when you were a child? Did you minimize or hide your true reaction? Blame others? Seek approval? Acquiesce? Retaliate in a devious way?

   Allow youself to feel the pain of *not* having been able to express your feelings as a child. Feel compassion for the child you were. Don't worry about whether the child "deserves" compassion, or whether the child had the right to feel one way or another. Focus on the feelings. Think about how you, as an adult, would respond to that child today.

5. Go back to the original problem and, with your new understanding of why you might feel so strongly about the situation, try to generate adult responses by thinking about how a calm, competent, self-assured adult would handle the disturbance. Consider the consequences of expressing your feelings directly. Ask both the agitated and clear-thinking sides of you what to do, and build on your response to *both* sources. Take your time. Listen closely to what happens inside you as you go through this process.

If you make a habit of using this Self-Renewal Practice each time you encounter unruly feelings, you will find yourself reacting better the next time a similar event occurs. The more often you do this exercise, the more you (and not your emotions) will be in charge of negative situations, and the more authentically you will respond to others who push your buttons.

Here is how one of my workshop participants completed this exercise:

1. Whenever my husband starts to criticize me for the way I look or how I parent the kids, I hold my ground for a while and then cave in to his demands or threats. I end up feeling horrible about myself for being such a doormat and I resent him for his mean verbal attacks.

2. I am afraid that if I stand my ground my husband will eventually reject me and leave our marriage. I don't really think he loves me, and I realize that he's just a "power broker," but I don't want to have to deal with being alone.

3. I can see my angry self yelling back at him, even kicking him. I can watch the irate, hurt part of me slam the door and leave him forever. How dare he abuse me? I have every right to be angry. I have every right to leave. My anger is justified. It would feel great to be as cruel to him as he is to me, but only at first. In the end I think I would feel bad for treating him as terribly as he treats me. I don't want to stoop to his level just to get even.

4. As a little girl I always felt that I had to give in to my parents' wishes. When they reprimanded they almost made it sound as if I had to be a good girl so that they could love me. "If only they really knew me," I would think to myself. "If they understood the real me they wouldn't spit on me." I often felt like running away just to show them how they had hurt me. I also thought about getting a new set of parents, parents who would love me. But of course I just behaved better; love on their terms was better than no love at all.

5. Now that I am an adult, I can afford to feel the anger that wells up inside me when my husband puts me down. My anger will protect me. It will let me know my own desires and needs more clearly, and help me stand up for myself.

   I want to learn how to welcome anger as my friend. I'll be happier if I can trust my anger and see it as a signal that abuse is coming from someone else—like my husband—or my own critical comments about myself. I hope to react to my husband more thoughtfully, not in the first rush of anger, but after considering what that anger means.

   As an adult I can afford to show my husband the real me so that he knows the person who is his wife. As I child I had to hide myself away. It is a risk even now to reveal myself, but I would rather lose this relationship than betray myself and stay hidden and paralyzed by my fears.

Learning to command new, more constructive emotional responses to disturbing situations doesn't happen overnight. You cannot hope to erase years of habit in one sitting. If you want to speed up the work, consider enlisting the aid of a competent and caring psychologist or counselor. A good therapist will help you through the tangled web of emotions and clarify issues you may not be able to see right away. If you find yourself with a therapist who tells you what to do or insists you see things his or her way, stop seeing that person. Therapy is about helping you find *your* way, not forcing you to subscribe to the views of someone else—that is what got you in trouble in the first place!

If you become comfortable with the hurt, angry, fearful child within yourself, you will be able to accept yourself as you really are, not just as how others see you or how you want to see yourself. There is a whole side of your personality that is lazy, selfish, and greedy, just as there is a side of you full of wonder, affection, and openness to new experiences. Carl Jung and his followers call your less appealing characteristics the *shadow self*. Once you welcome the shadow side of yourself into conscious awareness, you will find it easier to live with yourself. One man I know always had a difficult time getting out of bed in the mornings, and it bothered him immensely because he had a mental picture of himself as a real "go-getter." It was not until he acknowledged his shadow tendencies to hide from the trials of the day that he could reconcile his desire to stay in bed with his positive self-image. Not only has this man reorganized his life to allow himself to spend an "illogical" extra half hour in bed in the morning, but he is also less hard on himself in other areas. He claims that his enthusiasm for work has increased, and that he is happier in general.

It is much easier to accept the negative aspects of your shadow self if you also get in touch with the playful, spontaneous side of you, which may also be buried in the past. One way to do that is to shift your internal spotlight from *rumination to reverie*. Rumination creates a major barrier to emotional well-being by allowing pain from the past to contaminate how we feel in the present. Reverie allows us to apply the pleasurable feelings from the past to our present situations.

When you find yourself ruminating, return to the Self-Renewal Practice for unfreezing your emotions. But whenever you want a boost, push your *positive* buttons with a little reverie.

SELF-RENEWAL PRACTICE

Emotional Refreshment

1. Remember pastimes and play times that brought you joy as a child. List at least three of them in your journal. Try to feel once again the pleasurable emotions associated with them.

2. See if you can find any common threads in your joyful experiences. What do digging in the sandbox, performing a jackknife dive, and building a house out of sticks and leaves have in common? Sensuality (feeling sand, water, leaves)? Physical challenge? Repetitive emotions?

3. Think about what you gained from your favorite childhood activities. Did they energize you? Excite you? Relax you? Make you feel free? How did the joy you got from those activities affect the way you approached the world?

4. Consider ways to invite more episodes of joy into your adult life. Look for activities that replicate the characteristics you discovered in Step 2. You might ask yourself what kinds of activities provide you with time alone, time outside, play time, or the chance to be creative.

Many people find that playing childhood games, alone or with friends, outdoors or in, is a terrific way to tap into the joy and freedom experienced in childhood. Highly physical games, such as tennis or softball, seem to work especially well, since they also replicate the active side of childhood. Even something as simple as giving in to the urge to run or jump, call a friend, or buy ourselves a piece of candy can trigger a flood of warm feeling. The more often you engage in reverie, the more often you will experience spontaneous moments of connection with your pleasurable past, just as I did when I went for my walk in the field described at the beginning of the chapter.

Your personal button box is full. But to keep your collection valuable, you must take the buttons out periodically, examine them, give special attention to any that are in need of repair, and look for new buttons to replace or augment the damaged ones. Most important, take the prettiest and most special of them out of the box, and leave them out where everyone can see.

Name That Feeling

Kim, an architect, stood in her office, dumbfounded. Her boss, a petty and manipulative man, had just told her she was not going to get the raise she expected. Tears burning behind her eyes, Kim found the words to ask why.

"I don't like your attitude," the man replied. "We'll see how things look in another three months."

As Kim made her way home, her head spun. "I was really counting on that raise. Is he just being cheap? *Do* I have an attitude problem? God, it's going to look awful if I get fired."

At home, Kim plopped down on the couch and cried tears of bitter frustration as a mass of conflicting thoughts and emotions descended upon her. She searched her memory for any time she might have been unpleasant, curt, or unenthusiastic, but could find none. She was sure her boss had been unfair, but she also realized that since it was just the two of them in the office, he was going to be the one calling the shots. She spent the weekend in a frenzy of worry, depression, fury, self-doubt, and self-pity. In fact, the discussion with her boss bothered Kim for a long time. Six months later, she still found herself mulling it over as she went for her morning run, did dishes, or tried to fall asleep. She talked about it to friends, long past the point where they were helpful or interested.

When Kim told me this story, it was twelve years old, the problem long resolved: "I decided to give my boss what he wanted— attention—even though it cut into the time I needed to do my job well. I just smiled at him all the time, pretended to care when he told me his trouble and, when he wasn't around, did my work. After three months he told me my attitude had improved tremendously, and gave me my raise. But even though I think I handled the situation well, it still bothers me. I can't believe I let a jerk like that get to me."

I congratulated Kim on her ability to make a seemingly untenable situation work. Time and perspective had only underscored Kim's impression that her boss was a deeply troubled man, and that not getting the raise was no reflection on her work or her professionalism. It was clear to me, however, that Kim was still stuck in the emotional quagmire that had made the incident with her boss so painful. For all her intelligence and willingness to make the best of a bad situation, Kim had suffered more than necessary at the hands of her boss.

As Kim and I discussed how she could learn to deal better with complex problems such as the one that had hurt her so many years ago, she told me she thought she needed to be more like her boy-friend.

"Mike never lets stuff like that get to him," she said. "When Mike's boss yelled at him the other day, Mike just said to hell with him and forgot about it. I wish I could do that."

Kim and Mike approach their emotions quite differently. Kim dwells on her feelings to excess. She wards off experiencing her feelings through the clever mind games of analyzing, synthesizing, and rationalizing. Mike, on the other hand, avoids the emotional element of a negative situation altogether by completely shutting out all thoughts of it. What Kim was surprised to learn is that she and Mike both suffer from the problem psychologists term *alexithymia* (a-*leks*-i-*thigh*-mi-a), a Greek word that in its original form means "no words for emotion."

James Lynch, psychologist and author of *The Language of the Heart*, likens alexithymia to color-blindness. Just as those who are color-blind have no idea what they are missing, alexithymia victims "cannot tell you what it feels like to be sad, angry, or in love—except in rational terms." Perhaps the oddest irony of alexithymia is that people who have a professional need to understand emotions sometimes do not. Sigmund Freud, the founder of psychoanalysis, was plagued by acute alexithymia. Lynch surmises that though Freud was "brilliantly rational about his feelings, [he] himself may have had great difficulty expressing his own feelings, or for that matter, feeling those of his patients."

Like Freud, people like Kim and Mike often think they are emotionally healthy, the former because they can talk about their feelings and can "emote," the latter because they avoid getting enmeshed in what they consider to be troublesome and unnecessary emotions. But in truth, neither is able to perform the most important skill of mature adult emotional response—to link feelings to behavior—because they are both doing a great job of avoiding their feelings.

By keeping herself busy analyzing her situation, Kim avoided the truth: her boss had hurt her feelings. He had also scared her, because his actions showed that one of Kim's comforting beliefs—the idea that if you did a good job you would be treated well—was not true. Kim and I talked at length about whether her emotional armor was helping her in her career, and she came to an important realization.

"If I had just listened to my feelings," Kim said, "I could have saved myself a lot of grief. I would have been better off admitting right away that he hurt me, and just letting myself be sad. Instead, I agonized over it for two years. Listen to me—it *still* bugs me! What really gets me is that I was so unwilling to acknowledge that I had made some incorrect assumptions about the workplace. If I'd just admitted that life is not fair—and my feelings were *screaming it* at me!—I wouldn't have carried this problem around for so long."

Like most of my clients, Kim didn't realize that thoughts and speech can destroy our connection with our true feelings; her fancy mental footwork actually kept her emotions *walled in*. I asked Kim to consider what she would do now, were she to face a similar experience.

"I do not think I would act differently," she said. "I needed that job until I could find another. But you can bet that I'd take the time to mourn the loss of a favorite lie to myself, and I'd allow myself to get *angry* at that guy—though not to his face. I know I had a right to be angry, even if I couldn't act on that anger. If I did all these things to take care of myself, then my action would be savvy business strategy instead of a limp coping mechanism."

Mike was not a client of mine, but over the years I have seen many people with Mike's problem. While Kim's feelings are *walled in*, Mike's are *walled out*. Mike uses his highly evolved cerebral cortex (the portion of the brain responsible for thinking and verbal skills) to override his instinctual urges. In this way he is able to delay gratification, focus blindly on a goal, and pretend to himself that he is above something as base and unnecessary as emotion.

Like Kim, Mike must learn to listen to his feelings. In some ways he has it harder than Kim; she is at least used to talking about feelings. But once Mike can get over the hurdle of admitting he *has* feelings, he will be able to experience them in pretty much their raw state, without all the mental gyrations that put Kim in limbo.

As you might guess, the Kims and Mikes of the world often pair off in work and personal situations. Even though they do not get along, they use each other to play emotional "hot potato," blaming each other for whatever irks them.

Kim and Mike represent extremes on the continuum of alexithymia, but I have noticed in my practice that most of my clients have trouble expressing their feelings. Lynch himself estimates that 90 percent of adults suffer from alexithymia to some degree. The price of being chronically out of touch with our most basic emotions is being doomed to repeated incidents of inappropriate action. Emotionally driven people like Kim find themselves worrying constantly, whining, or pushing a confrontation; emotionally avoidant people like Mike tend to blow up at others unexpectedly, eat or drink too much, or become unusually inflexible on unimportant issues.

According to Dr. Hans Selye, the father of stress research, "it is not what happens to you that matters, it's how you react that counts." Since Selye's death in 1982, stress researchers have not only confirmed the validity of his ideas, but also defined the type of reaction that yields the best results in emotionally charged situations. The four elements of a healthy emotional response are:

appraisal → feeling → thought → behavior

Appraisal is an often overlooked aspect of emotional health. With appraisal, we assess the dangers and opportunities inherent in any circumstance that has triggered emotion. If you underestimate danger, for example, you may get yourself killed; if you overestimate it, you are likely to wind up unnecessarily fearful or angry.

Common sense is the best tool for deciding which emotions should be acted upon and which should be experienced and simply let go. If you think you have problems with accurate appraisal, ask yourself, "Would I want a friend in this circumstance to take it seriously?" and you will be more likely to get a commonsense response than a knee-jerk one.

Feeling may seem like the most obvious piece of the emotional-response puzzle. Tears, a knot in your stomach, a flutter of panic in your chest, and the uncontrollable urge to laugh or smile are healthy signs that your emotions have triggered thousands of neurochemical changes in your physiology. As we saw with Mike and Kim, how-ever, many of us are so uncomfortable with our feelings that we ignore our body's distress signals.

Emotionally mature people take autonomic stress responses as a sign that their feelings must be dealt with. They allow themselves to experience the feelings fully, even if they are painful. Only at this point can they follow the natural propulsion toward rational thought that leads to appropriate action (or inaction). For example, it is only after a widow admits the depth of her pain that she can allow herself to take appropriate action—mourning, taking some time off from work, being especially kind to herself. Neglecting to feel the hurt fully leads to the kind of inappropriate action—pre-tending nothing has changed, starting to date, getting angry at others—that will only make her more unhappy.

Feelings always manage to find a way out. You know that already: tension headaches, insomnia, mild depression, and "acid" stomach have plagued all of us at one time or another. Denied emotions even prompt our bodies to respond as though threatened. In the absence of some kind of physical release or stress management technique, your body remains "all dressed up with nowhere to go," stuck in a state of internal alarm. Recent medical studies show that seven out of ten people who feel sick enough to call their physcans are suf-fering from some type of unresolved emotional distress. We know from the research of cardiologist Robert Eliot, as well as from stud-ies of the "Type A personality," that *walling in* your feelings of anger is linked to heart disease. *Walling out* feelings of sadness over the death of a loved one has likewise been shown to be a predictor of cancer. In many ways, curing alexithymia is as important to your physical health as it is to your emotional well-being.

We also pay a price for squelching our natural responses to plea-surable emotions. Few of us are rewarded in societal terms for fully expressing joy. Imagine being able to tell a coworker how warmly you regarded her when she spoke up at a meeting, or feeling free to run down the street jumping for joy when you find out some good news! The side effects of joy suppression may not seem so dire until you consider how empty a life without joy can be. The empty-life syndrome may lead to severe depression, or to addiction to alcohol or cocaine or other drugs. Cognitive psychologists have recently hypothesized that the capacity to take pleasure in people, activities, and things is a primary factor in overcoming addiction.

If we pay attention to our feelings, we stay on the road to healthy, reflective *thought*. With informed thought, we can actually vary the intensity of our feelings, or shift from one feeling to another. For instance, by focusing on the long-term gains that will accrue if you tolerate the frustration of finishing a tough assignment, you can shift from feeling anxious to feeling eager—a subtle but powerful difference that will affect your work. Failure to feel, on the other hand, leads either to unproductive circuitous thought (which produces further anxiety) or to denial (and its companion, procrastination).

The fourth step in the chain of healthy emotional response is *action*. Once we have appraised, felt, and thought about how to respond properly to an emotionally charged event, we can act in the manner best suited to our desires. For instance, if Kim had not skipped feelings and gotten bogged down in circuitous thought, she would have been able to give her boss what he wanted without any negative emotional holdover. Had Mike not stopped at the appraisal stage ("This is not worthy of my attention"), he would have experienced his powerful emotions and thought about his problem. Then it would have been possible for him to confront his boss, find a new job, or take some other healthy step away from the bullying he so disliked. Decisions virtually fall into place when you make feelings part of the equation.

Alexithymia might be called the disease of the second stage of emotional response, and it is best cured by getting back in touch with the *five basic feelings* researchers worldwide have discovered form the foundation of emotional life: *love, joy, anger, fear*, and *sadness*. (The Chinese experience these five plus an additional one, shame.)

If you want to improve the quality of your emotional response, practice looking at your daily emotional load in light of these five primary emotions. Imagine the following scenario: You put together a top-notch written presentation, and your boss sends it back with "REDO" scrawled across the top in bright red marker. What would you do? Refuse to do it? Get right to work on corrections? Instead, take a walk to the rest room and ask yourself how you feel. Angry? ("It *is* a good presentation; she must have some ulterior motive here.") Ashamed? ("I'm upset that she doesn't think I've done a good job.") Embarrassed? ("Does anyone else know about this?") Now extend these feelings back to their most basic roots. Anger is relatively obvious (yet scientists tell us that anger is more clearly identified and acknowledged by men in our culture than it is by women). Shame? That's fear over what others think of you. (Research on fear reveals that women more readily admit to fear than men do.) Embarrassment? Fear again. Now extend that fear. What is the worst thing that could happen as a result of this problem? You get fired. And right now, the idea of getting away from that jerk doesn't seem all that bad, does it?

While it might seem a bit childish to admit to feeling afraid or sad—you may not have used those words since your preteen years —there is a kind of primitive comfort in doing so. When you were a child and said "I'm angry" or "I'm sad," there was an unspoken understanding that you wanted comfort—not someone else to fix it for you, and certainly not advice. Just allowing yourself to dwell on these feelings will help you to look at yourself through the same gentle eyes you would use to look at another person in pain.

Many clients of mine tell me that they are not sure they can handle the strong negative feelings they know will surface once they begin to *feel* their emotions. I can tell you in complete honesty that I have *never* had a client feel something he or she could not handle. As you know from the chapter on Mental Mastery, your brain is too clever to let you be hurt by information that is too painful to bear. But there's no need to hang on to unneeded defenses that are only a holdover from childhood development. Let your emotions grow up, too.

In Chapter 2, I told you the story of my brother's death, and how I had to let myself wallow in my grief before I could hope to live a normal life again. In Kim's case, she realized too late that failing to mourn the loss of her idealistic views had caused her years of unnecessary heartache. To get beyond your pain, you have to move through—not around—it. Think of your feelings as stray dogs. They are a lot easier to take care of once you let them inside and make them live by your rules instead of letting them run around you in circles begging to be fed. And once you name them, they are yours.

The three Self-Renewal Practices that follow are designed to gently cure alexithymia by reintroducing you to your feelings and helping you link them more directly and logically to your actions.

SELF-RENEWAL PRACTICE

Back to Basics

While visiting a friend recently, I sat down to read a book to her four-year-old. The book he chose, *F.A.C.T.: First Aid for Children Today*, published by the American Red Cross, contained a quiz, which I have adapted on page 150. In addition to being a terrific example of the kinds of emotional validation and training our generation (and others) missed out on, it is a wonderful exercise for adults because it allows us to cut our emotional teeth on problems that are not as complex as those we experience in the adult world.

There are no right or wrong answers to this quiz, of course; what is important is that you can clearly identify how a situation makes you feel. My preschool buddy answered the questions with no hesitation or self-consciousness.

SELF-RENEWAL PRACTICE

Clearing the Way

1. Take a minute and read about Rick's problem, and note in your journal which of the five *primary* emotions he is likely to be feeling:

   Rick is very proud of his daughter, who danced the lead role in the city ballet's children's productions for years. Although she says she still wants to take ballet, his daughter has been too busy lately with her friends to go to class regularly. Rick is angry that his money is being wasted.

		Happy	Sad	Scared	Angry	Surprised

❶ When me teacher tells me I have done a good job, I feel…

❷ When my best friend doesn't want to play with me at recess, I feel…

❸ When I fall off my bicycle, I feel…

❹ When my mom or dad tells me it's time to go to bed, I feel…

❺ When I lose my library book, I feel…

❻ When it's my birthday, I feel…

❼ When I fight with my brother or sister, I feel…

❽ When I'm playing a game, I feel…

❾ When I'm alone in my bedroom at night and I think I hear noises, I feel…

❿ When I pet a cat or dog, I feel…

Finish each sentence by circling the face that shows how you would feel.

2. Jot down as many ways as you can think of for Rick to "own" his own emotions so they will not cloud his decision-making.

3. Decide which of these emotions merit action, and which are simply feelings Rick should deal with on his own. How do you think Rick might resolve his problems?

4. Pick a problem of your own, and apply Steps 1 through 3 to it.

Here is how one person completed this exercise (be sure to complete it yourself before reading his answers):

1. Joy (that his daughter wants to keep dancing). Fear (that she'll stop). Anger (that she doesn't go to class).

2. I think Rick should listen to his fear here. He's afraid of losing his joy (watching his daughter dance), and is getting angry beause he thinks that joy is about to go away (his daughter might decide not to work toward becoming a dancer). I think Rick's anger at the money issue masks the fear (and maybe sadness?) that his daughter may only be dancing now to keep him happy.

3. Rick needs to deal with his fear on his own. It's his daughter's life, and while it must hurt for him to be disappointed, it's not right for him to expect his daughter to do something just to make him happy. Once he can put these other issues aside, he'll be able to approach the money thing with more perspective—as he would if his daughter kept losing her lunch money. "Use it or lose it, kid!"

4. My problem: I hate it when Duncan makes a joke at my expense.
   The emotions: Anger, because I think it's wrong. Sadness, that someone who loves me could treat me this way. Fear, that others will think less of me.
   Owning my emotions: I think the anger and sadness here are ways I'm choosing to cope with the fear that I am somehow worthy of ridicule. I know in my head that these jokes are no

reflection on me, but maybe they are a reflection of how Duncan feels about me (and so I guess I also fear that he doesn't respect me either). So it all boils down to my being afraid of rejection, by Duncan or by others, and I have no reason to think that either will happen.

Acting: I'm going to remind myself, every time another of those "witty" remarks flies out of his mouth, that it has more to do with his need to be accepted by others than my inadequacies. That way I won't leave every party feeling so bad. But I think I'll also remind Duncan, before each social event, that his jokes sadden me.

Note in the example above (and most likely in your own exercise as well) that it is often not until we get to the point of *owning* our emotions that they become really clear.

Getting back in touch with the basics of emotion is the first and most important step in managing negative feelings and will help immeasurably in your quest for other rewards on the path to Emotional Vitality.

SELF-RENEWAL PRACTICE

Speaking Language of the Heart

Clients tell me this Self-Renewal Practice helps to calm them down in emotionally charged situations and gets them back in touch with their emotions when they are so overwrought they go into emotional shutdown.

The first few times you do this exercise you might want to do it in your journal; after that you should be able to do it in your head.

1. Close your eyes and reflect for several minutes on any sensations you are having in your abdominal area. (The linings of the stomach and

esophagus are especially rich in receptors for neuropeptides, the chemicals that regulate mood states.)

2. Dwell on these sensations and see if you can link them with any of the five basic emotions: sadness, joy, fear, anger, or love or some combination of these. It's common to feel seemingly contradictory feelings such as fear and joy, or anger and love, especially in adulthood. Remember that emotional responses often defy logic and reason.

3. Match each emotion you are feeling with a biologically appropriate action. For example, you might link "running away" to the emotion of fear, or "clapping your hands and jumping up and down" to joy. When you identify an action that is triggered by a feeling, you create a language of the heart. Other feel-act sequences might include: anger → attack; sadness → weep; love → embrace.

4. Give yourself a few minutes to experience each feel-act sequence you identified. Some people do this by visualizing the feel-act sequence happening; others silently repeat to themselves a statement of their feelings and the corresponding action ("I feel so angry I could put my fist through a door"). Still others simply feel the emotion and then feel the emotional release of the action. Do whatever works for you. What is important is to focus on your feeling state and the action that would best express that feeling. *Do not "think" about your feelings.*

5. Once you have taken the edge off your feelings, put your brain to work again. Take a look at the specific trigger for your emotion, and come up with logical thoughts that express that emotion. Next, imagine words that express the feeling in constructive ways. You may want to create a chart like the sample below to help you create new thought-speak sequences.

These entries are excerpted from notes I took during consultations with my clients:

Feeling	Action	Thoughts/Speech
Angry	Put fist through door	*Thought:* I always get angry when my boss second-guesses me. *Speech:* Ask for more instruction up front and less criticism when I fail.
Sad	Weep	*Thought:* I am disappointed when people don't work out their differences. *Speech:* Express my concern over the stalemate and my hope for resolution.
Love	Embrace	*Thought:* When my spouse compliments me, I feel loved. *Speech:* Thank him out loud for the recognition. Tell him how much it means to me to know he respects me (and hug him!).

When you connect yourself consciously to your feelings, your thoughts and speech become *anchored in your emotional experience.* You are sizing up a situation in light of how you feel about it, not judging others. This approach improves your communication skills, because when you speak in terms of what you want or need, others listen without becoming defensive.

Biology and Destiny

My friend Gus works in a well-funded library, where he has access to just about every volume that comes in. Some years ago he told me about a book that examined the possibility of the existence of a mathematical formula for love, which involved a very complex equation something along the lines of "Divide your similarities by your differences, multiply the result by four, subtract three if you are the more attractive partner," and so on. While the idea of quantifying the feeling of love in this way is painfully unromantic (and probably more than a little ahead of our understanding of the way emotions work), there is some truth to the idea that when we love and hate we do so in a rush of neurochemicals that flow through our entire systems.

By far the most exciting new information on emotion comes from recent developments in psychopharmacology. Researchers seeking to cure mood disorders (such as depression, excessive anxiety, and loss of impulse control) have found that there is a specific biochemical reaction for every emotion we feel—and perhaps for every aspect of our personalities. Once a chemical is released by one cell and received by another, the process sparks an electrical impulse in the receptor neuron, and the whole sequence is repeated until it culminates in a feeling. Scientists have not only linked certain brain chemicals to certain feelings, they have also determined that brain cells are specialized to such an extent that they send and receive only certain of these mood-producing chemicals.

Contrary to what we might expect, however, our brains do not receive only one chemical bath. Each emotion is instead accompanied by a kind of biochemical cocktail. When, for example, your body gets a dose of the stress hormone ACTH (which triggers anger and fear in response to a perceived threat), it also gets a rush of what are called beta endorphins. Endorphins, the mood-elevating and pain-buffering opiates of the brain, are one thousand times more potent than their synthetic cousin morphine. So when your body is flooded with the chemicals of fear and rage, it has also flooded itself with the biochemical ingredients of pain relief and euphoria. Psychologist Charles Leventhal explains the neurochemical paradox:

It is clear that endorphins can serve as a window into our evolutionary past. In that past there is a world most of us are lucky enough never to have encountered, an environment in which we must fear a host of natural predators that could kill us at any moment. Imagine yourself as a small animal, a rodent or a rabbit, for example, in that dangerous world. What would you do to protect yourself and survive? One possible defense would be to escape visual detection in the first place, to freeze. While you were immobile, the protective coloring of your fur would blend into its surroundings. Your breathing would be rapid and shallow. Beyond this defensive posture, however, something else would be happening that would prove extremely advantageous toward your survival—you would be temporarily analgesic. The reason is that pain would ordinarily produce behaviors that would hurt your chances for survival, not help them. If you licked your paw, the predator would notice the movement. If visual sighting by the predator did occur, your next strategy would be to flee as quickly as possible. If you limped away on an injured leg, your escape would obviously be slowed. If you were to have any chance of winning an actual fight, an injury would be best ignored. There would be a powerful evolutionary advantage for a species, any species, to have developed a degree of analgesia in times of stress.

Even more interesting, experiments with laboratory animals and human beings suggest that *changes in behavior can alter emotional states*. That's right: the act of smiling itself, whether triggered by perception of delight or not, can increase the release of endorphins, and cause the smiler to experience happiness as a result. Similarly, the act of cowering, whether in response to a perceived threat or not, can prompt the production of stress hormones and the corresponding feeling of fright.

These discoveries, underscoring the hormonal element of emotion, shed new light on human anthropology. Consider the Asian practice of bowing to a superior. The bow is, in fact, a modified cower; by bowing you literally increase your fear of the more powerful person, which works to his advantage. Or think about the social habit of hugging a friend you have not seen in a long time. The powerful "love" chemicals released by a hug do in fact act as a kind of short cut to regaining emotional closeness.

Internationally known family therapist Virginia Satir taught couples to increase their positive feelings for each other just by shifting their physical postures. If one partner changes her clenched teeth to a relaxed smile, for example, she not only invites a more pleasant response from her husband, she also produces in herself an "all is well" feeling to replace the uptight, ready-to-run one she began with.

The exact reasons why behavior can trigger brain chemistry have not as yet been discovered, but what is undeniable is that the two are intricately linked.

Think about it. How many times have you pretended to have fun at a party only to find that you were, indeed, having fun? Perhaps you have unconsciously mimicked the posture of a sad friend (psychologists say that people engaged in meaningful conversation do this automatically) and been surprised at how sad you, too, felt after the encounter. And very likely you have noticed that your problems seem less bothersome after a good workout or a night's sleep. In all these cases, your actions are helping to change your biochemistry, which in turn is affecting your mood.

A terrific example of how our actions can change us comes from *Handwriting Analysis,* written by well-known graphologist Andrea McNichol (with Jeff Nelson). She explains that an experienced analyst can tell from someone's handwriting whether that person is sick or healthy, happy or sad, lying or telling the truth. Even more amazing, she claims that conscious efforts at changing *the handwriting alone* can effect changes in behavior. For instance, if you are the kind of person who tends to hold back from success, your handwriting is likely to reveal an unusually large right-hand margin. You can actually coax yourself toward success by reminding yourself to write farther into that margin, as successful people do.

Visualization, which we discussed in the chapter on Physical Vigor, works on the same principle. By taking on the mental trappings of our goal, we come closer to that goal. What is so exciting about emotions at midlife is that, knowing yourself as well as you do after forty, you can use your thoughts to shape your emotions just as your emotions have shaped your thoughts.

In the first half of life, most of us give ourselves wholly to our joy (feeling sad when the joy goes away) or our sorrow (missing out on much of what was good in the meantime). Our younger selves are, in effect, trapped by dominant emotions: the highs of youth are seductive and the lows appear inescapable.

In midlife, thanks to a decrease in the self-protective impulse and advances in crystallized intelligence, we are better able to *modulate* our responses to a situation. We also can experience a whole symphony of dominant and nondominant feelings at once. Being able to feel happy and sad, hopeful and despairing at the same time is the hallmark of mature emotional response. (The only people who seem capable of this emotional dichotomy in their younger years are those who have undergone and overcome huge hurdles—war survivors, world-class athletes, people who as children suffered severe emotional hardship.) This expansion in emotional capacity, coupled with our ability to trigger emotions via our behavior, gives us a chance at midlife to feel the way we *choose* to feel instead of being locked into some kind of emotional jail by the dictates of our brain chemistry. The next Self-Renewal Practice, which I have taught for over fifteen years, is designed to help you elevate your mood or modulate painful emotions whenever you feel the need to.

SELF-RENEWAL PRACTICE

Postures of the Heart

1. Select a particular emotion that you would like to experience instead of the emotion(s) that dominate now. You may want to promote calm over anger, or joy over sadness.

2. Assume a total-body posture (face, shoulders, hands, arms, stomach, legs) that reflects the emotional experience you desire. For example, if you seek calm, assume a posture that is in keeping with the way your body feels when you are at peace. Put your whole body, from your head to your toes, in harmony with the feeling you want to have.

3. Maintain that posture for at least three minutes, but allow yourself to shift positions as your mood changes. (I have observed that many people who seek calm spontaneously reach for deeper levels of physical relaxation to mirror their desire for peace, for example.)

4. Finally, check your emotional gauge. Notice how well you were able to create the emotion you sought. If you want to feel the emotion more strongly, repeat Steps 2 and 3.

Most of my clients benefit immediately from this practice, but it is interesting to note that people who are not sincerely motivated to change their emotional state do not achieve the same effects as those who are. In teaching customer service agents who handle phone complaints, I noted remarkable improvements in both mood and performance quality when the agents were truly interested in change.. Agents who assumed the posture for the purpose of manipulation did not enjoy the same results.

Another word of caution: postures of the heart should not be used to deny or mask important feelings that deserve to be felt and expressed. Try this approach when you need to move past negative feelings that might be impeding your ability to function well; you can always revive your initial, painful emotions at a later date when there is time to process them.

The next time someone pushes ahead of you in line or your plane arrives late, try smiling a sincere smile and see how quickly your frustration turns into a pleasant mood.

Increasing your ability to regulate your emotions and choosing which ones will dominate your experience is a prize of maturity well worth earning. A little practice in manipulating your own biochemistry will help you immeasurably in balancing the pleasure and pain that are part of life.

Liberating Laughter

Once upon a time there was a woodcutter who lived with his wife just outside a little village. Every morning he would set off into the woods, where he cut down trees to sell for lumber and firewood. Every evening he came home to find a clean house and a hot meal waiting for him. One day, the woodcutter returned home from work earlier than usual and saw through the window that his wife was engaged in a romantic interlude with the village pawnbroker. As he opened the door to the cottage, the woodcutter heard shuffling inside as the pawnbroker scurried to find a place to hide. The woodcutter opened the door.

How would you finish the story? What would you be feeling if you were the woodcutter? What should the woodcutter do?

The story of the woodcutter is a classic Japanese fable. The traditional version, as told in Allan Chinen's anthology *Once upon a Midlife*, continues something like this:

The woodcutter, a wise man, sees some humor in his situation, and decides to put the fate of the interloper into the man's own hands. The woodcutter strides over to his wife and embraces her, telling her he has wonderful news: the gods of the forest have bestowed upon him the gift of clairvoyance. All he has to do is look into a small hole in the center of a certain piece of wood, and he can see what other men cannot. He further reports that his new vision has revealed that there is something odd but extremely valuable in his bedroom chest (the pawnbroker, of course). Excited to demonstrate his newfound powers of observation, the woodcutter locks the chest and carries it to the pawnshop, where he places it on the counter. He announces to the shop assistant that he will sell him the chest and its contents for fifty gold coins. The woodcutter then strolls outside to smoke a pipe while the assistant considers the offer. From there the woodcutter can hear the pawnbroker screaming from inside the chest, pleading for the assistant to pay the ransom and win the pawnbroker's release.

With his marvelously clever solution, the woodcutter forces the pawnbroker—the archetypal miser—to literally *pay* for his transgression. Any worry the woodcutter might have had over losing face is gone, because villagers hearing about the woodcutter's dilemma would agree that his humorous and very fitting solution proved him to be the better man. Laughing at how he turned the tables on the pawnbroker makes it easier for the woodcutter to deal with his own pain, too. Furthermore, while the woodcutter is fifty gold coins richer, he has exacted his well-deserved revenge without compromising his own morals (as he would have done if he had killed the pawnbroker). Despite the obvious limitations of the story (such as why the wife is not held accountable for her actions—but that was the Middle Ages for you), it is a marvelous example of one of the most important rewards of midlife: perspective.

Were you able to see humor in the woodcutter's situation when it was first presented? The woodcutter used his wits to win; most of my clients admit they would have given the pawnbroker a powerful punch in the gut. Imagine being able to distance yourself enough from your feelings of fury and betrayal to come up with a solution as practical and emotionally satisfying as the woodcutter's.

One of the most amazing gifts of midlife is the ability to put some of our experiences into perspective. After forty-plus years, we finally give in to the overwhelming evidence that the world is confusing, that things do not always (or often) go our way, that we are just one little piece of the human pie. Most of us find we can give our concerns a kind of pecking order: having a healthy family is more important than having a healthy bank account; the clerk's rudeness was not really that big a deal. We may also find ourselves more capable of taking disappointments in stride, and more willing to try new approaches to the way we run our lives.

Some of us, however—especially those of us who have had to work very hard to make things "go our way"—have a difficult time letting go of the adolescent and young-adult tendency to hone in on areas of emotional turmoil. In other words, *we take life too seriously*, especially when it comes to issues involving strong emotional content—like a spouse's infidelity. Humor, irony, and paradox are useful in comedy, but they do not have much to do with our day-to-day lives. What well-adjusted older adults (over age sixty-five) have reported to social scientists, and what the woodcutter's story illustrates, is that a humorous perspective is useful in every facet of our lives, even the "important" ones.

If you can look at a situation from a humorous point of view, you gain some distance on it. Once you are able to *laugh* at your problem, your experience of the situation is no longer entirely negative. And as we have discussed, happy behavior (smiling, laughing, playing) promotes the production of endorphins, the brain chemicals that trigger happy feelings.

How many times have you looked back at a problematic circumstance in your past and laughed, only to wish you'd had that perspective about it at the time? There is a world of difference between intellectual understanding that "I'll be able to see a lot of humor in this in a few years" (typical of our development in our twenties and thirties) and the ability to laugh about a problem at the moment it occurs (which midlifers can learn to do), actually *shifting* feelings from negative to neutral (or positive). Humor gives you hindsight in the here and now, helping you decide how to handle emotionally charged events. The ability to see and employ humor also makes you more attractive; it is a lot more fun to be with someone who laughs than someone who whines and gnashes teeth.

Of course, humor, like anything else, can be taken too far. Laughing off what bothers you can also be a way of denying your most troubling feelings. The key is to use humor as a tool for gaining perspective, not as a crutch. The other limitation of humor is that for people just learning to use humor as a perspective enhancer, certain situations do not seem to lend themselves to laughs, or even irony. In that case it is fine, as my friend Stacy says, to let yourself be miserable, if you like, as long as you do not give yourself up to misery.

Many of my clients repeat the sentence "The situation is important, but not serious" to remind themselves that humor and perspective are where you find them. Perhaps you have caught yourself agonizing over something as important but nonserious as a dinner party—"What if the Joneses can't come? Will the market have cilantro? What should I make for dessert?"—then heard about someone else's tragedy and shaken your head: "And to think I was worried about my dinner!" The more perspective you gain, the less the dinner parties of the world will trouble your heart.

Almost any situation is ripe for humor. An Irish wake is one example of a ritual in which people seek some humor in tragedy. Freud believed that the ability to create humor from our lives was one of the best ways people could triumph over tragedy. The twentieth-century propensity for using sordid events—such as massacres, natural disasters, plane crashes, and the like—as fodder for the Monday-morning joke at the office ("Have you heard the one about . . .") is a good example of how humor can help us cope with situations too terrible for us to fully comprehend.

Humor is a sophisticated tool for resolving conflict as well. Telling the joke that follows is quite helpful at times when people are having trouble seeing eye to eye because of the negative stereotypes they assign to one another.

One day a string went into a bar, slithered up to a stool, and ordered a scotch and water. The bartender leaned over and whispered, "I'm sorry, sir, but we don't serve strings in here."

Embarrassed, the string went outside to think about what he should do. Before long he said to himself, "Hey, they can't do that to me! I know my rights," and slid back into the bar, demanding to be served.

The bartender spied him and gave him a menacing look. "I thought I told you: we don't serve strings in here!"

Humiliated, the string left the bar once more. Just as he was about to go in search of another bar, he got an idea. Ducking into the doorway of a nearby building, he wove himself into an intricate little ball. When he was done, he separated the strands at each of his ends so they appeared fluffy and full. Then he rolled proudly into the bar, selected a prominent seat, and requested a double scotch on the rocks.

The bartender had had enough. He walked over to the string, shook his finger at him, and roared, "Say, pal, aren't you that string?"

To which the string replied, "No, I'm afraid not [a frayed knot]."

(Get it?)

Whether you are laughing or groaning in the wake of that pun does not alter its positive impact. Either way, the silly string joke draws you out of your own problems and out of the conventional world of logic and human limitations. Physicist Fritjof Capra describes how a joke can be an example of spontaneous, intuitive insight in his classic text *The Tao of Physics*. Capra tells us that in the split second when we understand the punch line of a joke we actually experience what he terms a "moment of enlightenment." As Capra reminds us, this moment of enlightenment must happen spontaneously. The power of the punch line is lost if the joke must be analyzed or explained in order to be understood. In Capra's words, "only with a sudden intuitive insight into the nature of the joke do we experience the liberating laughter the joke is meant to produce."

Capra's study of Eastern mysticism, whose traditions are full of wit and humorous anecdotes, has convinced him that the most mature, enlightened men and women have great senses of humor. He quotes from the *Tao Te Ching* (a Taoist book of philosophy): "If it were not laughed at, it would not be sufficient to be Tao."

The string joke (one of my current favorites) takes us into the magical land of inner imagination and play, and helps us make fun of the foolhardy, false distinctions people construct in order to feel superior to one another. This type of humor deflates pomposity, pokes fun at the dark side of society, and says, "I am you, you are me, and we are all in this mess together, so we'd better find a new angle if we are ever going to straighten it all out."

Deep appreciation of "worldview" humor does not come into full bloom until adulthood. Mature adults, whose sense of self is typically much stronger than in earlier years, tend to be more secure, less likely to use humor to attack or manipulate than they may have been in the past. Their senses of humor are fun-loving, principled, and self-deprecating rather than biting and hostile toward others.

Philosopher-psychologist Gregory Bateson's study of the development of consciousness in cultures around the world suggests that midlifers particularly enjoy jokes poking fun at their own shortcomings and blind spots. Sophisticated satire that knocks the generation in power (our own, during midlife years) is appreciated most by those of us who are ourselves the subjects of ridicule. And what used to be sensitive personal areas (Am I smart enough? rich enough? good-looking enough? sexually attractive enough? thin enough?) can in midlife be cut down to manageable size through humor. A friend of mine who used to complain about his large, hooked nose now refers to his "Roman" profile with a proud grin. Another friend, a divorced woman who has worried for years about how attractive she is to men, has learned to accept her fifty-two-year-old, slightly pear-shaped exterior; she tells the men she likes, "Love me, love my three-baby belly!"

Laughing at our own foibles and dashed dreams is a sign that we are finally ready to admit we can live without perfection (ours or the world's) and that we are not now, never have been, and never will be in complete charge of how things turn out. All the jokes in life are ultimately on us for ever thinking or behaving otherwise. All we can strive for is a spirited, light-hearted perspective that allows us to be thankful for the roller-coaster ride of existence.

The Self-Renewal Practice that follows is designed to accommodate the idiosyncratic nature of humor. With your own taste in humor in mind, give these guidelines a try and see what you can do to change your perspective on sensitive issues.

SELF-RENEWAL PRACTICE

Humorous Hindsight

1. Select a recent incident that triggered in you *mild* feelings of anger, fear, or sadness. Briefly recall in your journal the specifics of the circumstance by reflecting on the people involved (if any) and what was said and done, in sequence. Consider your emotions at the time, and the feeling you took away from the encounter.

2. Now that you have some distance on the disturbance, use your hindsight to view yourself objectively. Evaluate what you did, said, and felt. Then look at your behavior with an eye toward humor, relating it to a person, character, cartoon, or story you find funny. For example, did you rush around so quickly that others might have likened you to the Road Runner escaping Wile E. Coyote? Maybe you argued with someone in the closed-minded manner of Archie Bunker. Perhaps your state of confusion mimicked Lucille Ball's zaniness in *I Love Lucy*, or you acted out of shallow self-centeredness just like bartender Sam of *Cheers*.

3. Ask yourself what lessons you can learn from viewing yourself from a more humorous angle.

   First, think about the emotions the situation evoked, and what you wanted to feel instead. Did the circumstance make you feel foolish when you wanted to feel respected? Unloved when you wanted to feel loved? Out of control when you wanted to be in charge? Wrong when you wanted to be right?

   Next, ask yourself if your behavior—now in its humorous incarnation—solved the problem or compounded it. Most less-than-satisfactory outcomes are the result of our humorously inept knee-jerk attempts to change the way we feel.

Now replay the scenario in your mind, and this time try doing the exact *opposite* of what you did the first time. If you were the Road Runner, try to be calm, physically and emotionally grounded. If you were Archie Bunker, make an effort to be open-minded. A Lucille Ball can try to clear her thoughts, a self-absorbed Sam can look at the needs of others.

Many people find it useful to incorporate their feelings into the scenario by telling the other person how they feel and acknowledging the ways in which the other person may be perceiving them: "I'm so tense I feel as if I'm running around in circles. I must look like the Road Runner!"

How did you feel during the replay and what were the results?

4. The next time you encounter a situation that typically puts you in an ineffective reaction mode, remind yourself of the humorous character you resemble. With compassion and humor, acknowledge your tendency to take on an unwanted role, and make a decision *not* to take it on today.

———————

A client of mine recently yelled at her teenaged daughter for expressing dislike for the kitchen wallpaper. While not an issue of monumental importance, the wallpaper conflict was representative of the type of "silly" flare-up that prevented peace in the house.

My client agreed to practice humorous hindsight any time one of her children voiced dislike over her decisions. These are the notes she shared:

1. I had been working all day wallpapering and rearranging the kitchen. Jamie walked in after field hockey, took one look at the room, and said, "Mom, this looks like throw-up." I stepped down off the ladder, threw the paste brush across the room, and screamed, "Don't you ever say those nasty words again. I have worked hard on this and don't deserve to be insulted!"

2. Looking back, I see myself coming unglued and going on a rampage. There I was flailing my arms about like a crazy woman. To Jamie, I must have looked dangerously out of control.

3. I really wanted Jamie to see and appreciate all my hard work: I wanted her to be impressed with me. Of course, the more I screamed, the less impressive I seemed. My reaction created the exact opposite effect from what I sought.

   I replayed the situation in my head, behaving as if I were unconcerned with Jamie's opinion of the paper (or me). In my mind, I actually smiled to myself over my first reaction, which was to throw things, and just kept on gluing the paper to the wall. Later, when I was less hurt, I had a talk with Jamie about how it feels to have one's work summarily denigrated. I told her that I felt like Roseanne [in the sitcom of the same name], and how ridiculous I knew that was. In this imaginary scenario, I felt better, and Jamie reacted with a simple apology (though she still hated the wallpaper).

4. A few days later I faced a similar incident, in which two of my children ridiculed me at a point when I wanted their appreciation. I immediately thought of "Roseanne on a Rampage" and said, "If you guys don't watch out, I might have to act like Roseanne on one of her rampages." We all laughed and went our separate ways, without a blowup. I couldn't believe it! I felt triumphant, and amazed that the mere image of myself as that Roseanne . . . character could shift my perspective so much that we didn't have an argument at all!

Humor is often all that is needed to take care of an emotional problem, because, through humor, pain is acknowledged and put in perspective. As Capra suggests, humor is one of those instant insights that put us on a new plane, able to experience negativity without necessarily needing to "process" it through behavior. You will find yourself responding to problems with a lighter heart and a more compassionate eye. And if you are like most of my clients, you will find yourself having a lot more fun.

VICTORIES OF EMOTIONAL VITALITY

In his book *Transformation*, Robert Johnson shares a wonderful three-stage model for the growth of human awareness. With *simple awareness*, we respond to our emotions as they happen, with little concept of the outer world and its restrictions. Children live at this level: they cannot function on their own in the outside world, but can experience pleasure and pain in the present moment. They wake up each morning unwounded by the events of the previous day, unworried about the potential problems of the next.

The person who has achieved *complex awareness* operates well in the outer world, able to make goals and strive toward them. But complex awareness also brings full knowledge of life's uncertainty and disappointment. A person in this stage is likely to be anxious, driven, angry, or lonely while following the dictates of the community. Most people reach the level of complex awareness in adolescence or young adulthood, but get stuck there, knowing too much to return to simple awareness but not enough to advance to the next level.

People who have achieved *enlightened awareness* have found a way to retain the simple joys of the first level while acknowledging the pain inherent in living life at the second level. They realize that they cannot return to the happiness they felt at the first stage, but they nevertheless manage to experience a full range of emotions, from the most pleasurable to the most painful. They own and cope with those emotions and have the perspective to realize that life goes on no matter what feelings may be flowing in the moment.

Johnson tells a little joke I have adapted here: Simple people come home from a tough day at work and wonder what to eat for dinner. Complex people come home from a tough day at work and are so focused on their troubles they forget to eat dinner. Enlightened people come home from a tough day at work and wonder what to eat for dinner.

What it means for midlifers to operate emotionally on the third level of enlightened awareness was expanded upon in a 1989 landmark study, "Emotions and Self-Regulation: A Life Span View," conducted by a team of psychologists at Wayne State University.

Gisela Labouvie-Vief and her colleagues found that those who reach emotional maturity display four types of emotional advancement:

1. The development of a more highly evolved language for emotions in which feelings are represented as dynamic, vivid, and uniquely personal experiences (rather than the more conventional approach in which feelings—like ideas or thoughts—are believed to be uniformly experienced)

2. A more explicit awareness that feelings, bodily impulses, and unconscious processes are useful in coping and should not be repressed or contained

3. An increased desire and ability to judge one's emotions by one's personal standards, rather than by external interpretations of appropriateness

4. Acknowledgment of personal responsibility for both generating and coping with emotions

Traveling the path of Emotional Vitality brings you a way to more fully become yourself. As you enrich your emotional responsiveness, you add immeasurably to your sense of being in harmony with life, your ability to stay productive despite disturbing upheavals, and your willingness to own your feelings and express them freely. You also put yourself on firm footing for gains in Interpersonal Effectiveness, Spiritual Serenity, and Personal Integrity.

CHAPTER 6

Pathway #4: Interpersonal Effectiveness

*We mark with light in the memory the few
interviews we have had with souls
that made our souls wiser,
that spoke what we thought,
that told us what we knew,
to leave us be what only we are.*

—RALPH WALDO EMERSON

I begin many of my interpersonal effectiveness workshops by asking attendees to participate in a simple experiment based on the findings of social psychologist Bernard Rimland. Read over the following set of instructions and, in your journal, write your responses to these questions:

1. In a single column on the left of your page, list the first names of ten adults *you know well.*

2. In a second vertical column to the right of the first, put the letter H next to the names of people whom you view as generally happy, and the letter U by the names of those you regard as generally unhappy.

3. Now evaluate each person with respect to whether you see him or her as selfish or generous in relating to others. In a third column, place the leter S, for "selfish," near the names of people

who you believe are unwilling to inconvenience themselves for others and who typically devote their time, energy, and talent only to advancing their own welfare. Then place the letter G, for "generous," adjacent to the names of the people who you believe put themselves out for others and who contribute their resources to advancing the welfare of others.

Be sure to finish writing your responses before reading any further.

If you are like 98 percent of the people in my workshops, you found that a person with a U (unhappy) designation was usually rated as S (selfish); in contrast, people you judged to be happy (H) tended also to be perceived as generous (G). Almost without exception, H and G are paired, and those who rate a U also rate an S. Rimland, whose well-controlled study surveyed almost two thousand people, reported that only rarely did participants list an individual as both happy and selfish.

Most people who attend my workshops are surprised at the strong correlation between happiness and generosity. It is not unusual, in the course of our discussion, for several in the group to admit that they had never realized how much of their own happiness was linked to following the "golden rule." For the most part, we view unselfishness as a trait benefiting only the recipient, yet caring for others, even at our own expense, increases our feelings of happiness.

Think about how you feel when you give someone a gift. Most people, even children, get great happiness out of selecting a gift they know the recipient will like, anticipating the recipient's joy, and seeing the happiness the gift brings. For mature adults, however, the satisfaction of giving a gift far outweighs the thrill of getting one. When we satisfy our distinctively human ability to be generous, we surpass the more fleeting gratification we gain from meeting other, less selfless needs. Psychodynamic and cognitive theorists contend that learning about others and putting their interests before one's own is a hallmark of maturity. Psychoanalysts Morton and Estelle Shane call the development of this authentic altruism the struggle for "otherhood."

All too often in my practice, I see problems that are primarily the result of a client's failure to realize this "otherhood." Couples, for instance, come to me seeking help for discord in marriages that were once joyful: a large porportion of midlife marital problems are caused by the couples' inability to reach out to each other in truly loving, generous ways. Similarly, many families are unable to feel compassion for their teenage members. Parents who cannot give their difficult-to-get-along-with adolescents the generous support and acceptance they need deepen the unfortunate schism between generations. In the workplace, managers complain that they lack the skills necessary to resolve conflicts. These executives have not yet found ways to give others what they need without compromising the demands of a do-more-with-less-and-do-it-faster workplace.

Adults who are willing to come out of themselves and approach otherhood during midlife find greater satisfaction in their relationships—with less conflict, better communication, and a stronger feeling of connection—than they did before. Many also report greater happiness overall.

THE CALL TO INTERPERSONAL EFFECTIVENESS

Every human interaction has the potential to bring great joy or great pain, sometimes both at the same time. When we look back at our lives from the vantage point of midlife, we realize that our most vivid and meaningful memories are of other people and the way we felt when we were with them. Most of us enter our later decades firm in the belief that relating to other people—emotionally, intellectually, or spiritually—is the most powerful solace we have in a beautiful but uncertain world.

At the same time, midlife can bring a good deal of upheaval in our ability to deal effectively with others. Our strengths and weaknesses seem to manifest themselves most strongly when we are thrown in the emotional cauldron with someone else. The natural turning inward that occurs around age forty gives midlifers a deeper self-awareness that necessitates renegotiation of some important relationships; the new perspective garnered at midlife may even portend the end of certain emotional attachments. Cultural imperatives that invite us to celebrate diversity or to love our neighbor as ourselves are not much help, either, and may in fact hinder us in our efforts to connect with others. No matter how convinced we are that the struggle to relate to others is worthwhile, it can be daunting to consider that we still have lessons to learn.

Some of the signs that a little interpersonal work is warranted are listed below.

Midlife Readiness Signals for Interpersonal Effectiveness
You may find yourself:

- unable to resolve, to your satisfaction, your differences with one or more persons
- sensing that you are "just not getting through" to someone
- curious about your gender role now that you have fulfilled all of society's dictates
- feeling nervous around old friends
- seeking new and different types of relationships
- afraid of being alone
- consciously or unconsciously provoking others in order to gauge their reaction

One of my clients came to me terrified that she would lose her friends after her divorce. Another felt unsure how to tell his parents about the important self-discoveries he had made in his midlife quest. Your own dilemmas might not be so specific; perhaps you are just feeling lonely, or misunderstood. Maybe you sense you are working at cross-purposes with some of the important people in your life. As you did in previous chapters, return to the Self-Renewal Inventory in Chapter 2 and look over your objectives in this area, then read about the rewards of interpersonal effectiveness that follow and see which are best suited to your situation.

As you put into action what you learn in this chapter, you will notice that your successes and failures are more immediate and obvious than they were in the last three areas. The response of an objective outsider will tell you quickly and in no uncertain terms whether your new approaches are working. Take care to be as patient with yourself in this area as you have been in the others; the direct evidence of failure you get with other people may be more hurtful than the missteps you make while working on your own. Be sure to treat others gently, too; they are probably as confused as you are on this new terrain. My divorcing client found that most of her friends were very supportive of her decision, but she noticed that others were not sure how to treat her. She took her time examining her options and desires, and once she found a comfortable vision of herself independent of her role as "wife," even these friends came around.

False starts in the area of interpersonal effectiveness are common. Sometimes they stem from overeagerness, other times from fear. Whatever the cause, be sure to take your emotional pulse regularly, and to return whenever you need to the Self-Renewal Practices in Chapter 5. Emotional and interpersonal skills are closely linked, because an emotion's impact is multiplied exponentially when shared, and because another person's treatment of us can have a strong effect on our emotions. Robert, the client who had a difficult time articulating some of the important changes in his life view, decided to spend more time reevaluating his emotions before he looked for a way to share them.

Putting your best face forward in midlife is not about giving people what they want; it is about presenting your true self in a way that others will respond to.

ADVENTURES IN INTERPERSONAL EFFECTIVENESS

Taking a good look at how you relate to others can be extremely rewarding, for it is in contact with others that we make our greatest emotional strides. Exchange of ideas feeds mental mastery, as well, and interpersonal contact is one of the most fulfilling ways in which we can express our physicality. Many of the rewards you read about in previous chapters—mindfulness, creativity, touching, and humor, to name just a few—have direct application to interpersonal growth, and will in turn be aided by your efforts to communicate better with others.

Perhaps the most exciting aspect of interpersonal work is how much just one little change can affect your relationships. Once you find the right path, your gains are likely to be swift and immensely satisfying. As you rejoice in your successes, resist the temptation to look at past relationships and say, "If only I had known . . ." The strides you are able to make today build on all you have already learned.

Relish the feelings you get from being with others, from comforting them and being comforted by them. Increase your capacity to learn from others with the neglected art of listening. And be sure to share your joy with others who will appreciate it.

Relating on the Third Level

A couple of years ago I planned to attend a weekend workshop for keynote speakers, but when a hurricane ravaged the scheduled location for the retreat, in Hawaii, the initial enrollment of fifteen dropped to three. Since it was not often that I carved five days out of my schedule for my own development, and since I was excited by the prospect of expert coaching and time for reflection, I hardly winced at the retreat's relocation to Pigeon Forge, Tennessee, and vowed to myself that this would be a great learning experience for me "no matter what." Little did I realize that my internal pep talk would be prophetic. Not only did I find new ways to improve my speechmaking, I also learned one of the key elements of interpersonal effectiveness.

Our first assignment was to deliver a portion of our keynote speech so that the coaches and other students could become familiar with our message and style.

Speaker number one approached the podium with a stack of note cards that must have been eight inches high and delivered a sample of his speech. Every sentence Charlie uttered was jam-packed with information, and he impressed us all with his thorough knowledge of his subject matter. Everyone agreed that he was a master at presenting fact-based ideas and strategies in an easy-to-understand manner. Throughout his talk, Charlie gave us an amazing amount of *substance*. But although his presentation was filled with reliable and useful information, it was a challenge to stay alert to his important message.

I was speaker number two. Not only did I have a great command of my subject matter, I was able to speak in an entertaining, humorous, and engaging style. The audience was impressed with my *substance* and my *sizzle*. But during my evaluation, one of the coaches warned me that I was missing one of the key ingredients of a high-impact speech. The feedback piqued my curiosity and I was eager to find out what the missing element could be.

I wished speaker number three good luck as he stumbled onto the platform, his seeing-eye dog guiding him. I was worried that this student would not fare well. Mark was unsure of his movements, and we were uncomfortable watching him from the start.

Mark began by sharing with us that he had barely graduated from high school. Our discomfort grew as it became obvious that his speech was lacking real *substance* and appealing *sizzle*. But then, halfway through Mark's presentation, an amazing transformation took place. The physically awkward young man before us captivated us by revealing the intimate details of the tragic events that had shaped his life.

Mark told us the story of the fire that had trapped and blinded him when he was twelve, explaining in a soft and clear voice how the flames had engulfed and burned him. His terror, even the sensation of the fire as it clung to his skin, seemed a vivid presence in the room; I could barely hold back my own gasps of horror. Mark described, in remarkable detail, feeling the intense heat of the flames that finally overwhelmed his face and plunged his eyes into complete darkness. He related the panic of being able to hear the flames still roaring in his ears—only now he had no vision of them.

Tears began to stream down my face. Mark went on to describe his hospitalization, surgeries, treatments, depressions, drug addictions, suicide attempts, and finally, his decision to live. I felt joy and deep pride for him as he talked about the peace he felt after coming to terms with his fate.

As the speech ended I heard sniffling, and suddenly became aware that Charlie and the coaches were all as moved as I was. This awkward young man had been able to influence his audience at the deepest human level simply because he was capable of revealing himself. He had brought his innermost feelings—about a tragic and life-defining accident, a terrible downward spiral, and the wrenching but heroic commitment to life—out in the open for all to see. Mark's presentation included the ingredient that my speech lacked: it had *soul*.

Mark's moving talk taught me that:

- how you feel about a situation is every bit as important as your understanding of that situation
- what you say about what happens is only half a description unless you articulate your emotions as well
- you are not operating as a whole human being unless you are willing to reveal your true feelings

By midlife, most of us have become masters at selective revelation. We might, for instance, discuss our self-doubts with our spouses, our excitement with our parents, and our financial concerns with our friends. Or perhaps we downplay our feelings entirely; at the most extreme end of this continuum we reveal them to no one. The fear that we will be disliked or not listened to has prevented many of us from speaking openly to others. It is all too easy, in the busy middle years, to hide behind a facade of contentment we do not really feel, or to compartmentalize ourselves emotionally—being funny with Joan, sad with Frank, even-tempered with the kids.

Although few of my clients express discomfort with the way they present themselves to others emotionally, the inability to "open up" is nevertheless a huge liability. Everything you feel comes through, no matter what you say, and not giving voice to your emotions sends out mixed signals that can make others react to you negatively. For instance, you're even-tempered with your children or perhaps with employees or clients, but they sense you are angry underneath. They withdraw from you, and then you in turn feel rejected, unappreciated, and frustrated. If you mask your angry feelings, you create tense, uncomfortable interactions. As discussed in the chapter on Physical Vigor, communications research has demonstrated that only 7 percent of our impact on other people comes through the actual words we use to communicate; a whopping 93 percent of the way others perceive us is based on our tone of voice, facial expression, and body language. Because your nonverbal modes of communication give you away, others know—sometimes consciously and sometimes subconsciously—when what you say or do is not in keeping with your feelings. For example, clinical research with adults in psychoanalysis reveals that a person's motives for being kind, generous, and caring may be either genuine or defensive (done perhaps out of a desire to be *perceived* as altruistic). Defensive altruism generates acts of generosity that are interpreted by the recipient as somehow manipulative and self-serving. The identical act, performed out of authentic altruism, evokes feelings of gratitude and joy in the recipient. While actions speak louder than words, motives speak louder than both.

If what you say (or do) and how you feel are clearly different, you are sending *incongruent* messages. Studies of emotionally disturbed children demonstrate just how dangerous these mixed messages can be. Social workers link many of the abnormal behaviors disturbed children learn, from mistrusting the world to failing to relate to anyone else, to parents who one minute professed undying devotion and the next minute abused the children mercilessly.

Even on a less extreme level, mixed messages can cause tremendous damage. If a mother says to her son, "come here and get a hug," and at the same time takes on a threatening stance or unpleasant facial expression, the child will certainly pick up the schism in the message and begin to doubt his intelligence ("She says she loves me, but I don't *feel* loved, so I must have misunderstood"), his lovability, or his sanity. Children, whose emotional links to primary caregivers are the breath of life, cannot turn off these incongruent messages; desperate for love and attention, they take what they can get.

Grown-ups, on the other hand, are usually not so desperate. When faced with two differing messages, they tend to focus on the negative one or tune out both. "Oh, Jackie, I'd love to come to your party, but I have plans that night," "I have feelings for you, Henry, but I'm just not ready to commit right now," and "No, I didn't get your message; my machine's on the blink" are all examples of messages that could be intended to preserve the speaker's sociable facade while getting across unpleasant information. Defensive emotional cover-ups, no matter how well motivated, make the listener feel terrible, while disturbing messages shared with heartfelt soul evoke feelings of respect and appreciation for the speaker's candor under tough circumstances.

What do you feel like doing when you receive mixed messages? Screaming and yelling at the speaker? Blaming yourself? Getting as far from the speaker as possible? Some combination of the above? None of us has survived to forty without receiving thousands of incongruous communiqués. How many times have you been hit by one and asked yourself, "Why didn't he just *tell* me he felt that way?" It shouldn't be so difficult to say, "I don't really like parties, Jackie. Maybe we can go out to lunch next week, just the two of us." Or "I'm not sure we see the same future for this relationship." Or "I'm feeling really low right now and haven't felt like talking to anybody."

Many of my clients tell me that the number one reason they shy away from expressing their true feelings is that they do not want to be perceived as whining or complaining all the time. If you find yourself pulling back for the same reason, first ask yourself why you are second-guessing everybody else's reaction to you. Perhaps you are underestimating the ability of other people to empathize. Eleanor, a woman who attended one of my communications skills workshops, told the others in her group that she ignored her friend Zoe for some time, until Zoe finally confronted her about it. Once pressed, Eleanor explained that she had been so depressed she had not felt like fit company for weeks. "Let me decide who's fit company," Zoe wisely replied. "Please don't deprive me of the chance to be a friend when you need one most."

The other factor to consider is *why* you feel sad, angry, or fearful all the time. You may need to go back to the chapter on Emotional Vitality and work through your feelings to your complete satisfaction. Interpersonal problems are often just emotional problems in disguise.

Speaking from the heart does not guarantee a pleasant discussion, but it does ensure that the interchange will be more emotionally satisfying for everyone involved. It also lays the groundwork for a more genuine and permanent resolution of any conflict and opens the door for the pinnacle of interpersonal relations: intimacy.

Human beings experience intimacy when someone listens to them and accepts them unconditionally as the center of their consciousness. Few feelings compare with that of having someone else's full attention and interest. And *the best way to activate the listening of others is to reveal how you feel.* Of the three levels of self-disclosure identified at my keynote workshop—substance, sizzle, and soul—only the third level creates an emotionally riveting bond between the listener and the teller. In the same way that we learn more from doing than watching, we learn more about someone else's experience by *feeling* the way they felt than by hearing all the facts and figures of their story.

Good mothering is perhaps the clearest example of simple intimacy. The mother gives her child acceptance and attention, absorbing the child's feelings as if they were her own. Of course, nature makes it easy for mothers to be intimate with children. Not only do mothers receive a felicitous dose of hormones after childbirth to start them off yearning to caress their babies and hold them close, but studies have also shown that women find babies' physical attributes—big eyes and heads, small and helpless bodies—impossibly appealing. The pupils of women in all cultures—both mothers and childless women—will dilate as a sign of their intense, positive attraction when the women are shown pictures of babies (among men, it is mostly fathers who have this reaction). While we cannot hope to return to infancy in order to get such automatic, absorbing attention from others, we do have available to us that other sneaky trick babies use to make us put down our newspapers and take note. Babies do not try to tame their emotions. They parade their feelings proudly, evoking from us spontaneous sympathy, laughter, hugs, and smiles. Bouts of anger, joy, fear, love, and sadness call forth a cacophony of screams, giggles, trembles, coos, and whimpers from this little guy or gal, and we love it.

In adulthood, sharing our feelings is much more complex. Not only are our emotions more varied, but, as we discussed in the previous chapter, we are liable to use the gift of language to control rather than express our emotions. Once we get back in touch with the emotions themselves, however, language can become a powerful tool for developing intimacy.

The Self-Renewal Practice that follows will help you develop an *emotional lexicon* to use when communicating with others in any setting. My clients tell me that it is a relatively painless way of beginning the tough process of opening themselves up to others, and that the success they have with it spurs them on to do it more often. (An added benefit is that self-revelation can increase your ability to make use of your emotions in decision-making. Recent research at the University of Massachusetts suggests that the better able you are to express the full range of your emotions, in the finest of detail, the better able you are to understand the full extent of your feelings yourself. This expanded emotional self-awareness guides you to make choices that coincide with your deepest emotions, not just those on the surface.)

A note about this Self-Renewal Practice: Yes, you are being asked here to do the complete opposite of what you did in the Self-Renewal Practices for alexithymia, and for that reason you should not attempt this practice unless you have accomplished some of your goals for Chapter 6. Skill in revealing your feelings presupposes that you know what those feelings are and have made some kind of peace with them first.

SELF-RENEWAL PRACTICE

The Emotional Vocabulary

1. Set aside about fifteen minutes to create an initial list of words to help you express the nuances of your emotional responses to whatever happens.

   In your journal, create six columns, five to correspond to the five basic emotions (love, joy, anger, fear, and sadness), and one labeled "Other." Next, begin listing any "feeling words" that come to mind, placing each in the column that is most appropriate. Do not worry whether you have categorized the words correctly; what is important is that the lists make sense to you. Some sample entries follow:

Love	Joy	Anger
Enraptured	Entwined	Aghast
Connected	Elevated	Belligerent
Benevolent	Thrilled	Frustrated
Erotic	Jubilant	Aggravated

Fear	Sadness	Other
Awkward	Miserable	Ashamed
Brittle	Dejected	Surprised
Fearful	Disappointed	Harried
Anxious	Brooding	Inspired

The best approach is to start with a small set of vocabulary words and use these words until they become almost second nature.

2. For the next week, whenever you experience a strong feeling, express that feeling using one of the words on your list (or another you do not ordinarily use). Anger might be described as frustration, disgust, or shame. What you first called love might be more clearly expressed as affection, admiration, or lust.

   Use your emotional vocabulary words whenever you have the opportunity. For example, use feeling words in the memos and letters you write. Make a special effort to express your feelings in greater detail when talking on the phone or in casual conversation. In addition, ask others to describe their feelings, and listen for any feelings they express spontaneously. Children are very good teachers in this regard.

   Notice any improvements in your ability to be persuasive and captivating, and to think more clearly and comprehensively. Do people respond to you differently when you say "I'm frustrated" instead of "I'm angry," or "I really respect you for that" instead of the overused "I love you"?

3. Continue to expand your emotional lexicon. As you get in the habit of expressing your feelings more thoroughly and precisely, add new words to your list, or reorganize them, if you feel the need. Do not hesitate to use a thesaurus at this stage.

   Many people who have practiced expanding their emotional vocabulary find that they enjoy this endeavor more than they expected. Far from being boring or tedious, this exercise becomes exciting from the very first time you find yourself engaged in more meaningful conversation. Feeling words enliven you, your message, and your listener.

Operating on the level of *soul* gives new dimension to the substance and sizzle of what you say; it is usually the missing link in communication gone awry. Do not wall yourself off from true intimacy by allowing "only so much" of your true self to be seen. The more you reveal of yourself, the more you will be able to connect with other human beings. Bonds born of soulful exchanges create profoundly intimate moments. Open yourself up to others and, as you begin to reap the fruits of vulnerability, you will find that others become more open with you.

Connecting Through Conflict
What do you see in the picture below?

What about this picture?

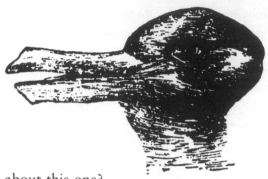

And what about this one?

What these drawings have in common is that they are all two drawings in one. The first picture depicts both the head of a Native American (in profile, with the nose to the left) and an Eskimo entering a cave (the Eskimo, shown from the rear, is wearing a hooded jacket). The second illustration contains a picture of a duck (with the beak to the left) and a picture of a rabbit (with the ears to the left). The last image is the famous vase-profile by Danish psychologist Edgar Rubin. If you view this illustration emphasizing background over foreground, you see a profile of two faces; if you concentrate on the foreground, you see a vase.

To find a second picture in these *ambiguous figures*, you must either shift your perspective—change your focal point, change your expectation, or change the angle from which you see the image—or simply stare at it long enough that it seems to transform itself into something else entirely. Clients tell me that the discovery of a second image in a drawing is surprising and pleasing. "How clever," they say to one another. "Which picture did you see first?"

Now imagine that you and a friend are doing volunteer work for the local art museum, and you have been given the job of categorizing pictures by subject matter. You come across the duck/rabbit drawing above, and neither of you knows it is an ambiguous figure. You see the duck. Your friend sees the rabbit.

"Guess this goes in the bird pile," you say.

"Huh? I think a rabbit would go in 'small mammals,'" says your friend.

At first, you express surprise over your disagreement. After all, the two of you usually see eye to eye. But soon your frustration begins to mount.

"Can't you *see* today?" you ask, exasperated.

"Yes," your friend responds huffily. "I see a rabbit."

No matter how emphatically you each state your case, your friend still cannot see the duck, and you cannot see the rabbit.

Finally you wise up. "Look," you say to your friend. "Let me show you. Here is the eye, here is the beak."

"Oh!" your friend cries, shocked. "I had no idea."

By *explaining* why you see things the way you do, you have managed to show to your friend that there is, indeed, a duck here worth looking at. You are satisfied.

Your friend, however, still sees a rabbit, and would like you to see it, too. So now it is your turn to listen while your friend shows you how to see the rabbit. Only when you *both* see both figures can you decide, together, where the picture belongs.

As you might guess, where the picture belongs is not the point of this story. What is important is that in order to come to an agreement, you and your friend must both feel that your views have been understood even if not agreed with.

Our museum story illuminates three of the fundamental truths of relating.

1. If you are involved with another person, you are also involved with another *equally valid reality*.

2. It is impossible for two people to work together effectively unless each sees and acknowledges the reality of the other.

3. Other realities reveal themselves only if we shift our perspective (or stay attentive long enough for them to spontaneously appear).

Many people have a rough time with the first truth. For most of us, the fascination with other perspectives does not extend beyond the clever artistic brain teasers pictured here. Struggling to see another person's viewpoint on more topical subjects—from politics to child rearing to how to spend the windfall from Aunt Grace's will—is not nearly as enjoyable or enlightening. Furthermore, just admitting the presence of another "right" answer means questioning our own perspective, and thereby admitting our potential fallibility. In a world that rewards us for being "right" about things, it can be difficult to acknowledge the limitations of our own vision.

The key to accepting the valid perceptions of others is remembering that we are all created equal. The other person has an equal right to his viewpoints. He may have information you do not have, or lack information you are privileged with. Regardless, his brain is different, his experiences are different, and it is quite plausible that he might take the same facts you do and come up with completely different ideas. He is not right. You are not right. There is no absolute "right." In Europe in 1491, you were right when you said the world is flat, not because you had a grasp on objective truth, but because everyone agreed that the world was flat. What is right is what we agree on.

Now let's examine truth number two. You probably know from experience that denying the validity of another's viewpoint gets you nowhere. In fact, the farther you get from the acceptance of the other reality, the more frustrated you become; failing to find common ground usually results in the use of force—crying, yelling, stomping, physical battle. But crying or aggression rarely solves the problem and usually escalates tension.

Rationally explaining your position might seem much wiser, but this, too, ultimately fails, because even if you do manage to convince a person, intellectually, of the superiority of your viewpoint, you have not acknowledged *his* viewpoint. Since his viewpoint reflects his feelings (which do *not* change, no matter how convinced he is intellectually that you are right), *it is his viewpoint that is the key to his happiness—and yours.* If you do not know the key to his happiness, you are operating at a great disadvantage. Unless you know what will satisfy him, you have no hope of getting him to satisfy you. To use a hackneyed adage, you must walk a mile in another's moccasins before you judge him (or his ideas).

If you still doubt the impact of perception on experience, consider the fact that experiments in quantum physics (a branch of physics that seeks to understand how the subatomic world works) demonstrate that even things as "definite" as scientific measurements are more a function of perception than fact. Physicists have found that by changing their *expectations* of the manner in which particles and waves will move they can actually cause these subatomic events to shift course. In other words, not even the laws of nature are immune to the power of perception. (Incidentally, these experiments are further support of the importance of visualization in achieving what you want.) I am not suggesting here that you simply visualize your "opponent's" viewpoint coming around to yours—though it would help—but that you realize the importance of individual outlook on individual outcomes. If perception is so powerful that it can change energy patterns, it is not something you want to ignore when dealing with others.

Which brings us to the third truth. If scientists can, in essence, cause electrons to shift course and even to shift form (waves become particles) as a result of their own individual preconceptions or perceptions, it would make sense that you, through changing *your* outlook, can effect less remarkable changes. And the best way to shift your perspective is to look at your subject through someone else's eyes.

Recently I consulted with a group of twelve managers. In a secluded conference room at their corporate headquarters, they huddled together like a football team, commiserating with each other over the tremendous conflict within their departments. One manager said:

"Last week two members of my department disagreed with

changes I had made in who would serve on a new task force. I could tell these two were disgruntled because they stopped talking in the meeting. No matter what I said, they refused to participate in the discussion. After the meeting, they went into one of their offices and raved on for more than an hour about how outrageous my new approach is.

"I can't believe how secretive and hostile adults can be. Don't they realize that I'm doing my best and only have the group's welfare at heart?"

After all the managers had their say, my clients turned to me, expecting me to give them a magic formula for making their subordinates see things "their way." Instead, I asked the managers to work on shifting their perceptions. For the next week, they were to stop viewing conflict as a headache to be eliminated at all costs. Conflict not only enables us to improve the situation at hand, it also provides learning opportunities that make us better managers in other areas. Then they were to look at the perceptions of their subordinates as *the* key to solving their problems, and talk to their employees directly about these perceptions. To the woman with the unhappy department members, I said, "These two must be feeling pretty dissatisfied with their jobs if they're acting like that in the office. I think you have something to learn from that. Why are they so unhappy? Is something in the physical or emotional aspect of their jobs getting in the way? Did they know something important that you didn't consider in your decision? I'm certain this is not your only departmental interpersonal conflict, but perhaps you can use it as a clue to how to get the whole gang back on the team."

One week later, the managers and I reconvened to discuss how relinquishing preconceived judgments for open-minded inquiry had affected department politics. Several admitted that they had had difficulty being inquisitive in a situation where people were acting so unprofessionally, but those who had been able to follow through were pleased with the results. Almost across the board, the subordinates had been thrilled with the chance to talk openly about their concerns over the way work was getting done. Many of the managers felt they had made great headway in learning how to manage their departments more effectively, and, surprisingly, several confirmed that they had already made steps to resolve disputes. The manager in conflict over the new task force proudly reported:

"I had a long talk with both individuals. I told them each what I appreciated about their work and explained that I was concerned that I had overlooked their input when making my decision. I also explained to them more fully why I made the choice I did.

"Then I got their input. I did what you said and tried to really listen to them, not just for opportunities to strengthen my argument, but to understand reality from their perspective. And as I listened I saw from their point of view how my decision would affect them, and I realized that their comfort with the decision was crucial to their being able to do good work.

"So I changed my mind. The long-term impact of their supporting the new decision far outweighed the benefits I had anticipated from my original, heavy-handed one. From now on, I am going to ask for more input—on the emotional as well as the productivity front —before I make up my mind."

As this example shows, *all that is usually required to improve any relationship is for one of the parties to shift into a more conciliatory, compassionate, and curious view of the other.* When one individual in a conflict is able to see the "opponent" as a worthwhile person with worthwhile opinions, resolution almost always occurs. In fact, the Harvard Negotiation Project, a series of investigations aimed at discovering the components of successful negotiations, has determined that learning to respect one's adversary is crucial to conflict resolution. In an effort to distill the success factors that were at play in the Camp David Peace Accord negotiations between Israel and Egypt, professors Roger Fisher and William Ury noted that the first step toward any fruitful negotiation is to "separate the person from the problem." In other words, don't confuse how you feel about the person (or the person's behavior) with how you view the issue. Conflict resolution is always more likely when you can be generous enough to extend to your opponent the recognition and respect that person seeks from you. (You should only forgo this approach if your adversary is operating out of evil motives. And while evil motives do exist, they are much less frequently a factor than we presume.)

The next Self-Renewal Practice helps you shift your perspective by showing you a way to focus on the *person* with whom you are in conflict, rather than on your goals and the manner in which your opponent prevents you from achieving them. Since we tend not to respect the opinions of people whom we consider unlikable, we need to learn to view our opponent not as an unattractive, unpleasant person but as an individual who possesses a combination of traits—some of which cause us to react positively, some negatively, some neutrally. It is only when we can see our opponents as real, multidimensional people that we can hope to build the other critical ingredient of conflict resolution: trust. Respectful listening builds trust, and when we trust people, we feel comfortable negotiating with them.

Most of us are raised with one objective in mind when it comes to settling a dispute: I win, you lose. The secret to the much-touted "win-win" negotiation paradigm is really: I learn, you learn, *we* win! The more you can learn about your opponent, the better able you will be to bring respect and trust to the table.

SELF-RENEWAL PRACTICE

Being Nimble in Conflict

Retraining yourself for battle takes time; this practice alone is designed to take about a month.

1. Select a person whom you view as an adversary. Pick someone with whom you have argued recently, or someone who has done something that has hurt, angered, frustrated, or frightened you. Then:

   - Write several sentences about your adversary *as though that person were someone you admire and trust*. Don't hold back. Go as far as you can go in describing the traits and talents you admire in that person. Be specific and honest.

   - Next, write several sentences about your adversary as though you loathe and distrust him or her. Be thorough. Leave no transgression or failing unrecorded.

- Now write several more sentences about your adversary, this time as though you have no feelings at all toward him or her. Be matter-of-fact. Assume an objective, detached, journalistic stance.

2. From time to time over the next several weeks, reflect on the admirable, "neutral," and negative traits you assigned your adversary. Think of yourself as getting to know this individual for the first time. (If possible, avoid intense, lengthy interactions during this phase of the process.)

3. Watch for any new insights you gain as a result of your more balanced point of view, and note them in your journal. Look especially for signs that you no longer feel great animosity toward the other person.

4. Once you have achieved a certain emotional distance from the person, you are ready to try approaching him or her anew. Remind yourself beforehand of the positive and neutral qualities you attributed to your former adversary. By emphasizing the attractive and neutral traits over the negative ones, you free yourself to see your former opponent's viewpoint more clearly. Furthermore, you will be able to demonstrate respect, giving that individual the opportunity to respond in kind.

The sample exercise that follows is adapted from one I completed when trying to come to terms with a coworker whose manner of giving feedback irritated me and sparked frequent conflicts between us.

1. *What can I say I admire about Jo?* Every time I look at Jo I see an energetic, longing child. She is beautiful, even captivating. She is extremely articulate. She is passionate and vigilant over what she considers important, even if it escapes others' view. She can get to the bottom of issues and see solutions. She is not afraid of speaking her mind or requesting hard work from others.

What do I dislike about Jo? Jo is fooling herself. She criticizes others to impress people and inflate her own self-worth. She is devious, indirect, and mean. She has a hard time honoring the work of others, and whines and complains and generally casts a negative shadow on every step of progress in the office. I hate her giggle and incompetence and lack of follow-through.

If I were just a neutral observer, I would say: Jo is a coworker of mine. She attends meetings, pays attention, and speaks up frequently. She is of average height and weight and seems intelligent and verbal. She raises issues and offers her own solutions. Sometimes she follows through. Sometimes she doesn't. Sometimes she seems negative, sometimes positive.

2. As I look back at what I wrote, I think I've done a good job of capturing Jo in different lights. . . . It's funny to look at Jo objectively. I'm so used to thinking of her one way. . . . Today I decided I should also add "thoughtful" to the positive list; she does try to take the needs of others into account, even if she can't manage to really do it. . . . (During those few weeks I purposely avoided intensive contact with Jo, and spoke to her over the phone only once.)

3. At the beginning, each time I had a positive thought about Jo I got a jolt of surprise. I was so accustomed to dwelling on what I detested in her behavior that I could hardly believe I was thinking about the same person. The contrast illuminated Jo's complexity.

   As I reflect on Jo's behavior more and more objectively, I am beginning to see that it is my own interpretation of her that converts her into "friend" or "foe." I never realized how much my thoughts affected what I saw in other people. I need to maintain this viewpoint so I don't overreact when she does something I don't agree with.

4. Today I invited Jo to brief me on a subject about which we had argued vehemently in the past. I have to admit I dreaded dealing with her, but, while extending the invitation, I made a point to think of Jo as articulate, passionate, and attentive to details. I

also complimented her on her ideas for our new account. Jo seemed pleasantly surprised, but I'm not sure she trusted my motives entirely. I was also pleased and surprised, because I found myself actually wanting to hear what she had to say—so much that I easily tolerated her communication style, which I had always felt was abrasive.

Of course, this exercise is not a cure-all. Though Jo and I had a much better working relationship as a result of my shift in perspective, I still found myself slipping back into frustration and even hostility over some of her specific actions. One day I overreacted to an accusation she made about me to a mutual friend, and I felt defeated in my efforts to balance my emotional reactions to this coworker. I had to remind myself that relating to Jo on a new plane would take time. I had plenty of evidence that I had made progress; this flare-up was just a reminder of how this particular conflict could throw me off guard. I told myself what I tell my clients: "Be patient with yourself."

The best evidence for the progress Jo and I achieved in relating to each other was that she began to confide in me about her personal life. As she discussed her teenaged daughter's late-night escapades and asked my advice, I was pleased to learn that Jo was a person who was able to admit she needed help. These interactions more than made up for the earlier setback.

Fortunately for us, empathy for another person's perspective comes easier in midlife than it does during earlier periods. Research on healthy adult development reveals that one key characteristic of maturity is the increased capacity to respect and even embrace another person's point of view. The vast improvement in my relationship with Jo is just one example of the satisfaction we gain when we can move beyond our rigid ideas and attempt to encounter others as people, not positions. Perhaps most exciting are the community —even global—implications of simply getting to know each other before we attempt to "solve" problems.

In my communications workshops, I ask participants to estimate the combined IQ of a group of ten managers, all of whom have individual IQs of 120 to 145. We all have a good laugh when I tell them the answer: 80. Even intelligent individuals have trouble with the "group mentality" trap. In order to avoid the hazards of hard-headedness and self-interest in a group setting where the issues at hand may appear to be impossible to solve, we need to undertake a *genuine dialogue* that will free individuals to do their best thinking. When each member of a group feels that his or her opinions and emotions are taken seriously, the group IQ can move beyond the intelligence quotient of any of the individuals, into what I call the *collective genius*.

Since 1992, the Dialogue Project at MIT has been conducting a series of practical experiments aimed at encouraging and exploring genuine dialogue between conflicting parties. Project director William Isaacs maintains that adhering to the true meaning of the original Greek word, *dialogos* (which literally translates as "speech flowing through"), is the key to successful negotiating. He encourages teams of managers and union representatives, physicians and nurses, and others to stop relying on familiar but nonproductive competitive dialogue and to engage instead in dialogue that relates the beliefs and emotions that frame their opinions. In a recent article published in the newsletter *The Systems Thinker*, Isaacs elaborates on the power of dialogue to unleash collective genius:

In the late 1960s, the dean of a major U.S. business school was appointed to chair a committee to examine whether the university, which had major government contracts, should continue to design and build nuclear bombs on campus. People were in an uproar over the issue. The committee was somewhat like Noah's ark: two of every species of political position on campus. The chairman had no idea how to bring all these people together to agree on anything, so he changed some of the rules. The committee would meet, he said, every day until it had produced a report. Every day meant exactly that—weekends, holidays, everything. People objected, but he persisted.

The group eventually met for thirty-six days straight. Critically, for the first two weeks, they had no agenda. People just talked about anything they wanted to talk about: the purpose of the university, how upset they were, their deepest fears and their noblest aims. They eventually turned to the report they were supposed to write. By this time, they had become quite close. In the corner you might have seen two people conferring who previously had intensely clashing views. To the surprise of many, the group eventually produced a unanimous report. What was striking was they agreed on a direction, but for different reasons. They did not need to have the same reasons to agree with the direction that emerged.

Remember the benefits of engaging in authentic dialogue next time you have an argument. Learning to relate to the person behind the opinions by shifting to a more positive point of view is the most effective way of ending the conflict. Your spouse's angry words are just an extension of his or her point of view—an expression of his or her *subjective* reality and feelings—nothing more, nothing less. Rising above your own feelings in this way requires the type of unselfish generosity we spoke of at the beginning of this chapter— the kind of generosity that also contributes to your own happiness.

Exchanging Anxiety for Assertiveness
"He's too distant."

"She's too clingy."

"He won't open up."

"She won't shut up."

If I had a quarter for every time I heard these refrains from couples, I would, as the cliché goes, be a wealthy woman. One person wants to bore in and talk a situation to death, and the other withdraws, pretending the issue never came up in the first place.

The standoff between a person who overrelies on *connecting with or clinging to others* (whom I have labeled the Type C personality) and one who overrelies on *distance and independence from others* (the Type D personality) is an exhausting, fruitless one. The more C demands attention, the more D retreats; the more D pulls back, the more fiercely C attacks. As you might imagine, there are less dramatic (but equally maladaptive) pairings: the Type C/Type C dyad, in which both people are overly attached, and the Type D/ Type D combination, in which both people are too independent, unable to find any common ground. When I witness the problems caused when two Cs go at it, I wonder, "Who is going to listen?" When I see two Ds in conflict, I wonder, "Who is going to talk?" And when I come across the classic attack/retreat of the C/D combination, I wonder, "Who is going to win?"

Evidence reported by developmental psychologist Carol Gilligan suggests that men in our culture usually harbor an independent self-concept, while women tend to hold a connected self-concept. In practical terms, these differences indicate that women define themselves in terms of their matrix of ongoing relationships, while men define themselves as independent and separate from their relationships. Gilligan and other researchers maintain that during early phases of human development (any point before midlife), individuals show an overemphasis on either one pole or the other, but that at more sophisticated levels of development (midlife and beyond), healthy, mature adults begin to integrate the independent self with the connected self. Of course, Type C and Type D conflicts do not always occur along gender lines; in my practice I have seen overly connected males and overly distant women. Furthermore, the C/D problem is not limited to love relationships. Troubled relating occurs between parents and children, employers and employees, even friends.

Though our individual C/D preference becomes obvious to most of us in our twenties and thirties, it is not until midlife that we get so tired of having the same fights over and over that we finally admit there may be other ways of solving the problem. Until midlife, most of us remain entrenched in our own behavior patterns, likely, as the saying goes, to try *harder* instead of *smarter*. In fact, studies have shown that adult humans are the only animals that will stick to a problem-solving technique that has lost its effectiveness. In contrast, countless animal-conditioning experiments with chickens and elephants show that after a certain number of attempts to jump a barrier, escape confinement, even avoid a painful electrical shock, the animals will give up trying.

We humans do get credit for persistence, if not for hardheadedness. Our problem is that we are going about it wrong. Our animal friends, on the other hand, are often completely incapacitated by failure. If the experimenter removes the barrier, boundaries, or electrical field, for example, animals still make no effort to achieve their original goal, even though goal attainment is now possible. Waiting for circumstances to change, however, is not usually a good option for humans seeking conflict resolution. It is not likely that some "experimenter" will magically render your previously unsuccessful communication efforts suddenly effective. Think of it as buying the lottery tickets of human interaction; it is possible, but highly unlikely, that you'll resolve anything without changing your approach.

Frankly, if we do not take a fresh look at communications problems at midlife, there is a good chance we never will: although older adults (sixty-five and beyond) *can* learn new communication skills, the prognosis for achieving great strides in interpersonal effectiveness diminishes significantly after midlife. Researchers who study relationship trends among older adults often cite age-related declines in physical ability, which hinder motivation, as well as deeply ingrained communication habits, as the major deterrents to improving relationships in the last stage of adulthood.

Although many of us sense that improving interpersonal skills is a do-or-die proposition in midlife, few couples seem able to figure out this particular interpersonal puzzle themselves. Despite years of trying to iron out the kinks in a relationship, many well-intentioned, otherwise clever people get stuck in their C/D, C/C, or D/D patterns. "If only she'd leave me alone," I hear from C/D couples, "everything would be fine." Or "I'm sure we could get back on track if he would just open up a little bit." C/C pairs tend to cling to one another, which both seem to enjoy when the relationship is working, but get into trouble when they disagree. "He just doesn't know how to listen," and "I can't make her understand me" are common complaints. The double-D combination consists of two Ds who exist on parallel planes, honoring privacy above all. Each waits silently for the other to do the emotional connecting. I might hear, "We're just not close," from this couple, or "I think the magic is gone."

Research suggests that the manner in which we resolve interpersonal matters can be traced back to our earliest experiences with others. As demonstrated in the section on healing emotional wounds in Chapter 6, we tend to adopt a relating style that worked for us as children, and to stay with it forever. In the case of the Type C/ Type D conflict, the roots of individual behavior appear to be based in the *bonding* experience of infancy, and have more to do with anxiety than they do with "communication" skills. Type Ds and type Cs convey the intrinsic message: I'm scared to death by you and don't know what to do about it.

There is no question that adequate bonding between the helpless infant and the all-powerful mother-protector (or other primary caretaker) is an essential ingredient in a baby's ability to thrive physically, mentally, and emotionally. Less-than-adequate infant-mother bonds have been linked to syndromes ranging from drug addiction to dwarfism. To infants, however, the initially symbiotic bond with mother creates a kind of primitive false impression that mother and baby are one and the same. The child does not yet discriminate between where the mother's identity ends and the child's begins. Successful bonding thus presents infants with a huge interpersonal challenge: separation from Mom. At the age of four to six months, every infant comes to the prelinguistic but nevertheless anxiety-provoking realization that "Mommy is not me. She is more important to me than anything, yet I cannot control her no matter how hard I cry or how often I smile." It must be like finding out that your arm is not yours at all, but someone else's. Correcting that initial relationship mistake is the first step a child takes toward becoming a person. Some psychologists believe that the mystery of why anyone holds on fiercely to intimate attachments, even destructive ones, may be tied to that original, terrifying separation.

Anxiety is a natural, deeply felt response to being emotionally or physically separated from another human being we have learned to count on. Some theorists contend that an infant facing this unpleasant emotion for the first time copes in one of three ways, based on cues he gets from the mother-rejecter. (We're not blaming mother here; mother-child separation is a necessary but difficult step for both.) If a mother uses separation as punishment in response to infant behavior that disturbs her (e.g., screaming, crying, wakefulness), then the baby may learn to rely on clingy-type (type C) relating in order to win the mother's attention. If a mother clings to a child in response to the child's attempts to *de*tach from her, the baby may learn to exaggerate distant-type (Type D) relating in order to avoid being engulfed by an overly possessive mother. And if the mother can modulate her own need to separate and attach according to the needs of her infant (which is difficult for even the most enlightened parent to do), the baby learns to relate without bias. This latter child is likely to become an adult whose ego boundaries are secure, and who is able to find emotional autonomy the middle road between emotional underdependence and emotional overdependence.

Some researchers believe that the intrinsic nature of the child, some inborn predilection to attach or separate from others, is more important than the role played by the primary caretaker in this personality-defining scenario. Regardless of how we developed our preference for the Type C or Type D coping tool, most of us tend toward one or the other of the ends of the continuum. It is only when we are comfortable with *both* ends of the spectrum that we can find the happy middle ground of effective relating.

Being able to let go of Mom and tolerate the anxiety of doing so puts infants in an entirely new relationship alignment, not only with their mothers, but with everyone else who matters to them. *I believe that there is a close connection between the ability to feel and tolerate this anxiety and the ability to enter mutually gratifying relationships.* Coping with separation anxiety means giving away some of our power over the valued other, some of our need to be in charge, and some of our insistence on gratifying our own wishes. In letting go of our basic selfish motives, we learn the rudiments of unselfish caring and relating.

Type Cs, who gravitate toward overconnectedness, seek undue amounts of reassurance or control in relationships, and may act domineering—or overprocess their feelings and opinions—in an effort to avoid the painful experience of rejection or abandonment. They seem to think that if others just *understood* their point of view, no separation would have to occur.

While it might appear that Type Ds are less anxious than those who hang on to others for dear life, just the opposite is true. Theoretical research and practical observation confirm that overusing detachment in relating is a powerful but dysfunctional attempt to quell anxiety of a different form. Complete withdrawal is a strong indication that the individual is so afraid of being engulfed by the other person's point of view or emotional state that running away appears to be the only solution. For the Type D, distancing is a last-ditch effort to maintain a sense of self. Individuals who make this type of interpersonal mistake report having been cared for by clingy, overly dependent adults while in their formative years, and having learned to temporarily turn off their attachment to, and concern for, their extremely needful parents.

Knowing why you have fallen prey to Type C or Type D errors will help you *know how* to catch yourself in the act and change the way you relate to others. But catching yourself is only half the solution; you must also be willing to risk being rejected or engulfed, whichever is more frightening to you. When you risk experiencing the pain that your coping method was designed to avoid, you eliminate your need to use it. In simple terms, if you can tolerate being rejected, you will not have to maintain attachments at all costs, and if you can handle being engulfed, you need not withdraw from situations in order to survive them intact. Only after you have come to terms with the possibility of abandonment or obliteration can you be truly *assertive* in voicing your true thoughts and emotions. Though it might appear that this problem, which is essentially emotional in nature, can be solved with private inner work, the dysfunction was born in the interpersonal crucible, and it is there that it must be resolved.

If you are a Type C person, you are a pro at bonding with others. You can find common ground in an instant and make strong attachments with ease. But you probably also find that:

- people tune you out.
- you put up with a good deal of abuse from others, who take advantage of your caring nature.
- you are afraid to tell people how you really feel, for fear that they will not want to be with you.
- you are uncomfortable spending much time alone.

To avoid these traps of overattachment, you need to incorporate a few useful Type D skills. What you gain from tolerating the anxiety of being rejected, relinquishing your overreliance on attachment, and becoming more separate or distant when the situation warrants is:

- a greater sense of autonomy and the ability to survive real or potential rejections;
- less tolerance for being abused by others;
- a willingness to stand up for your own needs; and
- a greater sense of relationship balance, marked by increased sensitivity to the attachment-separation needs of others.

If you are a Type D, you do a terrific job of staying "above it all" in emotionally charged situations. You refuse to let the emotions of others get you riled up unnecessarily, and you find your unflappable nature is appealing to others who need someone strong to lean on. However, you are likely to be upset that:

- people seem to think you are cold and uncaring.
- others do not respect your desire to be left alone.
- you find yourself agreeing to decisions or actions that do not please you simply to avoid argument.
- no one really understands you.

You have something to learn from Type Cs. Tolerating the anxiety of being overpowered or engulfed, relinquishing your overreliance on separation, and learning to stay close and more attached when appropriate will give you:

- a greater sense of autonomy and the ability to survive real or potential attempts to overpower or engulf you;
- more tolerance for dealing with conflict;
- a willingness to receive true love and generosity; and
- a greater sense of relationship involvement, marked by an increased awareness of the attachment-separation needs of others.

As nice as it would be to be able to balance the responses of your Type D husband or Type C mother-in-law, it is a whole lot easier to attempt to balance your *own* relating errors than it is to get someone else to change. At the very least, you get out of the D-C power struggle. At best, you will receive a tremendous reward for your efforts: others will respond positively to your assertive style and be able, in turn, to let go of some of their own separation anxiety. Try the following Self-Renewal Practice and see how much more balanced your responses are—and how much happier your interpersonal life is—when you put yourself on the line.

SELF-RENEWAL PRACTICE

Risk Being Yourself

1. Select a relationship in which you tend to commit Type C or Type D errors. Give yourself some privacy and time to reflect on several past unsatisfactory interactions you have had with that person. Assuming the role of impartial bystander, review what happened between you. Remember what you said, felt, and did (your behavior, gestures, posture). Pinpoint any evidence of dysfunctional behavior on your part and notice how your mistakes influenced the other person. Feel free to note your observations in your journal.

2. Now, mentally or on paper, rewrite the scenario you just envisioned, taking care to avoid your usual relating error. If you are typically a talker, listen. If you tend to let the other person do most of the relationship work, pick up the slack. In any case, make an effort to:

    • be clear and direct. Say yes when you mean yes, no when you mean no, and maybe when you mean maybe.

    • be open with your feelings, but not accusatory. Make "I" statements ("I can't handle it when . . ."; "I like to . . .") to demonstrate your willingness to take responsibility for your own emotional reactions, be they positive or negative.

- ask for what you want.

- accept the outcome of your discussion. Accept the right of others to deny your requests; acknowledge how the outcome makes you feel about the situation or the person. Admit your mistakes, offenses, and oversights.

- establish a next step, even if that step is a separation or a period of inaction. State what you will and will not do.

- finish your emotional "business," with or without the other person's involvement. If you do not do it face to face, you can do it with a confidant or a professional therapist, or in an imaginary conversation with the other party.

Do not be concerned about forecasting exactly what the other person in your scenario would do or say in response to your new, more effective relating. Just let the conversation continue spontaneously. What is of most benefit to you is practicing responses that boost your self-confidence and skill, not controlling the reactions of the other person.

3. Give yourself some time—days or weeks perhaps—to replay your effective relating scenario in your mind until it becomes almost real. Mental rehearsal will build your confidence and lay down a new set of interpersonal "tracks" in your conscious mind that will be easy for you to call forth in later, real-life interactions.

4. When you feel ready, or when the opportunity for interaction naturally presents itself, practice your new, more assertive relationship skills. Be gentle when you evaluate your progress—kindness to yourself is part of the self-nurturing you need to strengthen your ego boundaries. Celebrate any progress you make, and note how your improved interpersonal skills build your sense of self-identity and self-esteem. Enjoy the experience of dealing with others on your own terms.

The most wonderful aspect of this self-renewal process is that a little work in overcoming relating errors can bring about other inner changes that help an individual grow. A client of mine practiced this exercise faithfully for several months in order to become more assertive in her very troubled marriage. After paying careful attention to her own tendency to make Type C mistakes (mistakes that left her fearing his rejection, giving up her own needs, even enduring his physical abuse), Edie was determined to speak up for herself regardless of whether her husband could respond appropriately. In the midst of her struggle to improve her marriage, she had a significant dream:

> I was sitting behind the wheel of a blue convertible, driving as fast as I could safely drive, heading toward the Mississippi River and out of town. As I neared the bridge that led to another state, I saw a building I had never noticed before.
>
> This building stood tall among the warehouses on the riverfront, and I did a double-take as I passed it. I distinctly remember saying to myself, "How strange to see a church in this location . . . no, it's not just any church . . . it's made of adobe, and has a bell tower . . . it must be a mission. I wonder what it's doing there."
>
> Then, as I crossed into Illinois, I glanced one more time out of my rearview mirror at the mission. Looking at it from this new angle I could see a bright neon sign on its roof, its huge letters flashing the message LIVE WELL, LADY.
>
> I studied the message several times and then chuckled to myself —and commented, "That's not only a mission, it's a health club, too!" (While dreaming I must have associated the phrase "Live well, lady" with the fitness center called Living Well Lady.)

You do not have to be an expert in dream interpretation to decipher what Edie's unconscious wisdom was communicating to her in that timely, encouraging dream. Two of the most important benefits she reported after reflecting on the meaning of the dream were:

1. The self-confidence to separate from a relationship that could not meet her needs and to take charge of her own destiny by leaving her current "state" and traveling quickly but safely to a new and better one.

2. The courage to pursue the main "mission" in life, which is to "live it well," and to stay healthy and true to that commitment no matter how difficult it might be

As you have probably guessed, Edie decided to divorce her husband; she is now happily remarried and much more confident.

When you risk being yourself, you can master your greatest interpersonal fears. At the same time, you forge healthier, more rewarding alliances with others.

The Quest for a Soul Mate

Most people arrive at midlife still clinging to the notion that only a partner can fulfill their deepest longings to be loved. Many of my clients (even the married ones) admit that part of them is still searching for that lost soul mate—a kind of spiritual twin—who will make them feel whole. While some people are lucky enough to find such a partner, most of us do not, and the unrequited yearning for the "other half" of ourselves can cause us much loneliness.

Several traditional cultures, including American Indian, ancient Greek, and African, explained that yearning via their creation myths in which *complete* people—those with both masculine and feminine energies—once existed. But because of some human transgression, usually a failure to obey the laws of God, these people were torn asunder, divided into male and female halves. According to these legends, the two halves of the essential self have been seeking ever since to reunite. The sex act, with its physical merging of the masculine and feminine, was thus both the perfect metaphor for and vivid proof of the undeniable attraction between the masculine and the feminine.

Cross-cultural researcher Arthur Waley describes the origins of the feminine principle, "yin," and the male principle, "yang," in his treatise *Three Ways of Thought in Ancient China* by retelling a very different creation myth. Waley introduces us to Lao Tzu, an ancient Chinese sage, who claimed to have completed a spiritual journey to the beginning of the world. Upon his return, Lao Tzu told Confucius, another ancient Chinese philosopher, that he had witnessed the primal forces of female and male energy at the initial moment of creation:

> The mind is darkened by what it learns there and cannot under-
> stand; the lips are folded, and cannot speak. But I will try to embody
> for you some semblance of what I saw. I saw yin, the female energy,
> in its motionless grandeur; I saw yang, the male energy, rampant in
> its fiery vigor. The motionless grandeur came about the earth; the
> fiery vigor burst forth from heaven. The two penetrated one another,
> were inextricably blended, and from their union the things of the
> world were born.

What is most striking about this particular creation myth is that neither the masculine yang nor the feminine yin could exert its powers in isolation; each requires the presence of the other in order to exist.

For centuries, men and women have been fascinated by the essential and powerful differences between the sexes. Through art, philosophy, mythology, and science we have labored diligently to divine what characteristics of thought, emotion, spirit, body, and behavior are most typically female, and which biological, social, and psychological traits are indicative of "maleness." What *does* it mean to be a man? A woman?

In the dawn of the twentieth century, Swiss psychologist Carl Jung argued that each person's view of "masculine" and "feminine" is tied to a powerful *collective awareness* of these energies. To represent the mental blueprint he believed shaped our understanding of the male/female dichotomy, Jung distilled the protagonists of myth and legend into what he termed *archetypes*, or recognizable symbols of psychological and social behavior. Taken collectively, the archetypes for traits traditionally viewed as "masculine" make up what Jung called the *animus*; archetypes for the "feminine" characteristics make up what he termed the *anima*. According to Jung, all human beings are capable of expressing both masculine and feminine archetypes to some extent.

The chart that follows describes several archetypal patterns of feminine and masculine energy identified by Jung in his clinical research.

Feminine Archetypes	Masculine Archetypes
The Mother—nurturing others' lives physically, emotionally, mentally, spiritually	*The Father*—judge, protector, provider, lawmaker
The Companion—skilled in the arts of intimacy, friendship, and mutuality	*The Hero*—single-minded, strong-willed, capable of extraordinary feats
The Solitary—possessing personal independence, motivation, and courage	*The Youth*—enthusiastic, tireless, busy with projects
The Visionary—in touch with the future and able to call it forth	*The Sage*—wise, experienced, able to appraise self honestly

In early adult life, most of us embrace either the anima *or* the animus, and there are strong societal rewards for proving our mastery in the arena indicated by our gender. The girl playing Mommy and the boy playing warrior are the most basic examples of the ways in which we instinctively align ourselves with our "proper" gender roles. But Jung (and those who have furthered his theories) documented a type of unity principle at work in the most psychologically healthy individuals: an unmistakable tendency to attempt to resolve the tension between the polarized forces of feminine and masculine energy. Jung observed that the urge to resolve these inner tensions occurred most often at midlife, spurring a quest for *inner androgyny*.

Middle-aged men who continue maturing find themselves less preoccupied with the competition for power, control, and prestige that so fiercely motivated them in earlier stages. They focus more on improving relationships, and on the emotional side of existence in general, arenas they would previously have considered too feminine. Women, on the other hand, turn away from the more submissive forms of relating encouraged by most societies and turn toward satisfying their unmet needs for adventure, independence, and self-assertion. Clinical evidence confirms that if maturing adults successfully unify their internal masculine and feminine drives, the battle of the sexes as it is conventionally waged in our families, offices, and culture diminishes.

Tribal cultures the world over are rich with examples of the inner androgyny that can be found later in life. Shamans are known to vary their dress according to the ritual, dressing in feminine clothes when they intend to use traditionally female traits and donning masculine garb when the skills they need are more typically associated with males. In this way, a tribe's spiritual leader honors the powers of both the feminine and masculine forces, invoking whichever ones the situation calls for.

Even Muslim society, which is founded on extremely patriarchal traditions, can spawn dramas depicting midlife shifts in sex roles. In one such story, "Stubborn Husband, Stubborn Wife," recounted by A. S. Mehdivi in his anthology *Persian Folk and Fairy Tales*, we are introduced to a middle-aged wife who is disgruntled by her husband's unwillingness to complete household chores and to a husband who is convinced that his wife is out to emasculate him by requiring him to engage in "women's work" (a theme with obvious universal appeal).

As the tale unfolds, the husband is determined not to be dominated or fooled into performing "feminine" tasks. His wife is just as relentless in her determination to share the household duties with her husband. In an argument over who should milk the cow, the husband and wife agree that the first one of them to speak will lose the bet and have to perform the dreaded milking chore.

As the day passes, the husband is approached by a traveler who, in stopping for a drink of water, admires the husband's treasure of silver and gold artifacts. The husband presumes his wife has sent the traveler to lure him into speaking first. So as not to fall into her clever trap, the husband stares silently at the stranger. When the husband appears to be mute, even deaf, the stranger decides to test the husband's reaction to him, stealing some of the precious artifacts. The husband remains steadfast in his silence as the traveler removes every one of his valuable worldly possessions and rides away.

Next a woman barber passes by the doorway where the husband sits smugly awaiting his wife's return. He is proud of himself for resisting the temptations of the traveler. The barber asks the husband if he would like a shave. The husband is certain her invitation is just one more ploy on his wife's part to entice him into speaking, so he is silent. The barber takes this passivity as a sign of ascent and shaves off the stubborn husband's beard so that his face is smooth and pink and bears no resemblance to his previously manly appearance. The barber is so taken by the dramatic change in the husband's face that she playfully paints his lips red before she departs. Throughout the ordeal, the husband keeps his bargain and never speaks a word.

Sometime later, the wife, who has spent the day in seclusion and is unaware of the misfortunes that have befallen her husband, arrives home. Immediately she sees the devastation and is crushed over the losses her husband has endured. Quickly she explains that she has not tried to trick her husband into speaking. In keeping silent to win, he has lost their fortune and his masculinity along with it.

The wife rushes out into the desert in a valiant effort to regain their lost fortune. She does so by flirting with the man who swindled her husband. Returning home victorious, the wife finds her kitchen in perfect order and her husband hanging the laundry out to dry. She questions him about his "strange" behavior and he replies, "I lost my face, my fortune, and my wife because I was a stubborn fool."

The wife, feeling a wave of insight and empathy, takes the wet laundry out of his hands, saying, "This is woman's work!"

The story ends with the husband and wife having a good laugh over how stubborn they both have been, the husband in his refusal to take on feminine responsibilities and the wife in her insistence that he do so. His belief that he should undertake nothing but masculine enterprises has in fact led to the loss of manly attributes for the husband, and the wife's pushing her husband to help her ease her burdens has eventually led to the necessity of her taking on the scary and difficult new role of provider and protector.

Ironically, as this tale illustrates, it is only after we become adept at both masculine and feminine pursuits that we can hope to have a deeply satisfying relationship with a member of the opposite sex, and especially a spouse.

In our present culture, we have few examples of midlife androgyny. Data from a 1990 national survey entitled *The Quality of American Life* showed little evidence that men in their middle years had embraced more feminine roles, or that midlife women had taken on masculine ones. If we are, indeed, predisposed by nature to acquire opposite-gender roles during midlife, some powerful deterrent must be at work.

Many individuals I see in my practice have suggested that societal pressure for a male to "be a man" or for women to "stop acting so mannish" is no help, but several feel that our materialistic society has broken the true spirit of masculine and feminine ideals. Can you name someone whom you think of as a "real man"? (And I do not mean someone who makes women swoon because his pecs are so big.) Can you name a "real" woman? Without a clear, attractive, and consensual definition of masculine and feminine it can be difficult to claim the rich androgyny that should be a reward of our later years. Consider the traditionally feminine and masculine characteristics listed below (I have adapted them from a wide array of research investigations into the gender roles as viewed by both Eastern and Western cultures):

Traditional Feminine Sources of Power	Traditional Masculine Sources of Power
Receptivity	Proactivity
Vulnerability	Protectiveness
Nurturance	Leadership
Vision	Strategy
Intuition	Analytic ability
Being	Doing
Sensitivity	Toughness
Aestheticism	Practicality
Tolerance	Courage
Relationship orientation	Goal orientation

In the second half of this century, it would appear that we have focused on certain specific strengths of each gender, but ignored others. Men in our culture, for example, tend to be proactive, goal-oriented, tough, and practical, but I can count on one hand the number I know who are protective or courageous. And while I come across many women who are aesthetically inclined, relationship-oriented, and sensitive, I know very few who are tolerant, honestly nurturing (without their own agenda in the forefront), or visionary. Furthermore, if we use financial recompense as a measure of how much we value each quality, it is clear that we reward masculine traits far more often (and better) than we do feminine ones. Realizing this, many women have done a fine job of incorporating the use of analytic reasoning, goal orientation, and toughness into their corporate lives. But as we have discussed, none of these traits exists in a vacuum. If, for example, everyone adopts "masculine" traits in the workplace and no one uses "feminine" characteristics, the masculine traits lose their power and their meaning: strategy needs vision to be complete; toughness needs sensitivity.

In a society lacking respect for the full spectrum of male and female behaviors, most of us admit to being confused about how to act out the gender roles nature assigned us. Androgyny may, in fact, seem the easy way out. But true androgyny is not the absence of gender; it is the ability to incorporate the *strengths* of both.

One of the marvelous advantages of midlife is that the maturity you have gained often enables you to skip a step or two in your personal development. At this stage of your life, for example, it does not make much sense for you to run around looking for your lost manhood or womanhood (if it is indeed lost). You would do best simply to decide which of the *human* qualities you lack and work to attain them.

The integration process of inner androgyny is no easy task. Psychologist John Sanford illuminates the challenging nature of the quest for inner androgyny in his book *Invisible Partners*:

There are opposites within us, call them what we like—masculine and feminine, anima and animus, Yin and Yang—and these are eternally in tension and eternally seeking to unite. The human soul is a great arena in which the Active and the Receptive, the Light and the Dark, the Yang and the Yin seek to come together and forge within us an indescribable unity of personality. To achieve this union of the opposites within ourselves may very well be the task of life, requiring the utmost in perseverance and assiduous awareness. . . .

Jean Bolen, Jungian analyst and scholar of Greek mythology, also believes that this integration of opposites is our ultimate personal goal. In her book *Goddesses in Everywoman*, she states that becoming our most mature selves actually "ends in the union of opposites," and that reconciling these opposites is a matter of making the most of "the human potential with which we start."

Bolen, like many psychologists, maintains that the seeds of *every* masculine and feminine quality reside in each of us already. According to this theory, men are perfectly capable of behaving "like women" if they want, and women can take on as many masculine characteristics as they desire. To someone unsure of his gender role, the idea that he is some sort of emotional hermaphrodite can be quite unnerving. (Many therapists believe that discomfort with this concept is at the root of homophobia.) But as we saw with the story of the stubborn Persian couple, it is only when a man acknowledges the feminine instincts within him that he becomes truly masculine. By the same token, a woman who takes on appropriate masculine attributes finds herself more thoroughly feminine. In other words, that mythic "other" you yearn for may simply be the other side of *you*.

Striving to realize both the masculine and feminine aspects of your soul involves more than putting aside time and energy to try new personas in the mirror; it means using these heretofore hidden sides of yourself when you relate to others. If you have been the protector for your children, for example, approaching inner androgyny may mean you decide to switch to nurturing, when appropriate, instead. I can hear the moans now: "I'm glad you're supportive, Dad, but I need more than hugs here. What about the hundred bucks?" (This dialogue takes courage, too!) If you have always prided yourself on your sensitivity to the needs of others, you may find resistance when you adopt "toughness."

The scariest element by far of inner androgyny is the way it affects sexuality. Androgyny in sex is not bisexuality, but rather the ability to bring traits from both genders into your love life no matter whom you love. If you have always considered your performance as sexual aggressor the measure of your sexual self, taking on a passive role can be as frightening—but also as exciting—as a first kiss. Will you like it? Will you be accepted? Sex therapists who counsel couples complaining of arousal difficulty (or problems maintaining excitement) report that an authentic sex-role reversal in lovemaking can be especially helpful in midlife. Moving out of strict gender roles is one of the best ways to rekindle passions that may have been doused by overwork, waning hormones, or children.

Midlife biology invites all of us to be more sexually androgynous. The felicitous biological changes in male and female sexuality in the second half of life can mean greater understanding, excitement, and satisfaction for both partners, provided a couple is comfortable moving out of the sex role stereotypes that fueled the fantasies of their twenties and thirties.

Men who at twenty enjoyed instantaneous sexual arousal at the mere sight of an attractive person find that at midlife they require more time to become fully aroused. Studies also show that middle-aged men are more aroused by a strong emotional attachment to their partner than they are by how attractive the partner is. With time and emotion as critical components of male arousal, it becomes easier for men to enjoy a more receptive, less dominant sexual role.

In contrast, midlife women report feeling much more freedom to be sexually aggressive, because many are past child-bearing years. Furthermore, most studies indicate that women reach their biological sexual peak during their late thirties and early forties (with only a minimal decline in sexual desire after that, especially if estrogen levels remain sufficient). The blessings of these shifts naturally provide opportunities for women to become more sexually assertive if that approach is beneficial to the sexual exchange.

Fortunately, by midlife, most of us are ready to accept the anima or animus hidden within, in both the sexual and social arenas. We may even sense it trying to emerge—when we begin to chafe at the roles we have taken on, when we notice ourselves reacting "out of character" in new situations (such as becoming a grandparent or managing employees in a new job), or when we start to feel that a particular period of our lives has passed. The natural desire to incorporate more opposite-sex traits into our behavior is a sign that we are ready to move beyond gender roles and into full personhood.

The more androgynous you become, the more you have to offer to others—in bed or out—and the less you will feel that yearning for a mythical "other" who can fulfill you. If you can balance yourself, your psychic neediness will disappear, opening you up to the best love of all: the love between equals.

Advance yourself in your quest for inner androgyny by practicing the following interior dialogue.

SELF-RENEWAL PRACTICE

The Intimacy Within

1. Take a few minutes to review the list of twenty sources of interpersonal power on page 210. Write down the name of each of the twenty characteristics in your journal. As you write, decide whether that particular source of power is one you have cultivated in yourself. If you view it as one of your personal power sources, place a check mark next to it. If you believe that the particular trait is not present in your interpersonal repertoire, or could use some work, place a box ☐ beside it.

2. Select one current strength and one current weakness. You may choose them at random if you like, or you may pick a strength and weakness that need balancing: receptivity and activity; toughness and sensitivity. Some people select a specific weakness that has been giving them trouble, such as courage (to stand up to the boss, perhaps), and a strength, such as sensitivity (maybe you find yourself drained by others' demands), that needs to be downplayed.

3. Imagine how these two characteristics might actually appear if they were personified. Give each one a concrete identity in your imagination by conjuring up a face, body, costume, and persona for each. For instance, if you choose *visionary* as a strength, you might think of it as a wise, grandmotherly figure holding a crystal ball; if you choose *goal orientation* as a weakness, you might see it in your imagination as a young, energetic boy busily constructing a city of Lego blocks.

4. Let the two imaginary people you have created converse with one another. Just begin the conversation and let it flow. Chronicling the dialogue in writing is helpful so that later you can reflect on its meaning.

   Initially, you will have to concentrate on what one entity says to the other, making up messages that they trade back and forth. Once the dialogue gets going, however, you will notice that the characters seem to take on a life of their own, and you will not have to work so hard to put words into their mouths. (Some people actually report feeling as if they are "in the audience," watching two actors engage in a riveting dialogue.)

   Do not worry if the dialogue wanders a bit, or if the actors stray out of character. Attend to the essence of what they reveal.

5. Notice how your archetypal masculine and feminine characters assist and complement one another, and how curious and accepting they can be, actually encouraging the other to succeed.

The sample dialogue that follows is one I tried this week.

> Nurturing character: "You know me, I'm everyone's friend. I go out of my way to connect with people, to anticipate and meet their needs. I am happiest when other people enjoy my presence. I make Kathy Cramer popular and lovable."
>
> Analytical character: "I'm glad to talk to you again, you are a joy to know and your power is very strong inside the personality we both share. I am still weak, but very important, too. My purpose is to see life and others and Kathy Cramer as honestly as possible.

My contribution is to remember all the experiences and to connect the past to the present and to the future."

Nurturing character: "You know, I could use a little help from you. More often than I'd care to remember, I seek approval and love from people who are not good for me. In my blind desire to please and to support others, I often wind up wasting my energy and diverting my attention from those who bring meaning to my life and who are most significant to my happiness."

Analytical character: "I'd be happy to assist you, but you have to give me more air time. Let me take the lead. Sometimes you jump in so quickly, or dominate a situation. Just sit back and let me survey what is involved. I'll take time to listen and to determine whether that person in that context is important for you to nurture."

As I reflected on this dialogue, I became more convinced than ever that I need to cultivate and trust the powers of analysis so I can make more discerning appraisals of others (and myself). All I have to do is to allow "him" to grow stronger and more dominant.

Achieving inner androgyny is one of the best shortcuts to expanding your human potential. If you can overcome your mental barriers to this important life-enhancing tool, you will have come a long way toward tapping into the rich reservoirs of gender power.

VICTORIES OF INTERPERSONAL EFFECTIVENESS

Caring, concern, and a healthy connection to the people in your life may be the strongest indication that you are a well-adjusted, mature adult. That's what a large sample of middle-aged adults said when they were interviewed in a 1989 University of Wisconsin survey seeking information on what contributes most to psychological well-being during the midlife years. The study, conducted by psychologist Carol Ryff, revealed that both men and women hold a strong belief that adults who are "other-oriented" are mature, while people who are "self-centered" are immature. Furthermore, almost 70 percent of the survey respondents rated their families as the most important thing in their lives at present; slightly more than one-third felt their jobs were most important. When asked what experiences from the past were most positive, respondents ranked marriage and family first and second.

A loving family is, for most of us, the place where we feel comfortable in disclosing ourselves, where we care enough to exercise compassion during conflict, where we can risk being autonomous in relating, and where we are first called upon to find our opposite-gender sources of personal power. It is within our families—whether they be made of blood ties or newer emotional bonds—that we can most easily learn the lessons of interpersonal effectiveness, which carry over into every relationship we undertake. Although confronting your shortcomings in relationships is painful and embarrassing at times, the alternative is worse: people in midlife who do not work at better relationships end up isolated and disenfranchised from themselves.

In contrast, people who hone their capacity to be first-class relaters reap unanticipated benefits. Increased ease with others, greater happiness with ourselves, and a deeper understanding of humanity are the bonus prizes of interpersonal effectiveness. The rewards garnered in this chapter are also the basis for spirituality; connection with others is the first step toward connection with the greater whole that unites us all. Interpersonal effectiveness is also a key component of personal integrity, which is defined in part by how much we respect the integrity of others. Most important, as we continue to grow and mature as adults, strong interpersonal skills ensure that we attract warm, caring people as our companions on the journey of life.

CHAPTER 7

Pathway #5: Exceptional Competence

All of my life I have tried to avoid ruts, such as doing things my ancestors did before me, or leaning on the crutches of other people's opinion, or losing my childhood sense of wonderment. I am glad to say I still have a vivid curiosity about the world I live in. . . . It is as natural for me to believe that the richest harvest of happiness comes with age—as to believe that true sight and hearing are within, not without.

—HELEN KELLER

Two years ago, my small business mushroomed. Suddenly we had more opportunities for training and consulting than we could keep up with. I was thrilled with our growth, but I found that I was working twelve hours a day and spending three or four days a week out of town in order to keep up with the demand.

Although I was willing to make sacrifices for the good of the company, and was aware that I would eventually be able to delegate much of my work, I nevertheless felt the ill effects of constant pressure. I fell into bed each night exhausted, unable to remember what city I was in. My husband began to complain that I was neglecting him, and I noticed conflicts at the office that were due in large part to my continued absence.

Six months later, when I was finally able to pass the baton to several other professionals now certified to teach the most popular of our workshops, I had some time to reflect on the time that had just passed. I realized more than ever before that the skills I had developed over the past fifteen years were the keys to my ability to sustain peak performance when the pressure was on. I also realized that if I wanted to continue to make top-notch contributions, I would have to be more careful to guard my own physical vitality (which I put at risk during extended periods of stress) and my relationships with people I love (which I unilaterally had put "on hold" when the need arose). In short, my life was out of balance.

As I slowed my pace and rebalanced my life, my marriage grew stronger, my relationships with others improved, and the morale of my colleagues improved. Yet something was missing. I had a nagging sense of unease and felt a bit sad. It was a constant battle to tend to details. The slightest mistake (on my part, or someone else's) frustrated me intensely. I could not understand why I felt so uptight and depressed when my marriage, my business, and my health had never been better.

After a few weeks of being grump-of-the-month, I sat down and did a Life Map, like the one outlined in Chapter 1, for depression. I discovered that each time I had faced this feeling in the past, I had conquered it by reprioritizing. With my brother Jim's death I had made the decision to take care of my body. With failures, I determined to try harder, or I formed new goals. Suddenly it became clear that I had been focusing so hard and so long on the goal of making my life run smoothly that I had failed to appreciate the fact that my life *was* running smoothly. I had not celebrated, nor had I developed any new goals. I was, in effect, going through my life on automatic pilot.

A bit of research showed me that exceptional competence is another of those tremendous presents nature hands us at midlife. We have been performing many of the same tasks for years, and by now have become quite good at them. In much the same way that the loss of self-consciousness frees our brains to perform amazing mental feats, exceptional competence frees our time and attention so we can focus on the important goals of the second half of life. All of the studies on successful aging show that in order to thrive, midlifers experiencing the wonder of exceptional competence must confirm or readjust their priorities and develop a vision, just as they did when they were young. The goals of youth are more societally bound, more concrete. In midlife, our goals are based on individual rather than cultural need: we have to fashion our visions ourselves.

Rejuvenated, I set about the difficult but fulfilling goal of designing the rest of my life.

THE CALL TO EXCEPTIONAL COMPETENCE

There are several clear signals that you are ready to embrace the joys and heartaches of exceptional competence. One of the most obvious of these is boredom. Some people experience boredom only with certain tasks. Others are ashamed to admit they find other people, or even their own *lives*, boring. Feeling the weight of too many tasks is another common sign that it is time for you to cease being a "beast of burden" at work and at home. But the biggest tip-off that you need to travel down the pathway is that your life lacks sufficient meaning. Other readiness markers are listed below.

Midlife Readiness Signals for Exceptional Competence
You may find yourself:

- noticing a decrease in the amount of time or energy it takes you to perform important tasks
- wanting to make huge changes in your life, from leaving your spouse to switching careers to moving to Tahiti
- feeling more physical exhaustion with less emotional satisfaction when doing routine work
- lacking interest in work, hobbies, people, or ideas that used to excite you
- believing that all your hard work did not get you what you really want
- dreaming about new challenges and opportunities
- being more open to the opinions of others, as well as other lifestyles and values
- sensing more poignantly the world's problems—poverty, the ozone layer, war—and feeling more determined to do something about one or more of them

For many of us, maximizing the benefits of exceptional competence does not seem particularly pressing; rarely do the signs of exceptional competence incite deep feelings of angst. But the slow death we die of boredom or from lack of a meaningful framework for our own lives is actually more harmful to midlifers overall than the inability or unwillingness to deal with the mental or physical aspects of aging. Depending on how you approach it, the gift of exceptional competence can either be a plateau on which you are stranded or a resting place on the mountain that leads to inner peace.

In part, traveling the pathway of exceptional competence means celebrating your achievements in all areas of your life. Now is a good time to go back to your SRI scores (from Chapter 2) and congratulate yourself for your many strengths along all the pathways. Also take another look at your exceptional competence score and reevaluate your goals before you look at the rewards in this chapter. Above all, do not compare your successes and failures to those of others. Doing so will only deflate or inflate your view of yourself unnecessarily: you will underestimate the value of what you have done, or you may end up with a false sense of superiority that will squelch your motivation. Each of us develops at his or her own pace and according to his or her unique needs and interests.

ADVENTURES IN EXCEPTIONAL COMPETENCE

As your life's new direction becomes clear, you may find that your day-to-day life changes much more than it did on other pathways. I recall one man who completely overhauled his work schedule to accommodate his hobbies after he began this journey. Other people do not change their schedules much at all, but shift instead the way they approach or perceive their lives. Be confident that no matter what direction you decide upon, the many skills you have already mastered will be of great help in getting you where you want to go.

Accepting your great competence at midlife can make your work and personal lives sizzle. Knowing you can rely on your established abilities frees you to accomplish amazing feats of creativity, productivity, and what many psychologists call generativity: being able to give away what you know. It also enables you to prepare for the exciting adventures of spiritual development. With the rewards of exceptional competence, you can learn, achieve, and contribute in ways that far surpass what you have been able to accomplish so far.

Rainbow of Roles

By midlife, we have all become expert at doing more than one thing at a time. We can talk on the phone while doing paperwork, make an important deal over lunch, or cook dinner and discuss the day with our spouse simultaneously. We are also many different *people* at the same time: worker, partner, friend, parent, child. The demands of playing so many important roles often mean we end up composing a grocery list at a board meeting, practicing a presentation while raking leaves, and listening to self-improvement tapes on the way to work. Role conflict, role overload, even role ambiguity (how am I supposed to behave in my role as a stepparent, temporary worker, or lay minister?) are part of the terrain of midlife.

A common complaint from people who attend my seminars is that they feel at odds with the number or quality of their roles. Many people who have the responsibility for caring for aging parents experience a conflict between being competent and loving caretakers and doing a good job in their other important roles of spouse, parent, and employee. Other clients tell me that they are still so busy with work at midlife that they have less time than they thought they would to pursue their own interests. For many of us, blended families, shifting finances, and unclear societal expectations make it difficult to prioritize all the many things we do.

Ironically, research shows that occupying a number of highly important roles during midlife can actually buffer anxiety, enhance self-esteem, and increase your sense of control over your own life. Researchers at Brandeis University found that women who occupied multiple roles, which they deemed to be *positive*, including paid worker, wife, and mother, showed greater self-esteem and overall psychological well-being than did women with fewer or more negatively experienced roles. Furthermore, if you experience a disturbance in one role, the rewards of other roles can compensate for the loss and lessen the impact of the blow. When your child leaves for

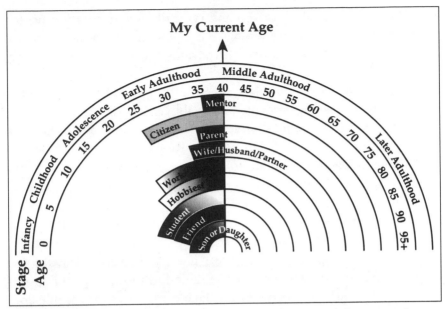

Rainbow of roles across the life span: a modification of the original career rainbow reported by Donald E. Super in 1976

college, for instance, you may feel sad that your role as parent has changed forever. Besides the promise of a different but equally satisfying relationship with your child, however, you will now have more time to give to developing any of the other roles that may have been put "on the back burner" while your child was at home.

In the 1970s, psychologist Donald E. Super, the "Dr. Spock" of healthy role development, proposed a stage theory of career growth that charted an individual's career from the years of *exploration* in adolescence to the years of *establishment* in young adulthood through to the most productive, creative years in middle adulthood, which he termed the *maintenance* stage. According to Super, we need to trace the development of *all* of our roles if we want to make the most of our work and our lives. We also need to make conscious decisions for future role management. Super developed an ingenious model for role growth, which I have adapted here. This particular rainbow belongs to a forty-one-year-old man.

Our earliest roles are determined by our family lives. We are born into the role of daughter or son and typically live in that groove for the rest of our lives; even when we move away from home, create our own families, and survive our parents' death, there is a deeply felt part of us who will always be a child.

As we move further into the outside world, we cultivate other roles, such as friend, student, and hobbyist. Our natural talents, interests, and personalities drive our role development, while the opportunities and obstacles of our situations provide role boundaries. Some of us are fortunate to experience a productive chemistry of inner and outer imperatives that create wide, deep "role grooves" and encourage free-flowing growth. Other people are not able, because of undue external constraints, to follow their inner drive. When the forces that propel us from the inside collide with those that shape us from the outside, we end up in roles that are too shallow and too narrow. Once we reach adulthood, it would appear that we have more opportunity to place ourselves in favorable context where our talents and interests can be maximized. Unfortunately, however, inadequate role definition in youth often carries over into adult life, because most of us stay in the same role grooves as we age.

In midlife we can, in fact, deepen and widen even our earliest roles. I devised the multileveled Self-Renewal Practice that follows to help clients alleviate the strain of roles that compete for time, energy, and emotional commitment. It also uncovers ways to deepen the meaning we glean from our roles.

SELF-RENEWAL PRACTICE

Re-Creating Roles

1. In your journal, create a set of "core values," nouns that represent for you the most important aspects of life. These might be anything from leisure to physical activity, and can be values you now have or ones you wish to have more of in your life. List anything that you consider essential to your happiness and fulfillment.

    The values listed below are those most frequently identified by my workshop participants. Feel free to borrow some of these if you want, but be sure you list some of your own.

Intellectual stimulation   Respect
Creativity   Honesty
Autonomy   Affiliation
Intimacy   Challenge
Altruism   Beauty
Security   Meaning
Personal power   Achievement

Do not worry about the way you word your own core values; just write them down in a way that makes sense to you. "Helping others learn" is just as good as "teaching."

2. Draw yourself a role rainbow. Add or delete roles as needed to ensure that your chart reflects the roles most salient in your life. Be sure to let the starting points for each role correspond to your own development. (You may, for instance, have started your hobbies later in life than the man in the example.) Don't forget to note your current age.

3. Consider each of the roles in your rainbow, one at a time, to see how each has varied in importance over the years. For example, the role of student may have been crucial to you in adolescence and early adulthood, but less so before and after those stages. For other people, this role peaks between ages thirty and forty, as they master new job-related tasks.

Once you have a good idea of the course you have run to date with each of your roles, amend your rainbow to reflect variations in role intensity. Colored pencils or crayons work best for this part of the Self-Renewal Practice, but lighter and darker shades of regular pencil will do.

If you are using colored writing instruments, select a color for each of your roles. Match any color to any role; the idea here is to make the roles stand out individually. Now shade each "ribbon" of the rainbow, using pale shading to reflect times when a given role was not particularly important to you, and dark shading to show periods during which the role was intensely important. Create as many different gradations of shading as you need to for each role. Shade each role only up to the dotted line that represents your age.

4. Evaluate the relative importance of each role by counting how many of your core values you experience in each role. Select one role at a time and prepare a chart similar to the sample below. Be sure to list values you *do* get rather than those you wish you would or think you should.

Role	Core Values	Importance Index
Son	Intimacy, altruism, meaning, respect	4
Friend	Respect, affiliation, honesty	3
Student	Intellectual stimulation, creativity, meaning, challenge, autonomy	5
Hobbyist	Challenge, control, meaning, beauty	4
Worker	Security, power, respect, achievement	4
Husband	Intellectual stimulation, intimacy, respect, meaning, affiliation, honesty	6
Parent	Respect, power, intimacy, meaning, challenge	5
Citizen	Respect, meaning, altruism	3
Mentor	Respect, honesty, achievement	3

Next, rank your roles according to their Important Index scores. Next to the importance scores, give a rough estimate of the percentage of your focus and attention each role actually gets. The person in the sample responded this way:

Role	Importance Index	Percent of Attention
Husband	6	15%
Student	5	5%
Parent	5	15%
Son	4	5%
Hobbyist	4	5%
Worker	4	40%
Friend	3	5%
Citizen	3	5%
Mentor	3	5%

5. Look for any imbalance in the columns. In general, people are happier when their Importance Index ratings and Percentage of Attention ratings are similar. Incongruities tend to breed role dissatisfaction. In the example above, the man who values his role as a husband would note that only 15 percent of his attention is devoted to that important role. Could this disproportion be the source of any unhappiness with the role as he is currently experiencing it? In addition, the amount of his focus that goes toward work is way out of proportion to the importance he assigns it.

   Write down any ideas you have for bringing the attention column in line with the importance column by reducing the amount of focus you give to a role or by increasing the number of core values you derive from it. My client, for instance, knew before he came in that his role as worker was way out of whack, but he also knew he needed to continue to perform at that level to maintain his earnings. After completing the rainbow and lists above, he chose to upgrade his work core-value quotient by generating more opportunities for altruism, intellectual stimulation, challenge, and meaning at the office. He also decided to apply some of his interest in intellectual stimulation and challenge to finding ways to be more productive, so he could have more energy to devote to his family life and to personal learning, both of which were important to him.

6. Decide how important you want each of your roles to be in the future. Perhaps you want to create new roles, or downplay old ones. Shade the "future" area of the chart according to your preferences.

7. Keep the rainbow in mind as you go about solving the problems that crop up in daily life. When circumstances or people change, roles change too. Whenever you sense role conflicts, overload, ambiguity, or emptiness, look again at whether the particular role involved provides you with what you value most. Sometimes it is important to cycle back through each step of this Self-Renewal Practice to pinpoint the exact source of your problem.

A terrific example of role strain is that experienced by parents whose grown children, out of economic necessity, are living at home. These parents find that they can ease tension if they give less attention to parenting: making older children responsible for feeding and clothing themselves, for keeping their own schedules, even for living in only certain quarters of the house reduces the percentage of attention parents spend in a now less-valued role. Investing one's parenting with a greater number of core values, such as intellectual stimulation or affiliation, also can resolve problems between parents and more mature sons and daughters.

In order to get the most out of our complex collection of midlife roles, we must make conscious choices. People who commit to continually recreating their roles discover a newfound sense of personal control and greater satisfaction in all the roles they choose to play.

Hidden Assets

Do you earn enough money? Does any of us? I don't think I earn enough. Despite the fact that I live well, I can think of all sorts of reasons more money would be useful. I'd like to take a long vacation, for one, and I'd like to pay someone to do the chores I'm tired of doing. Then there's the live-in masseur I want to hire to massage my troubles away. And that's just the beginning.

Sit back for a second and imagine you have just won ten million dollars in the lottery, or that a long-lost relative has graciously left you ten million dollars in her will. In your journal, write the answers to the following questions.

1. What is the first thing you would do? Tell your boss good-bye? Leave home with no forwarding address?

2. What long-term changes would you make? Would you go back to school? Move to a tropical island?

3. Would you be happier because of new found financial security and experiencing those long wished for escapades?

Studies have shown that lottery winners are, in fact, no happier than the rest of us. Furthermore, most winners do not make major changes in their lives. Their standard of living rises, and some find themselves willing to take financial risks they were not comfortable with before (such as starting a new business), but their new wealth does not increase the amount of joy they get from their lives. In fact, many lottery winners report that their happiness diminishes slightly in the wake of their windfall.

What is interesting about these studies is that they prove that *financial security—that brass ring we all grab for—is not a key to happiness.* Think back to your first job. Didn't it always seem that if you could just make 10 or 20 percent more you wouldn't feel so strapped? When you got the raise in pay, were you happy? Even now, don't you have a sense that another ten thousand dollars or so would increase your ability to relax and enjoy life?

Money fails us in our quest for security for two reasons. The first is that money, or its value, can be taken away. Stock markets crash, governments collapse, wars erupt. That green stuff we value so much might someday turn out to be completely worthless. Second, security itself, as we define it, is unattainable. Even if we had all the money in the world, along with the promise that money would retain its value, we still would never get to that magical "relaxed" place for the simple reason that there are no guarantees in life. You or your loved ones could get hit by a car tomorrow, or we could be invaded by Martians. Even millionaires worry, because, as we all know, money cannot buy love, and money cannot buy immortality.

All we really need money for is food, shelter, and clothing. Anything more—gourmet ice cream, a four-bedroom house, stylish apparel, even a television—is simply something we *want*. I don't mean to suggest that we shouldn't want these things, only that we should recognize that they are not essential to our lives.

Now think about your job—the activity at which you spend most of your day—and, in your journal, answer these questions.

1. Why do you do your job? To earn enough money to feed, house, and clothe your family? To take care of your children so your spouse can be free to earn? To save enough to realize your dream of boat ownership?

2. What gives you the most on-the-job satisfaction?

3. If you could change three things about your job, what would they be?

In his research on adult development, psychologist Douglas H. Heath identified what contributes most (and least) to job satisfaction. The chart below summarizes his findings as I have interpreted them.

Most Significant Contributors to Work Satisfaction	Least Significant Contributors to Work Satisfaction
Tasks that mirror interests	Salary received
Chances to achieve one's full potential	Feelings of competence
Assignments of increasing difficulty	Amount of energy required
Opportunities to use most highly developed skills	Amount of time demanded
Sense of identity reinforced by work responsibilities	Status derived from work and relationships on the job

Note that the characteristics in the right-hand column are related to *extrinsic* rewards, while the items in the left-hand column describe the *intrinsic* rewards of the work itself. It is not that we do not strive for money, status, feeling competent, and the like—we do. Human nature makes us all strivers. What the chart tells us, however, is that if extrinsic outcomes are all we gain from working, we will not feel very satisfied.

The intrinsic rewards of your work, or of anything you do, for that matter, are your hidden assets. No global monetary fluctuation, no office politics, no invasion by little green people can take away your enjoyment and satisfaction in what you do. *Your best security is the ability to get the most satisfaction from whatever tasks come your way.* Ironically, those of us who get the most satisfaction from our work tend to be top performers who have plenty of self-esteem—two qualities that are associated with increased earning potential!

Midlife offers us the opportunity to remake work in ways that make it more relevant to our most heartfelt needs and desires. In the chapter on mental mastery, we talked about ideas for keeping your mind engaged when tasks were less than stimulating. The next step is to find a way to extend the number and quality of "satisfiers" in everyday life. Most people over the age of forty are surprised to learn that they are skilled enough, experienced enough, even secure enough in their earning power to enable them to transform the work they do to make a living into more than just working for a paycheck. At the very least, midlifers are able to see that no matter how much money they make, it is important to pursue satisfaction somewhere, too.

Few of us have more than a vague idea of what our personal satisfiers are. We are in the habit of gauging our work primarily by the worth it commands on the open market, not by how well it matches our inner urges to grow. Give the Self-Renewal Practice that follows a try, and look for several opportunities in the next week to practice activating your personal satisfiers.

SELF-RENEWAL PRACTICE

Increasing Your Assets

1. Select an activity that you engage in on a regular basis that brings you a lot of satisfaction. Take care to select a rich, complex activity. Growing a garden and investing in stocks are examples of complex activities for midlifers; boiling eggs and driving a car are not.

2. In your journal or on a tape recorder, and without any self-censoring, describe what you do while taking part in that activity. Give as many details as you can about the various components of the activity. Outline the specific strengths and skills you bring to it. Explain why you enjoy each element of the job, and how the parts and the whole of the task bring you satisfaction and meaning. (If you have a partner, ask if he or she will listen closely as you tell why you derive such satisfaction from the particular job.)

3. Reflect on what you discovered in Step 2. Alone or with you partner, review what you said and make notes about the specific skills, preferences, and kinds of satisfaction that were revealed in your extemporaneous comments. (Here is where a partner can be a great help; he or she is likely to be more objective than you are, and therefore more insightful. Allow your partner to speak, uninterrupted, about what he or she sees as your satisfiers. Take notes, and mark with a question mark any ideas you disagree with, to be discussed later. Be as open-minded as possible; you may be delighted to learn of strengths you did not know you had.) Generate a list of "core satisfiers" that are consistently rewarding.

4. Look for instances in everyday life that confirm your identified satisfiers. As you become more confident in the power of these strengths to add satisfaction to your life, capitalize on these competencies in other situations. For example, you might want to request assignments at work that require you to use your most well-developed skills. Or you may want to invent new ways of addressing certain duties and interests that incorporate your hidden strengths.

You will probably find it helpful to read about the experience of one of my clients, Jane, before you try this Self-Renewal Practice yourself. Jane was seeking more satisfaction in her work as claims manager for a large insurance company. After I walked her through the practice, she breathed new life into what had become a dull, routine job—and gained newfound self-esteem, as well.

1. **Kathy:** "Jane, tell me about one of your favorite pastimes or hobbies. What activities are involved? What do you enjoy about it? What kind of satisfaction does it bring you?"
   Jane: "Well, my favorite hobby is being a Girl Scouts troop leader. When I'm with those children I lose all track of time and completely forget the problems at work. I enjoy planning their activities because I know they will be so happy to try to accomplish another project. I actually get inspired by their energy and enthusiasm. An evening of Girl Scouts is like a big

dose of joy for me. We work hard, play hard, and go home feeling like a team."

2. **My notes:** "Interests and skills Jane demonstrated by her comments: teaching, leading, giving back to the community, mix of fun and learning, self-development, loyalty, discipline."

3. **Kathy:** "Jane, in that brief description of your favorite pastime you revealed a number of your competencies and interests. Listen to what I noticed and see if you agree or have anything more to add." I read Jane the list of observations I had recorded in Step 2 of this exercise.
   Jane: "I can't believe you got all that. I guess being a Girl Scouts leader involves more than I realized. The only thing I might add is that scouting helps me balance my life. Without it I would be too focused on work. So I guess that means I know how to stay in balance."

4. **Kathy:** "Can you think of any way to integrate some of the skills you use in scouting into your work as a manager?"
   Jane: "I will have to give this some thought, of course, but off the top of my head . . . let's see . . . maybe I could think of some ways to make those deadline-driven projects more of a game for the staff. If I approached specific projects that way we might all feel less stressed-out by them. What keeps standing out in my mind is to somehow introduce more fun into the job. Our administrative work is really quite boring and tedious most of the time. Maybe I will ask my group for some of their ideas. They may think I'm out of my mind to suggest that we could have more fun on the job. Maybe I'll just make some changes in how I present the workload and set some playful objectives and see what happens."

The first few times Jane broached the idea of creating a gamelike atmosphere in the office, her staff sloughed off her suggestion. But Jane was convinced that morale and productivity would increase if she could create a more teamlike feeling. Eventually one of her subordinates decided to back the idea—reasoning that the staff should be willing to try any new approach that might relieve the pressure and revive spirits—and her support broke the group's resistance. The entire staff came up with a game in which anyone who complained or criticized others while the pressure was on to meet a deadline had to ante up one dollar. The complaint/criticism dollars were to be held in a kitty to pay for a group celebration once the deadline was met.

As the kitty grew, so did team spirit. Magically, negative comments became more jovial and less demoralizing. The person fined was able to easily (but not entirely painlessly) "erase" any debt of negativity with his or her dollar. The celebrations were modest, but afforded everyone a well-earned lift. Jane was thrilled at the group's new camaraderie, and reported that her days on the job were now filled with the same satisfactions as her evenings of scouting.

Jane's successful transference of satisfiers from scouting to the workplace is an example of the power of hidden assets. Because her plea to change came out of a sincere desire to increase *satisfaction* (rather than financial recompense, or power), she was able to lead her subordinates toward increased happiness on the job, which translated nicely into increased self-confidence and productivity. Note that she did not confuse her efforts with shallow management practices such as passing out smile buttons or having "morale" meetings; people sense a manipulative motive when it is present, and give only as much as they think they have to to appear to be a team player.

In every complex activity that delights you are buried intrinsic sources of satisfaction that can be carried over into other areas of your life. Make a habit of using your hidden assets in all your endeavors, and you will find your workday as fulfilling as your time off. The next reward shows you another way to elevate satisfaction while increasing competence.

The Hazards of Peak Performance

Every single one of my friends has a complaint about his or her job. One's job is too dull, another's is too hard. Those whose jobs are stimulating complain of overwork, while those whose jobs give them a strong sense of competence report that their days are filled with tedium and lack of meaning. None of this is news to the folks at Northwestern Mutual Life Insurance, whose national survey report "Employee Burnout: America's Newest Epidemic" shows that 62 percent of those polled claimed to be exhausted, and seven out of every ten people blamed job stress for their health problems and lack of productivity.

How you feel about your job is key to making the most out of your midlife competence. If you generally find yourself in situations that are fun but too demanding, you are most likely a *learner*; if everyone agrees that you do your job very well, but you experience little joy from it, you are what I call a *performer*. If you are not sure of your natural preference, complete this short self-test to determine which area you prefer in your quest to feel and be competent.

SELF-RENEWAL PRACTICE

What Makes Effort Fun?

Down the left-hand margin of a page in your journal, list the numbers 1 through 7. Then read each of the seven pairs of statements below and decide which of the two statements is most true for you, marking "a" for the first statement and "b" for the second. No answer is better than another; all we are doing here is gauging preferences.

1. a) I like to pursue activities that express my natural talents.
    b) I like to pursue activities that spark my interests and passion regardless of my natural talent.

2. a) I enjoy operating from within my comfort zone.
    b) I enjoy operating outside my comfort zone.

3. a) I have a low tolerance for making mistakes.
    b) I have a high tolerance for making mistakes.

4. a) I believe there are set limits to my capabilities.
    b) I believe my capabilities can continuously expand.

5. a) I look for permanent solutions to problems.
    b) I look for temporary solutions to problems.

6. a) I enjoy doing what I am already good at doing.
    b) I enjoy practicing to become good at doing something.

7. a) I count on certainty and predictability in order to perform well.
    b) I count on uncertainty and surprise in order to perform well.

Count up the number of "a" answers, which indicate a preference for performance, and the number of "b" answers, which reflect an interest in learning. If your total scores for learning and performance are *three or more* points apart, you show a definite preference. A one- or two-point difference shows you tend to like some aspects of each task experience, which will make it easier for you to enjoy both ends of the competence spectrum, though you may also find yourself hampered by the weaknesses of each.

Many people who take this quiz find it difficult to separate what they intrinsically *enjoy* from what they have been rewarded for. Educator Robert Fritz, in his book *Creating*, explains that our educational system is designed to produce performers, not learners.

> Often guidance counseling is based on the assumption that people cannot learn in areas where they do not begin with natural aptitude. A student's life direction is often decided by her aptitude. Many suffer the tragedy of spending their lives in careers they never truly cared about, all because of some aptitude they happened to demonstrate in high school. In fact, many people adopt the premise that they must tailor their desires to their talents and abilities. Growth, change, expansion, independence, learning, inventiveness, and self-generated progress all become difficult when you remain in the performance mode.

Fritz points out that during the first half of life many people are unable to see that their vocations and hobbies are works in progress that add meaning to their lives, rather than ends in themselves. If you suspect you may have been "educated" away from a natural inclination toward learning over performance, take the test again, but this time put yourself in your six-year-old mind-set. How would you have answered the questions in elementary school?

The outside world rewards task demonstration, not task acquisition, and both performers and learners base their sense of self-worth largely on how well they perform. Performers tend to focus too much on the things they do "well," and to shy away from learning situations in which they are sure to experience some short-term failure. They are likely to get stuck in ruts, and often become complacent and bored. Learners, on the other hand, fail to make the most of the performance mode, frequently out of fear of boredom, but often out of fear of long-term failure. Most of us know at least one "perpetual student" who hung out at high school or college long after graduation, or who went on to pursue many degrees but not a career. Some learner types are career jumpers, trying out many fields of endeavor in order to avoid failure in one; still others stick to one vocation but follow their own interests to the point that they are not as productive as they could be. Certain learners actually see learning itself as a kind of performance. Learners are often dreamers, unwilling to commit to the complacency of performance. Ironically, natural learners who push themselves to perform (usually in a job) are just as likely as performers to get bored.

During midlife, especially, it is tempting to get stuck in the performer mode, in part because the outer world rewards performance but also because we fail to realize the inevitability of entropy. No one ever told us that peak performance had a downside of decline. John R. O'Neil, president of the California School of Professional Psychology and author of *The Paradox of Success*, explains the importance of self-observation during periods of peak performance:

Think of this process as a trek up a winding mountain trail. Veteran trekkers periodically step off the trail to size up the work done and the task ahead. During the respite, they explore certain questions. Is the rate of energy being expended appropriate for this point on the trek? Are sustaining satisfactions being derived or has the venture lost meaning? Is the summit still ahead or have they strayed from the right path?

O'Neil reminds us that the happiest and most productive people are those who make good use of both their intrinsic interest in learning and their spontaneous enjoyment of performance. Both task modes—learning *and* performance—are essential to exceptional competence. The intricate connection between the two can be represented by the S-shaped function. The sigmoid curve was first identified by Jonas Salk in his studies of fruit fly reproduction patterns, and has since been found to represent many biological patterns, including that of energy and growth. It also describes the pattern by which humans learn any task. I have combined the main messages of both Salk and O'Neil on the graph below.

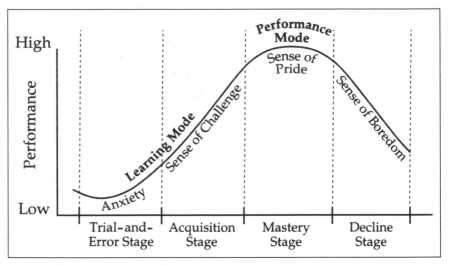

Stages of Competency Cycle

Notice that, initially, performance level is low. Awkwardness and mistakes produce anxiety ("I may never master the task"), which is compounded if others are concerned over the task competence as well. Whether you are trying to become a competent bike rider or competent artist or competent rocket scientist, the learning mode brings on feelings of *incompetence* that then develop into a sense of challenge as performance, with time and effort, improves.

Mastery peaks while you are in the performance mode. In this part of task development, the sense of challenge is gradually transformed into a sense of pride. Performing a task you are now good at is exhilarating. The emotional high you feel from success at a difficult job is one of the best gifts life has to offer.

Unfortunately, performance-mode bliss has its limits. The day comes in every endeavor when your masterful performance yields more boredom than exhilaration. Boredom can turn into disenchantment, with its concomitant lack of concentration and desire, and a noticeable *decline* in mastery and satisfaction. O'Neil warns,

> The primary reason for stepping aside from your present trail is to determine what current efforts are delivering in the way of learning satisfaction compared to the needs you uncover. If you have reached the place on your present learning curve where increased effort results in diminished returns it is time to change curves.

Think about learning to make an omelet. The first time you do it, you usually end up with a strange mishmash of unevenly cooked eggs. You may be a bit demoralized. The next time you try, though, you do a bit better, and you are eager to attempt it again, to see if you can do still better. Over time and with effort, you manage to make an omelet you can be proud of. You thrill in making omelets for all your friends. You feel good about your accomplishments and yourself. You are the Omelet King (or Queen). But after a while, making omelets begins to feel "old hat," no longer challenging or exciting. You may stop giving your omelets the care you once did. Maybe you even forget an ingredient or two. Unless omelet-making becomes fun again (maybe you should try exotic fillings), you might stop doing it altogether.

If you do not make it your business to invest in a task with ever-evolving challenges, the law of entropy will take over and transform what was once an activity that brought you pride and joy into a routine effort devoid of satisfaction. Once you have reached peak levels of mastery in whatever task you choose, you cannot simply go back and start over—you've already developed the skill. What you have to do is to ride the wave of performance as long as it is exciting for you, then *move to a new curve*. Performers do best if they wait as long as they can, then jump onto a shallow curve that allows them plenty of performance pleasure and little frustration.

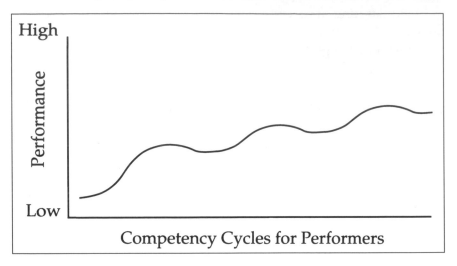

Learners must take care not to jump to a new learning curve too soon. It is important from a psychological and practical perspective that gains in learning ultimately culminate in productivity. This may not occur if one jumps to a steep challenging curve just after mastery peaks.

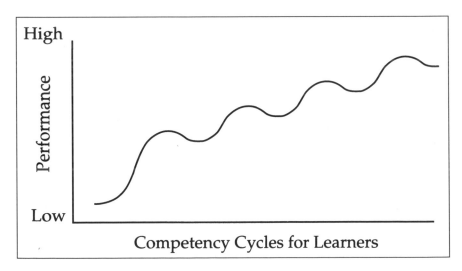

The next Self-Renewal Practice will help you explore your competency preferences in several areas of your life and decide how best to achieve the learner/performer flow that keeps you moving toward your goals.

SELF-RENEWAL PRACTICE

Key Competency Curves

1. Spend about five minutes reflecting on the areas of competence you need to achieve important personal or professional goals. Consider the skills that are critical in doing your job, fulfilling volunteer commitments, carrying out family duties, and pursuing your favorite hobbies.

2. In your journal, make a list of these "key" competencies. For example, one of my clients made the following list:

   > Supervising other people
   > Strategic business planning
   > Playing golf
   > Making persuasive speeches
   > Cooking meals
   > Gardening

3. Reproduce in your journal the S-shaped curve displayed in the Stages of Competency Cycle graph and decide where each key competency belongs on the competency development curve. Place a skill in the initial part of the curve if you are still in the trial-and-error stage. If you are somewhat more competent at and challenged by another skill, map it in the steeper portion of the learning curve. Competencies that bring you the excitement of masterful performance should be placed near the peak of the curve. Any skills you have mastered that no longer bring you much pleasure should be placed along the declining line. In our sample, my client mapped out her competencies this way:

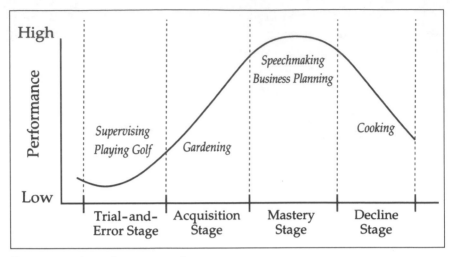

Stage-mapping of competencies

4. See if there is any pattern to how your key competencies map out. Do they all cluster in one mode? Does work tend to fall in one mode and your personal life in another? A clustering of competencies in the learning mode is especially frustrating for a performer, who might want to make more use of performance-mode competencies to offset anxiety. People who show a majority of key competencies in the decline mode are generally happier when they move onto another learning curve in one or more of the areas of decline. Check your learning-performance comfort level in each field of endeavor.

5. Identify the key competencies that are most in need of attention. For learners, that means any competency that has peaked or is approaching mastery. Performers generally prefer to work on competencies only after they have begun a steady decline. It is also a good idea for performers to reprioritize a bit if several key competencies are in the learning mode. For example, if my client were a performer, she might decide to forgo golf until she felt more secure with her mastery of supervising. If, on the other hand, she is a learner, she might decide to get on a new learning curve for cooking—go the gourmet route— or stop cooking altogether (by having another family member cook), if it is not a competency she wants to continue to rely on.

6. For any competency in need of a new learning curve, create a set of "stretch" goals that provide more enrichment or challenge to the endeavor. For example, my client selected speechmaking as an area where she wanted to expand her competence, so she decided to pursue speaking in front of progressively larger groups of people.

   For any competency you feel anxious about, see if you can find a way to use other, more masterful competencies, to help you feel more confident. My client decided to ask her subordinates to help "rate" her speeches as a way of increasing her employee interaction (an area that needed work) in areas she already felt competent.

Midlife gives us a second chance to make the most of our abilities. With some effort, we can find new ways to strike a comfortable balance between learning and performing, enjoying the skills we already have and developing those that can take us to new levels of productivity and happiness.

Destiny Bound

In my senior year at a semicloistered, Catholic, all-girls high school, the nuns charged with our education frequently asked us to consider if we had a *vocation*, or calling. They were referring, of course, to a calling from God to join a religious community.

My classmates and I spent hours trying to figure out if we were destined to become nuns and serve God through a life of prayer and good works. How would I know if I had a vocation? Would I actually hear God's voice? Would there be some sort of sign? Did the fact that I could see myself as a nun mean I *should* be one?

Struggling with that decision at seventeen, I thought you either received "the call" or you didn't. And since I was pretty sure God wasn't calling, I went on with my life. I didn't realize then that *everyone* has a call, to his or her own particular destiny, and that each of us must make peace with that inner voice over and over again throughout life. I have searched my soul many times, in college, during the early years of my career, and right up to today, as I am writing this book.

We have all heard of people whose destiny announced itself early on. "I knew from the time I could talk that I wanted to be a singer." "I never wanted to be anything but a firefighter. My mom says all I did from age three on was 'save' people!" For most of us, however, discovering what we are born to do is no easy task. Neither is pursuing our destiny once we have found it. But those individuals who are at this very moment living out their most deeply felt life scripts (and we all know at least one person in this category) prove to us that such alignment is possible, and wonderful.

Whether your calling is baseball or farming, raising children or writing books, making machines or helping others feel good—and whether you believe the calling is the result of some cosmic force or simply the "real you" struggling to get out—how you reconcile your survival needs with your inner urges to "give to the world" is one of the most important factors in your happiness and sense of self-worth. Do a little soul-searching with me now. Look at the two sets of quotations that follow and see which best fits your life.

> "I thought my career would be more satisfying than it is. At this point, I go to work because I have to."
> "I'm scared to go to work part-time, but I also don't want to miss being there for my kids."
> "My job seems so meaningless. I wish I could do something more important or useful."

> "If I die tomorrow, I'll be glad I did what I'm doing today."
> "I love this work with my whole heart and soul."
> "I'd pay for the chance to do this job."

How would you characterize *your* current life's work? Not the day-to-day ups and downs of your job (discussed in the "Peak Performance" section of this chapter), but the overall quality of your experience. Does one year roll into the next, not much different from the one before, or does each year bring exciting challenges and achievements? When someone asks what you do, do you respond proudly, positively, or offhandedly, apologetically? Do you wake up each day excited to begin your day, and go to bed each night satisfied that the goal you are struggling for is worthwhile? *Does what you do fit who you are?* Another of the rewards in this chapter, "Hidden Assets," encouraged you to extend what joy you found to other, less interesting endeavors. Are your many assets, hidden and otherwise, being wasted?

These questions are not navel-gazing, fluffy, or esoteric ones; they get to the heart of what it is to be a mature adult. Your answers to these inquiries tell you whether you are living a meaningful existence. "Meaningful," of course, is different for different people, but in general, a meaningful life is one lived according to one's most deeply held values, truest talents, and unique capacity to leave this world—which includes family, neighborhood, workplace, church, profession, children, the environment—a little better off for one's having been there.

The urge (and ability) to leave a positive mark on the world is nature's way of elevating us to the plane of self-discovery. Most of us have a vague sense of what we were "born to do," one that we push to the side in the face of many "I shoulds" and "I wants." These latter goals, grounded in the mundane concerns of approval-seeking and ego gratification, are not nearly as compelling as *acts of destiny*, which are generated when what we have to offer coincides with what the world needs from us.

Unfortunately, most people feel so consumed by their jobs and their extracurricular activities *the way they are currently constituted* that they bypass the opportunity to cultivate new ways of contributing what they want most to contribute. Many of my clients protest that they are unable to shift gears and adopt a new life vision because they cannot disappoint their families, jeopardize their financial security, or otherwise rock the boat. These valid concerns warrant serious attention; no one should abdicate their obligations. On the other hand, we owe it to ourselves and our world to apply our hard-earned know-how and know-why to advance a good greater than our own.

Midlife opportunities to "follow your bliss" (as mythologist Joseph Campbell has described) or to marry your "deep gladness" with "the world's deep hunger" (as theologian Frederick Buechner calls it) often come disguised as rude wake-up calls. Losing the ability to feel productive or to earn an income, experiencing the loss of the "empty nest," skill obsolescence, or just plain bad luck often catapults people into examining what it is they would really like to be doing for the next twenty or thirty years. Other times, the stirrings of destiny at midlife are much more subtle. Glimmers of what it is that could make life more meaningful, or efforts more fruitful, come and go like daydreams. Sometimes your inner longing to shift gears makes you feel lighthearted or a bit devilish, tempting you to play hooky or do something a bit crazy.

Midlife movements toward destiny are almost always scary. Life in the safe lane has kept you out of harm's way, so far. It takes courage to make the leap of faith necessary to follow your heart. For most of us, it also takes time, forbearance, and a willingness to risk what is for what could be. The Self-Renewal Practice that follows is not for the fainthearted, but rather for those who are searching for the courage and the wisdom to do what they were born to do.

SELF-RENEWAL PRACTICE

Living Legacies

1. Select at least five people whom you admire and respect and who benefit (or might benefit) from your presence on the planet. Try to choose people from different spheres of your life—someone from your family, someone from work, someone from the community at large —as well as people who might be representative of a larger group of people upon whom you could have a positive effect. (Choosing a particular child, for instance, might reflect your impact on a whole classroom of children; a certain coworker might represent many such coworkers.)

   As you write the names of these people in your journal—making sure to leave enough space beneath each to write several lines— think of these individuals as "stakeholders" in your destiny. Tell yourself that they have a *vested interest* in your following your path toward joy.

2. Now, step inside the mind and heart of each stakeholder in your destiny, one at a time. Spend a moment or two getting in touch with that person's attitudes, values, and personality. Recall the particular speech patterns, behaviors, and values of that individual.

   Once you feel a deep connection with that person, imagine that *you* have died and that the stakeholder is talking about what your life has meant to him or her. Assume you made a contribution to that stakeholder's life, and feel what that person would be feeling on the occasion of your passing. Under that person's name in your journal, write down the praise and appreciation that person would have for you.

   Use the sample comments from one of my clients, John, to guide you in framing your responses.

> My wife: "John loved me and brought out the best in me. He stretched me and believed in me when I lost confidence in myself."
>
> My friend: "John always made me laugh. No matter what happened to drive me crazy I could always call him on the phone and know he would take time to cheer me up with his great sense of humor."
>
> My employee: "John was the greatest boss I've ever had. He told me everything he knew about the business, gave me credit even when he had a hand in the success, and never passed the buck when it came to taking the heat for my mistakes."
>
> My neighbor: "John treated me with respect as I was going through drug treatment. He spent hours listening to my story and supporting me in fighting for my life. Without John's help, I might not be drug-free today."
>
> My colleague: "John was the most creative, energetic, land-on-your-feet politician I've ever seen. Just when you were afraid he might be defeated in a bid for office, somebody somewhere would come out of the woodwork and sing his praises for helping this community in his silent, personal way. John made me proud to be a man."

3. Review your "eulogies" all at once, and try to detect any themes or patterns. Notice the particular character traits and talents your stakeholders admire about you. (In our sample, John found themes of caring for others and helping them to develop themselves. He also saw that others valued his hard work, honesty, and empathy.)

   Examine your current life and see how close you are right now to living up to the praise others would give you. Are you doing a good job fulfilling the needs of people whom you find highly valuable?

4. Now imagine that each stakeholder is being interviewed about the contributions you have made to the wider world. Speak from their viewpoints, and make notes in your journal about the contributions they attribute to you. Again, be spontaneous in your responses. John's notes read something like this:

   > My wife: "John gave his children a deep sense of security that started with his confidence in them as individuals, his love for me, and his abiding belief that life is worth living."
   > My friend: "John made all his buddies remember not to sweat the small stuff."
   > My employee: "John led our industry in becoming sensitive to market needs and in doing business without compromising his humanity."
   > My neighbor: "John ensured that St. John's drug rehab center had a successful fund drive for twelve years running."
   > My colleague: "John broke the back of the faction of the community that wanted to cut taxes for education. His term on the school board brought this community a new passion for creating a first-class school system."

5. Think about the legacies you have "left behind." Allow yourself to feel satisfaction about the positive, personal imprint you made on the part of the world you touched.

6. Now, and over the next few days, allow the results of this exercise to stimulate you as you make plans to more purposefully realize the destiny you have just previewed. Return to this practice whenever you

feel stuck, bored, or uncertain that you are following the dictates of your destiny.

———————————

For many of you, this Self-Renewal Practice may be the hardest one in the book. Most of us resist singing our own praises out of modesty (false or real) and the belief that self-aggrandizement is narcissistic and selfish. Let me assure you that this important, private effort at finding the way back to your own personal path is anything *but* selfish. Looking at yourself from the outside in is often the best way to be objective about the lessons life is offering you. Almost everyone who completes this exercise finds that afterward, his or her vision of how to lead a meaningful life—and how he and she would like to be remembered—changes significantly.

Several of my clients have also avoided this practice on the grounds that "you don't have to make a contribution to the world in order to lead a meaningful life; just being yourself is enough." To a certain degree, they are right: it is not the extent or even the value of your contribution that adds meaning to your life, it is your willingness to expend effort for the sake of bettering the world that counts. No doubt there are those who act with the intent of making a positive impact and never do. There are those who operate out of genuine concern for the next generation and inadvertently do harm. These errors notwithstanding, if you want to have a sense of belonging and peace, it is your job as a midlife adventurer to *match your inner drive to become your best self with how you can benefit the world.*

Making the effort to concern yourself with more than your own needs is rewarding. Dan McAdams, a professor of psychology at Loyola University, has researched the life stories of hundreds of adults to ascertain the degree of generativity they attain. McAdams defines generativity, which I mentioned earlier in this chapter, as the desire to have an impact on the world and to commune with others. His results revealed that, overall, midlifers who demonstrate strong generative concerns tend to be happier and more satisfied with their lives than those who are not highly generative.

The real barrier to trying this Self-Renewal Practice is fear. Fear of failing, fear of success, fear of financial losses, and fear of the unknown all hold us back from our destiny. Fear is a deterrent to growth and change throughout life. The only reason any of us finally risks anything is that the potential rewards outweigh the potential strain. Think of some risks you have taken in the past. The promised benefits must have been worthwhile enough for you to move through your fear and go for the prize. Leaving home for college or a job, asking for a date, and traveling to a new city or town are all risks you have taken because the possible reward was greater than the possible failure. Studies show that the act of risk-taking itself—independent of the success or failure of the venture—increases one's self-esteem.

Carlos Castaneda, author of *The Teachings of Don Juan*, cites fear as the overriding challenge to be met in all significant human endeavors. He contends that moving beyond fear to taking goal-directed action is the primary requirement for evolving into a full-fledged person. Erik Erikson, one of the first psychologists to address development patterns in adulthood, warns specifically against the midlife stagnation fear can engender. His theory proposes that each of us makes a fundamental choice at midlife, conscious or unconscious, between stagnation or generativity. Unless we face the reality that fear can stifle generativity, it is easy to rationalize our failure to follow our own destinies as simply "doing our duty." But if your "duty" is in conflict with your inner drives, it is probably masking fear. That fear is easier to handle if we recognize that generativity is a choice we make anew each day. Generativity (and fear) is best taken one day at a time.

There is no getting around fear. It has to be faced head on. In the same way that you need to welcome your masculine side in order to be feminine, that you must see yourself through the eyes of others to see yourself clearly, that you have to accept the possibility of rejection or annihilation when relating to others, you must move *through* your fears, whatever they may be, to get to your ultimate destiny.

Remember a time when you faced great fear, perhaps on the high dive before you jumped, in a waiting room before an interview, on a podium before a speech. Remember how you felt as you neared the moment of truth—exhilarated, anxious, full of energy—and the wonderful release you experienced once you reached the point of no return. What a relief to be past the fear barrier, on your way to success or failure, but nonetheless on your way!

Read the next story, written to me by a client at the end of a session on the rewards of living out your destiny. Use this man's analysis of how fear had once paralyzed him as inspiration as you break into a whole new way of approaching your life and your world.

To most people, I must have looked pretty rock solid perfect. I was Mr. Middle America in everything; age, job, class, intelligence, income, aspirations. I was fifty years old, married to the same wonderful wife for twenty-three years, had three great kids and and a nice home in the suburbs, was a leader in my church, had spent twenty-eight years with a Fortune 100 company, and was good at my job, with no major vices or debts. So why was I so miserable?

For as long as I can remember, I've been afraid. Who knows why? Because my father left to be a soldier in the war when I was three and I feared he was never coming back? Because we moved from town to town in my youth and I was constantly forced to be the new kid on the block? Was it the first curveball I saw and couldn't hit in high school? Was it the shame of quitting the college football team tryouts? Was it not transferring to Missouri University's journalism school when I dreamed of a writing career? Maybe it was selling my soul to the company store for twenty-eight years in a career I never wanted. Whenever it started and whatever the reason, fear was my constant companion. Nameless, faceless, futile fear. It's a lousy way to live.

I've often thought there are just two kinds of people in the world: yes people and no people. What seems to separate them is the "fear factor." Yes people aren't afraid. They grow and prosper. No people are dominated and paralyzed by their fears. They shrink and shrink and die a little every day.

When your decisions are always full of fear, I'm convinced you deny the best that is in you. That's a sin against yourself . . . and probably the biggest sin of all.

The struggle to overcome my fears began the day I finally realized who my opponent was. One day I saw the enemy and he was me. I was the one who was standing in my own way. But that knowledge in my head didn't make me brave enough in my heart to give up my job security and jeopardize my family's well-being. True, I wanted to be different and do something else, but what? And would that something else put bread on the table?

What followed was years and years of compromise. I made attempt after attempt to find fulfillment and satisfaction. Within the confines of my company and my church, I tried mightily to become the person I wanted to be. Truth is, there were some great times and many good times, but all in all, it was a bad time. I was living a lie. A dignified, well-paying lie, but still a lie. And I wasn't the only person paying the price of that lie. So were my wife and three children and others.

As I reached the fifty-year milestone, it became tougher and tougher to resolve my personal dilemma. How could I take the risk and make a break when I felt weaker and less in control every day? Even doing the job that I liked and was very good at became an exercise in tilting at windmills.

Suddenly, without warning, the universe intervened. The company offered an early retirement plan that was designed to eliminate thousands of upper-level managers just like me. From a planning standpoint, I wasn't ready. I thought I would be working there until the bitter end, so I had plenty of daydreams, but no real "fall-back" plans in place. From a financial standpoint, I wasn't ready either. The early retirement plan was attractive, but not nearly good enough to put my three kids through college unless I could generate supplemental income.

Without any question, early retirement was the hardest, most gut-wrenching decision I ever had to make. And it had to be made in sixty days with practically no one to help. Sure there were hordes of financial planners who wanted to help me place my money. And there were several good retirement seminars offered by the company. But there was no one to talk to about the deepest, most important issues involved . . . my personal, internal, emotional issues. Especially my fears.

Now I was forced to come face to face with that monster, FEAR, that I had been running from, hiding from, all my life. What did I really want to be, and could I pull it off? On the one hand, my job always had been a great security blanket that I could pull over my head and hide beneath. On the other hand, it was smothering me. I was only fifty years old. My physical health was good even if my emotional health wasn't. My three children all needed to finish college and get started in life. My wife wanted to spend as much time as she could with her children before they flew the nest. And what did I want? I still didn't know.

I agonized. Decisions never were easy for me, especially major ones. The bottom line finally got down to this: Did I want to be sixty-five years old and have to ask myself, "Is that all there is?" My answer was a resounding "No!" But this time it was a positive no. This might be my last chance to find the best that was in me. No more compromises. No more living a lie. No more suffocating security blankets. Somehow, I had to become a yes person. Surely, it wasn't too late. But how?

When I said yes to the early retirement offer, my family was brave and supportive, but inside, they were scared to death. So was I. No more fat paychecks twice a month. No more respected title and all the cushy comforts of the company. I was on my own, and what in the world was I going to do?

After answering want ads and sending out résumés, I learned quickly that the recession was not just a story invented and blown up by the media. The recession is real, and it has sharp teeth that can tear your heart out. The job market had little or no interest in a fifty-year-old ex-manager with my credentials. So now what?

The question got me back to the real question. What did I truly want to do with my life? Miraculously, a door opened. My career had given me expertise in the design, development, and delivery of education and training programs. In what seemed a coincidence, I had recently been introduced to a small, entrepreneurial company that provides education and training programs to help individuals and organizations overcome adversity and accomplish success. Their business is success stories . . . informing, inspiring, and enabling them. I realized that success stories are what I've wanted to tell all my life. Now this company was offering me the opportunity to make a second career doing exactly that. The universe works in mysterious ways.

As an associate with this company, I am committed to helping individuals and organizations overcome adversity and find success. In the process, I can do the same for myself. Now I know that my journey has a goal that is real and personal and important to me. Before, I was just wondering and wandering. Now, I can see my destination, I'm committed to getting there, and I've been given a realistic way to make it happen. Equally satisfying is that every day I'm enjoying the journey.

For the first time in my life, I have the satisfaction of knowing that what I'm doing is what I am supposed to be doing. That doesn't mean I have no more fears and adversities. My real income is less than 25 percent of what I had been making in my corporate job. I am sacrificing now to reap my financial rewards later, and I know deep down that all worthwhile journeys require adversity and struggle. They are part of the process. In fact, they are necessary to achieve growth and gain. And finally, I understand that success is not about "knowing" success, it is about "feeling" success. Certainly, what I'm feeling is not "perfect," but it is definitely "rock solid" enough for me to build the rest of my life upon.

Victories of Exceptional Competence

For the generations born prior to World War II, midlife brought a sense of security, accomplishment, and generativity lived out of specific, narrow roles established in the first few years of adulthood. Most adults lived out their midlife years of exceptional competence as role models for younger employees of the companies they had already served for more than twenty years, or as role models for further generations of homemakers. For those of us born in the baby-boom era, the victories of exceptional competence are greatly expanded. We have the chance to expand the number of roles we assume; to breathe new levels of satisfaction into how we approach those tasks; to strike a comfortable balance between learning and performing; and to match what we were born to do with what the world needs most from us.

We enjoy these additional opportunities thanks to the way technology and the information age are reconfiguring our work settings (from hierarchical to virtual organizations), mandating ever-advancing job skills, rendering traditional career advancement patterns obsolete, and otherwise changing the nature of how work gets done. The other main source of opportunities comes from within. Ours is the first generation to whom self-actualizaton is perceived as a right and responsibility, rather than a luxury. Investigations into why midlifers of our generation make career changes reveal that job shifts more often emerge out of a desire for self-discovery, new challenges, and changing interests than they do out of negative circumstances such as job loss or incompetency. In fact, career development researchers have pinpointed a renewal phase in the course of midlifer's career development.

Traveling the road of exceptional competence will spur your mental mastery, your physical vigor, and your emotional vitality. With your roles in synchrony with your values, everything you do has greater meaning.

In his novel *Siddhartha*, Hermann Hesse vividly portrays the process of revitalizing oneself at midlife. For Siddhartha, career disillusionment gives birth to an inner voice that awakens his soul. "How strange it is," Siddhartha says. "Now, when I am no longer young, when my hair is growing gray, when strength begins to diminish, now I am beginning again like a child." Hesse explains that his heroic adventurer "had died and a new Siddhartha had awakened from his sleep. He also would grow old and die. Siddhartha was transitory, all forms were transitory, but today he was young, he was a child—the new Siddhartha—and he was very happy."

CHAPTER 8

Pathway #6: Spiritual Serenity

GOD HUNGER

When the immutable accidents of birth—
parentage, hometown, all the rest—
no longer anchor this fiction of the self
and its incessant I me mine,
the words won't be like nerves on a stump
crackling with messages that end up nowhere
and I'll put on the wind like a gown of light linen
and go be a king in a field of weeds.

—MICHAEL RYAN

Just as researchers have charted the course of healthy mental, physical, emotional, and social development across the life span, contemporary scientists and theologians have recently attempted to map out how human beings grow spiritually. Theologian James Fowler, in his book *Stages of Faith: The Psychology of Human Development and the Quest for Meaning,* presents a six-stage model of spiritual development, paralleling one's chronological age and social roles, which I have distilled below:

Stage I, Intuitive-Projective Faith: Imagination, combined with the beliefs of the parents (often articulated as "stories"), creates in a child powerful, fanciful images of love and hate, good and evil.

Stage II, Mythic-Literal Faith: Greater socialization and mental skills, as well as initial entrance into the outside world and the attendant desire for security, give the school-age child a very literal belief in the basic, immutable order of the universe and a strong sense of right and wrong.

Stage III, Synthetic-Conventional Faith: The adolescent, experimenting with who he or she is, begins to develop a defensible, comforting, personally crafted ideology.

Stage IV, Individuative-Reflective Faith: As individual belief is tested in the real world, young adults reconsider and redefine spirituality, often relinquishing the narrow views they were taught as youngsters and embracing the universality of spiritual principles and practices; this expansion of spiritual viewpoint may allow them to find spiritual meaning in art, music, nature, and more.

Stage V, Conjunctive Faith: With the pain of disillusionment in middle age comes the recognition that "truth" as perceived by others is just as valid as one's own "truth"; that the world is full of paradox; that in many ways the enemy of one's happiness is the enemy within. Those who come to terms with these difficult realities enjoy a deeper sense of awe and mystery of life; a wise understanding of the collective myths, religions, and traditions; and the potential to be a spiritual leader.

Stage VI, Universalizing Faith: Adults in later life who come to terms with death and their place in the cosmos enjoy an abiding sense of love and compassion for all of life.

The notion of an ever-evolving spiritual dimension may be relatively new in cultures dominated by Western and Middle Eastern religions such as Judaism, Christianity, and Islam, but it is centuries old in cultures where the Eastern religions—Buddhism, Hinduism, and Taoism, for example—are practiced. According to the ancient spiritual traditions of Tantric yoga and Kundalini yoga, a person moves through an ascending series of physical/mental/spiritual centers to become more enlightened and united with the cosmos.

In his book *Yoga, Immortality and Freedom*, religious scholar Mircea Eliade offers a comprehensive explanation of the precepts of the yogic system, which is practiced from India to Tibet to Mexico. The seven centers of growth, called chakras, are said to exist along

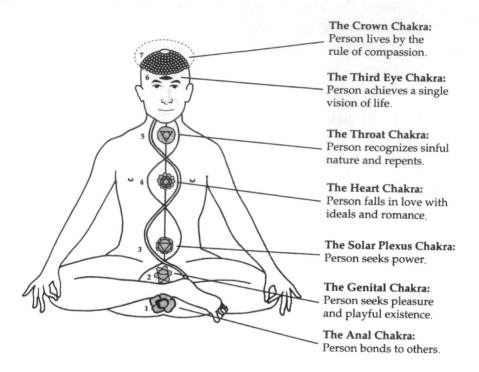

The Crown Chakra: Person lives by the rule of compassion.

The Third Eye Chakra: Person achieves a single vision of life.

The Throat Chakra: Person recognizes sinful nature and repents.

The Heart Chakra: Person falls in love with ideals and romance.

The Solar Plexus Chakra: Person seeks power.

The Genital Chakra: Person seeks pleasure and playful existence.

The Anal Chakra: Person bonds to others.

seven different locations in the spine and brain, beginning at the base of the spine and culminating at the crown of the head. Proponents believe these energy centers to be related to every aspect of life (physical health, mental development, personal power). In this chapter we are concerned with the path of enlightenment and spiritual transformation proposed to exist along the chakras. Learn about the progression of spiritual development as it has been linked to the body chakras by examining the illustration above.

You may note several parallels between the spiritual-development models of Western/Middle Eastern and Far Eastern. Perhaps you found yourself somewhere in one or both of them. Most of my clients and friends admit feeling stuck, spiritually, in what could be called Stage IV or Stage V of Fowler's model; others might be better described according to Tantric tradition, with a great imbalance in their chakras that prevents them from fully receiving the gifts of any of them.

THE CALL TO SPIRITUAL SERENITY

The signs that you are ready to grow in spirit appear in the form of both curses and blessings. You may experience severe episodes of disillusionment with life, or periods of profound awe and reverence for the miracle of existence—or both at once. The ups and downs calling you to spiritual serenity will continue as you walk down this frustrating and fulfilling path.

Midlife Readiness Signals for Spiritual Serenity
You may find yourself:

- taking more time in your day to reflect on the meaning of events
- feeling despair over the injustice and evil that seem everywhere in the world
- longing to find a way to cope with your personal beliefs about death
- struggling to understand why so many good people suffer
- seeking a comprehensive and more satisfying life philosophy
- yearning for more opportunities to enjoy solitude and silence

Some people who notice these disturbing feelings panic, worried that something is severely wrong with them. They feel "too old" to be searching for answers to the mysteries of life, death, and the meaning of existence, especially if they dealt with these issues in the past. In fact, this midlife anxiety is exceedingly normal; people who profess to be spiritually *content* as they enter midlife are generally sound asleep at the wheel. If we don't struggle to find more satisfying answers to these fundamental questions during our midlife journeys, we risk facing old age with fear and anger as our main companions. If, on the other hand, we can begin to wrestle with these questions (realizing, of course, that we're unlikely to find any definitive answers), we open ourselves to a spiritual awakening that makes the second half of life a deeper, richer experience than we imagined possible.

Before you begin your adventures on the pathway of spiritual serenity, return to Chapter 2 and check your answers to the "spiritual" portion of the Self-Renewal Inventory. Amend them, if necessary. Then take another look at the spiritual development theories of James Fowler, and the Tantric yogis, in order to get a clear picture of where you are on this particular path.

ADVENTURES IN SPIRITUAL SERENITY

I have been struck over the last decade by the many different ways people are able to breathe new life into their spiritual lives. Some study sciences with the hope of gaining spiritual insight from recent findings about the way the subatomic world works. Others return to the traditions and teachings of the religion they were taught as children, and reexperience those rituals and writings at a deeper spiritual level. I've known people who rediscovered spirituality after they gave themselves up to the glories of nature, and those who studied many religions with the idea of creating new belief systems of their own. There is no limit to the methods by which you can tap into peace and meaning. Truth is where you find it.

Rest assured that your spiritual journey has many rewards independent of the answers you seek. Through spirituality, you can make leaps of understanding that defy the limits of your mind; connect with others, and the world around you, at levels never before experienced; and eliminate much of the fear and doubt that plague your emotional life.

Take your time on this pathway—there are people who dedicate their whole lives to the important pursuit you are about to undertake. Although you may find you can share with and learn from other spiritual journeyers, the answers you find are meant for *you*. Feel the experience fully, and live what answers are offered.

From Human Doing to Human Being

One morning at the end of last summer I awoke with my husband's arm around my waist and my schnauzer, Shadow, curled up behind my knees. Not wanting to disturb either of my bedmates, I opened my eyes slowly, enjoying the lazy comfort of a day when I didn't have to be anywhere or do anything. I found myself staring across Lake Aspen at hundreds of oak trees, which were bunched up like huge stalks of broccoli. At first glance I noticed that, overnight, the lush foliage on the far bank had lost a slight touch of green. I blinked several times, trying to bring the picture into focus. The change in color was so infinitesimal that I was amazed at my own powers of observation.

I am privileged to wake up, snug inside our A-frame cabin, on special weekends and holidays. Under ordinary circumstances I am jolted awake by an alarm clock and hit the ground running. For most of us, in fact, the world clamors for attention the moment we open our eyes. But there is another way to wake up—the way of my September morning. Seventh-century Asian monks call it the way of the NEN.

I first ran across the term NEN while reading *Freeing the Creative Spirit* by Adriana Diaz. Guiding us to our deepest wells of experience, Diaz reveals that in their spiritual practice the Asian monks used the word "NEN" to describe the shortest time fragments people experience, moments so brief that they are, for all practical purposes, timeless. According to artist and creativity scholar Fredrik Franck, the *first NEN* is the initial instant in which we perceive something. It is made up of nothing but pure experience, free of our judgment or thought. The concept of NEN has modern proponents. Novelist and writing teacher Natalie Goldberg, in her book *Writing Down the Bones*, explains that she believes our greatest creative energy has its source in what she calls "first thoughts"—that we can best capture the essence of an experience in the first instant our minds flash on it. "First thoughts," "NEN," and "beginner's mind" are all terms that refer to conscious experience uncontaminated by intellect.

Give yourself a "first NEN" experience right now by reading the rest of this paragraph and then trying what I suggest. Close your eyes. After a minute or two, turn your head in any direction, and open and close your eyes quickly. In this brief glimpse, you provide yourself with an initial NEN awareness. Specific objects may actually appear unrecognizable from this new perspective. Your mind absorbs what you see nonjudgmentally, nonrationally. Most people report that in the blink of an eye they experience line, shape, color, light, and form, along with a slight afterimage that seems to glow in the darkness behind their closed eyes.

Although NEN experiences such as these can provide refreshing "perspective" breaks in our busy days, extended "first NEN" experiences are far more beneficial. If you are able to suspend most of your thought and simply "be" in the here and now for five to twenty minutes, you achieve a state of deep physiological relaxation, often called the alpha state by researchers who distinguish relative degrees of alertness by transducing brain chemistry into electrical impulses that can be graphed and observed on an oscilloscope. Brain researchers have named the lowest level of alertness—i.e., the deepest state of relaxation—the alpha or first state. When you allow yourself to relax to this degree, you replenish your adaptive energy supply, increase your capacity to be creative, and put yourself in the position of thinking more effectively when you do return to the "doing" mode.

NEN means dwelling on the now, on only what is happening ("Jake is angry"; "snow is falling"). When you experience NEN, you exist in what I call the *human being* mode. Most of the time, of course, we adopt the *human doing* approach, and actively seek to understand and influence what is happening ("Why is Jake angry at me?"; "I'd better shovel"). In our human doing mode we live in a realm twice, three times, or four times removed from the initial impression we get in NEN awareness. For example, after I saw that small shift in the color of the leaves at Lake Aspen, my brain intruded: Are you sure? How could you possibly have perceived a change so subtle as the paling of leaves?

The NEN experience is one of the easiest ways to bring spirituality into your life. Regular NENs usually lead to a feeling of greater "connectedness" to others and the world, and to a kind of day-to-day spirituality that gives our lives balance and purpose. My Lake Aspen NEN, for example, held an important lesson for me. It put me in the center of nature's living-dying paradox, showing me that to exist as part of nature is to be living and dying all at once. Had

I allowed my logical, thought-dominated second and third takes of the forest to prevail, I would have missed the wisdom the extended NEN was offering me.

SELF-RENEWAL PRACTICE

Extending the First NEN

1. Be on the lookout for a moment in your daily life that you believe to be worthy of an extended NEN experience. Attractive objects, providential circumstances, and nature scenes lend themselves especially well to extended first NENs.

2. When a NEN opportunity presents itself, stop whatever you are doing and go into the mode of the first NEN. Suspend your judgment, resist thinking thoughts. Just allow the sights, sounds, smells, textures, and rhythms of the experience to move through you, dominate and guide you. Let whatever happens be in charge.

   Stay focused in this first NEN for as long as you choose.

3. When you have moved back into a more thoughtful mode, reflect on your initial NEN experience. Ask yourself what you can learn from the particular NEN. Do not try to invest the NEN with meaning. Let it speak to you.

4. Find ways to weave the lessons you learned, and the pleasures you derived, into the human-doing mode. Some people generate symbols or actions (such as deep breathing) that remind them of the way they feel in the NEN state.

   But even without conscious effort, NEN experiences have a way of infiltrating your memory, storing themselves in your every cell. After you seek and find a few good NEN experiences, you may notice that NEN moments begin to find *you* when you least expect them, providing you with a sudden rush of terrific NEN feeling that renews you and reminds you there is another way of being.

Here is how Jack, one of my clients, was able to benefit from this type of NEN practice. He had come to me for coaching after a series of minor career disappointments.

Jack's NEN scenario:

Yesterday morning I was driving my rental car back to the airport to catch my flight home when I ran across three abandoned railroad cars scattered willy-nilly around a blazing campfire. This old guy was stoking the logs with a crooked branch and pouring himself a cup of coffee from a blue tin pot. I pulled off the highway to get a better look at this cowboy and his setup. I watched him from behind some brush for almost twenty minutes. The whole scene mesmerized me.

Jack's NEN reflections:

Watching that cowboy in his self-styled homestead brought home to me the meaning of freedom. His freedom reminds me of my own freedom, to travel as I was that day from one city to another, to play a round of golf, to enjoy a barbecue with my family and then a glass of wine with my wife. I am free to live, to start and then to stop and see whatever I can see.

Jack's NEN integration:

I went out this morning and purchased a toy train car, and I put it on my desk where I can see it every day. It reminds me that I have the freedom to chart my own destiny, just as that cowboy does.

Jack spent several months establishing a specific agenda that matched his renewed sense of freedom. He enrolled in several graduate classes at the state university, became a coach for an inner-city basketball team, and began a long-term research project. Jack believed that taking initiatives like these would make him less susceptible to the changing tides at work. In the course of taking charge of his life again, he realized how out of touch he had become with the stimulating, yet ordinary, aspects of his days. He had been running on fast forward for so long that for years he'd seen nothing more than a blur. Suddenly he found himself relishing his family, his surroundings, even many of his tasks. Reengaging his first NEN awareness was of great help in Jack's quest for more meaning in his life. Practicing this self-renewal exercise will help you, too, to discover the lessons embedded in our everyday experiences.

Another method for triggering extended NEN experiences is to set up situations that shatter your logical expectations or prevent you from forming opinions and making judgments. Putting yourself in an illogical context, such as holding a strategic planning session deep in the forest or renewing your wedding vows while soaring in a hot-air balloon, invites pure experience into otherwise "thoughtful" situations. My art instructor unwittingly created an extended NEN experience for me when she suggested I might improve my painter's eye if I turned the object I was painting upside down. I was skeptical, but intrigued enough to try it.

I selected a Renaissance master's depiction of the Nativity as my subject, turned the color plate over, and began to paint. Because my subject was upside down, nothing I was painting seemed familiar. The figures and buildings and animals that I could name instantly when they were right side up were rendered unrecognizable by my new perspective. I had no ordinary guideposts to inform my brushstrokes, no hints of how to depict depth, movement, or emotion. And yet somehow this topsy-turvy masterpiece was guiding me; not by the conventions of painterly realism, but by the dictates of pure form and color and space.

I felt as if I were viewing the incredible, rhythmic interplay between line and color for the first time. As I moved my brush between palette and canvas, I was at one with all I saw. The master's work was somehow luring my paint onto my canvas on its own, without any effort on my part. I painted feverishly for three hours, without a word or stray thought.

When I repositioned my canvas and took a step back to see what I had created, I was stunned. There before me was the most technically proficient and artistically sensitive painting I had ever produced. This beautiful painting had emerged because, for just a little while, I had been able to suspend all thought. In doing so, it seemed as though I'd actually stopped time, too. In this realm of upside down, I learned to trust and follow the essence of what actually makes it possible for us to see anything.

What was most astounding to me was the way the experience made me *feel*. I was filled with the kind of calm yet spirited enthusiasm that I remember feeling as a child. Literally translated from the Greek as "en-theo-ism" (being filled with God), enthusiasm is not the same as enjoyment. When you experience enthusiasm for what you do, you are one with it. Merging with the canvas when you paint, the racquet when you play tennis, the feelings of a character when you read a novel are all ways to get beyond yourself and into the bare beauty of human existence. Athletes in their peak moments describe strangely transcendent episodes, which some refer to as "going into the zone." These are moments when body, mind, and spirit converge with the momentum of the game, and astounding physical accomplishments are produced without strain or struggle. Some women report that giving birth to a child is an extended NEN moment wherein vibrant pleasure and intense pain combine, connecting the mother to the essence of ecstasy.

Some of my clients, especially those whose religious belief is very strong, fail to see the importance of personal experience when it comes to developing one's spirituality. But personal experience is, in fact, the most fundamental ingredient of connection to something greater than ourselves, no matter what you believe that "something greater" to be. In *The Coming of the Cosmic Christ*, theologian Matthew Fox explains that the first great meaning of mysticism is experience itself. Fox takes us back to a quotation of fifteenth-century teachings of Kabir, a creation mystic of India who championed experience as the prime source of spiritualizing when he argued, "I say only what I have seen with my own eyes—and you keep quoting the Scriptures!" Kabir goes on, "Experience, O seeker, is the essence of all things."

With compelling intensity, Fox implores us as contemporary spiritual seekers to turn to the experience of the Divine rather than theory or settling for *knowing about* the Divine. "Taste and see the Lord is good," says the Psalmist in the wisdom tradition of Israel.

He warns us that there is no such thing as vicarious mysticism—no one can experience life and divinity on our behalf.

Your own spiritual connection may not be as strong as you would like, but its seeds are there. Almost all of us have a list of peak episodes of decision, action, or reflection that are memorable for their ability to transport us out of the realm of ordinary experience. Certain extended NEN experiences, like my art lesson, or Jack's encounter, are so full of joy, pain, meaning, or life-altering information that they become defining, transforming events. I call these experiences *holy moments*. Some holy moments are surprising and enlightening; others trigger shock and disillusionment. Some I have heard described are:

- Experiences in nature, such as withstanding the terror of fierce storms, or witnessing the breathtaking beauty of mountains
- Being struck by the profound words of a child
- Surviving a near-death experience
- Meditating on a flower
- Standing up for human rights
- Suffering a debilitating illness
- Losing a loved one to death
- Reading someone else's mind
- Dreaming a prophetic dream

Ask yourself what was special about your own holy moments. What truth was communicated to you? What did your soul receive from the experience? (Refrain from asking questions such as "What am I doing?" or "What do I need to learn?"; the answers to "I" questions satisfy the ego, not the soul.)

As a human being, you are capable of reflecting on the mysteries of life and of celebrating the magnificence you find. When you are able to actively replay your holy moments at will, you find that your connection to the deeper, more meaningful side of life becomes part of your daily existence rather than a once-in-a-blue-moon stroke of luck. When you discover the power of your holy moments, you discover a well that will renew your spirit and keep you fully alive.

Devour your holy moments; they are one of the best ways to nourish the soul.

From the Devil to the Divine

According to a 1989 *Life* magazine article, more Americans believe in the existence of an evil spirit they call the Devil (over 70 percent of the population) than believe in the existence of a good spirit they call God (less than 40 percent of the population). In his recent book *The Cry for Myth*, eminent psychologist Rollo May cites this study as evidence that we are, as a society, moving from "faith to fatalism."

The trap of fatalism is quite compelling at midlife. By age forty, many of the men and women I counsel have seen, in their companies and their communities, a full range of self-serving, power-hungry, unethical, and immoral behavior undertaken in the name of the organization, the city, the state, and the nation. They have witnessed the destructive power of human frailty. It is natural for midlifers to become numb, disenfranchised, or themselves corrupted by the influence of evil. They may feel helpless to correct, or even operate morally in, a system so pervasively warped by evil.

Several of my clients and friends also voice hopelessness over the way their children are growing up. In a world that suddenly seems filled with drugs, alcohol, guns, and life-threatening sexually transmitted diseases, many parents feel that the very survival of an entire generation of children is threatened.

A wave of destruction has also put our planet at risk. The global economy is failing us, too; we seem unable to stem the tide of money flowing away from those who need it and into the pockets of those who merely want more of it. Everywhere we look we find a mind-boggling number of ethical questions about how we should be using our resources and our time.

With so much hate, violence, greed, and wrongdoing around us, it can be difficult to see much good in the world. Dispirited, too many of us simply throw up our hands in defeat. We do not necessarily give ourselves over to evil, we begin to feel it is futile to fight it. We begin to *expect* bad things to happen.

It doesn't matter whether you believe the forces of "good" to be

God, a great creative energy, love, destiny, or simply a path to harmony with others, and "evil" to be Satan, a tremendous destructive force, hate, death, or a way to gain power over others. What is important is that you recognize that our attitudes—including our fatalism—are at the crux of the world's problems.

Imagine earth *without* evil, a planet that is 100 percent good. Being "human" would have no particular meaning. Since the dawn of complex human consciousness, humankind has believed that what separates us from other mammals is our freedom to make our own choices. Choosing to "be good" would be meaningless unless goodness existed in tension with its polar opposite: evil. Just as male balances female and dark opposes light, so good and evil exist side by side. Every situation, every institution, and every person has the seeds of both good and evil within it. What makes "good" and "evil" is what we choose to do with our lives. Your *intent*, rather than the action itself, is paramount. (As discussed in the last chapter, behavior undertaken for good does not always bear the fruit of its intent, any more than evil motives always bring evil outcomes.)

Religions of every persuasion prescribe some kind of human reconciliation of good and evil. For example, the Barong dance in the Bali-Hindu tradition recognizes the interplay between the two forces that pervade human experience. The vast array of Christian ceremonies surrounding repentance and salvation, as well as the theme of temptation, acknowledge the universal inner struggle between the devilish and the divine within us.

A wide range of schools of psychology also recommend owning up to one's tendencies toward good and evil, in the belief that coming to terms with both inclinations is a means to healthy emotional, social, and spiritual development in adulthood. Jungian depth psychology, which we touched upon in Chapter 5, suggests that many of our evil tendencies remain hidden, even from ourselves, until midlife maturity provides us with the imperative to confront them. In psychoanalysis, a cousin of Jungian theory, individuals must identify the early abuses to their well-being, which were unwittingly inflicted by well-meaning parents and sustained in the child as unconscious complexes.

Even the newer schools of psychology, which downplay the possibility of warring factions of good and evil in the unconscious, recognize that a person's conscious belief in the threat of "evil" or the benefit of "good" can have a huge impact on the individual and society. Psychologist Rollo May theorizes that the individual struggle to prevail over the feelings of evil powers that invade each of us produces the tension that gives birth to both moral action and creativity. According to May, this inner struggle is at the heart of our sense of personal freedom.

You may remember from the chapter on Interpersonal Effectiveness a discussion of new revelations in quantum physics regarding the power of expectation to change the behavior of subatomic particles and energy waves. Many modern thinkers, physicist David Bohm, psychologists Jean Achterberg, and Julian Jaynes among them, extend those findings into a belief that "what you think is what you get," literally. If they are right, we are actually bringing more of that evil on ourselves by focusing on negative thoughts, negative news, or the evil in others.

From a religious, psychological, and practical standpoint, it stands to reason that *we have a vested interest in changing our attitudes, even if evil seems too powerful to oppose.* Before we can hope to conquer the evil that is "out there," we must face the part of us that gives in to these vices, that allows us to lose hope in the face of negativity, that is still the conscienceless, selfish animal we were at birth (and still are somewhere deep inside). Typically, those of us afraid of the evil within *project* those traits onto others in the world.

Therapists and spiritual counselors have long understood that projection is the easiest way to avoid dealing with our own darker traits, impulses, and actions. Psychologist and author M. Scott Peck, in his book *People of the Lie*, defines projection as pure scapegoating. Peck suggests that spiritual growth requires the acknowledgment of one's own imperfection. He links the destructive power of evil to the inability to admit personal sinfulness, and the corresponding tendency to see others as bad instead.

Fortunately, inner exploration means more than facing personal weakness. Looking closely at oneself also allows for rediscovery of spiritual strengths. As you follow the steps of the next Self-Renewal Practice, remember that the specifics of your belief system are not as important as the power and peace you can attain through living them out. Each action we take and each thought we think is a choice between good and evil.

SELF-RENEWAL PRACTICE

The Divinity and Devils Within

1. Make two columns in your journal, one for evil tendencies and the other for good tendencies.

   For the purposes of this practice, consider your evil tendencies to be those that urge you to deceive or hurt yourself and others, and your good tendencies to be those that motivate you to be honest and loving toward yourself and others. Spend about ten minutes noting the good and evil characteristics that most apply to you. Review these sample lists for ideas:

Evil Tendencies	Good Tendencies
Dishonesty	Generosity
Jealousy	Sincerity
Lustfulness	Humility
Selfishness	Ability to love unconditionally
Inflexibility	Ability to forgive
Power orientation	Forthrightness

   Note that you may possess tendencies that are polar opposites of one another (such as selfishness and generosity). It is common to harbor two tendencies and lean toward one or the other as the situation appears to warrant.

2. Select one of your good tendencies and one of your evil tendencies and reflect on each, one at a time. Recall at least one recent situation in which you gave in to each tendency. For example, you may have given in to your tendency to be inflexible by unreasonably refusing to change your plans to accommodate a friend's request, or you may have displayed your generosity by giving your time and attention to someone in need.

Take a few moments to review each scenario in some detail, so that you can easily identify the tendency's presence in your feelings, thoughts, and actions.

3. Now, personify the evil and good characteristics within you. For the purposes of this Self-Renewal Practice, try to look at the two tendencies you chose as entities that exist independent of your participation. Generosity, for example, is a force that you tap into at will, one that operates for good apart from the instances in which you yourself act generously. Inflexibility is, likewise, a discrete, negative force that is available to anyone.

Now visualize your chosen evil tendency. First give it a color, then a shape in which it can conform itself to your body. You might, for example, see your self-serving inflexibility as a gray-green cloud over your head, or a black-and-orange aura, or a brown halo with daggers in it. Do the same with your good tendency. Perhaps you see generosity as a sky-blue band around your heart.

4. In your mind's eye, recreate one of the times you fell into the "evil" trap of your chosen negative tendency. Face your dark behavior—and its personified form—squarely. See the destructiveness it sows in yourself and others. Allow yourself to feel sad, or sorry, or embarrassed that you "gave in" to the negative energy. Feel the strength of whatever emotions arise as you remember participating in evil. (If you have trouble dealing with these emotions, go back to Chapter 6 and reacquaint yourself with the precepts of emotional vitality.)

Now, see yourself discarding the mantle of evil. Throw off the halo, dispel the aura, blow away the cloud. Then decide what tendency you would rather have chosen in that difficult moment. Perhaps you would choose *the ability to feel joy* in place of *inflexibility*. Give this joy power a color and a shape, and take on its mantle. See yourself facing the original situation differently, behaving, thinking, and feeling out of this new mode.

5. Now take a look at your good tendency. Envision yourself enveloped in your divine tendency. Relive the moment you most recently made use of it, and notice how that particular power for good affected you,

others, and the situation. Recall how its positive energy guided your feelings and actions. Allow yourself to feel whatever uplifting emotions arose. Rejoice in the fact that you operated as a channel for the universal forces of goodness, truth, and love. Vow to choose that path again.

6. In your journal, or in discussion with a trusted companion, outline for yourself your basic beliefs about good and evil, God and the Devil, positive energy and negative energy. Try to come up with a framework that takes into account the day-to-day struggles we all face. If you are not sure or want to change what you believe, commit to seeking out answers you can live with through research or soul-searching.

Consider understanding of good and evil a work in progress; return to this Self-Renewal Practice often. Most people find this practice enlightening and affirming. Used on a regular basis, it will help you in the inner quest for peace.

Celebrate each time you choose good over evil. Acting morally gives you a greater sense of control, and of hope. Remember that battling the Devil in one's psyche—and winning—reduces the forces of destruction that wound the world.

> Since wars begin in the minds of men, it is in the minds of men that we have to erect the ramparts of peace. [UNESCO Charter]

Surrender to Suffering

An advertising executive I know has had a number of assistants in recent years. All of them entered the company with solid skills, lots of enthusiasm, and high expectations. But advertising is a grueling field, and employee burnout is rampant. After about eight months, each realized that smarts, hard work, and long hours just weren't enough to get ahead in such a competitive field. One assistant, Lena, a graduate of a top women's college, had a fantastically high IQ and spoke fluent Mandarin, but resented having to work so hard. Unhappy that her brilliance was not being rewarded in the manner she expected, she began to bad-mouth her boss and was transferred into another department. Ford, an incredibly diligent and easy-to-work-with young man who was hired to replace Lena, whined that he "just didn't have what it took" and moved into a different but equally high-profile field, only to be disappointed again.

Surprisingly, Sandra, assistant number three, who attended a less prestigious university than either of the other two and who was the least promising of the three on paper, proved to be a winner. She worked hard (but never to the point where she felt used), played by the rules (written and unwritten), and was forthright in voicing her expectations. She had had several modest successes and already received one promotion when it became clear that personnel changes in the company would render her further promotion impossible. Suddenly it seemed as if all Sandra's hard work had been for naught. Though she expressed bitterness and anger over the storm cloud that suddenly hung over her career, after a few days Sandra actually seemed happy with the disappointment life had offered her. She bounced into work each morning, surprising coworkers with her assertion that she'd find that proverbial silver lining. Two months later, with her boss's help, Sandra had found a position with a firm whose clients' needs exactly matched her own interests, and she got a substantial raise in pay. Four years after taking her first advertising job, Sandra has earned the same job title as her erstwhile boss.

Of all the paradoxes that help us detach from the ordinary plane of existence and connect with the spiritual plane, *suffering that breeds a greater engagement in life* is perhaps the most intriguing. How on earth can a profoundly hurtful experience make anyone live life more fully? That *any* pleasure, or good, can come from pain seems impossible for anyone to believe other than mothers in childbirth, martyrs in ecstasy, and those who, with a strong belief in life after death, lose a loved one.

Yet suffering can be *redemptive* for all of us. Sandra is not a saint, yet she has what Lena and Ford lack: the ability to turn suffering to her own advantage, not just at work, but in life. Because Sandra approaches her painful experiences with an open mind, she is able to make the best of them, learn from them, and get beyond them. Lena and Ford, on the other hand, experience *nonredemptive* suffering, or suffering in vain. They learn nothing from their anguish.

Anthropologist Angeles Arrien outlined a marvelous prescription for redemptive suffering when she suggested four rules for vital living:

- Show up.
- Pay attention.
- Tell the truth.
- Don't get attached to the results.

In our example above, Sandra *showed up*: she faced the inevitable losses of her life head on. She *paid attention* to the nature of the workplace and to her feelings, which she translated into action when appropriate. She *told the truth* by admitting to herself, and to her boss, both the reality of what was happening and how much suffering it caused her. Most important, she *did not become attached to a particular outcome*. Contrast Sandra's outlook to that of Lena, who remained attached to her belief that the company *owed* her a particular kind of job experience, or Ford, who fixated on the idea that this particular company was "not right" for him. Neither of them was *open to possibilities other than what had been imagined*. Following Arrien's four rules in the face of suffering leaves us open to whatever gifts may be available to us as we endure the loss of something we cherish, be it an object, a person, a belief, or a dream.

The fourth rule is the toughest one to live by. (Remember Kim, from the chapter on Emotional Vitality, whose emotions were so out of whack that it took a major confrontation before she realized that her expectations were holding her back.) If we want to receive the true benefits of our life experience, we must empty ourselves of expectations. As the medieval mystic Meister Eckhart reassures us, if we hope to be filled with the gifts of life, we must first make room for them:

There,
>   where clinging to things ends
>   is where God begins to be.
If a cask is to contain wine,
>   you must first pour out the water.
>   The cask must be bare and empty.
Therefore,
>   if you wish to receive divine joy and God,
>   first pour out your clinging to things.
Everything that is to receive
>   must and ought to be
>   empty.

Few of us open ourselves to redemptive suffering before middle age. The first half of life does not typically present us with the kinds of grave losses that provoke the profound suffering most of us must experience before we open ourselves to events beyond those we wish and plan for. At midlife, however, the truth behind illusions such as "I am in control," "If I work hard, I will succeed," "Life is fair," and "If I am a good person, nothing bad will happen to me" hits us square in the face. As much as we would like to hold on to these beliefs, it becomes increasingly hard to do as we experience serious career disappointments, problems with our children, financial difficulties, the death of parents or friends. Just as a raging forest fire can level everything that stands in its way, consistent or deep inner suffering can obliterate the very illusions that fanned the flames of suffering in the first place.

For illusions do hurt us twice. They hurt us when they cause us to take action whose logic is based in false ideals; we then suffer the consequences of our bad decisions. Arguably, they hurt us more the second time around, when we have to face the pain of losing the (ineffective and untrue) principles that have guided us. Fortunately, through redemptive suffering, we can survive the loss of these illusions, discover important truths, even experience spiritual growth.

Even one episode of deep suffering can destroy our damaging illusions. Before I met him, my husband, Grady, experienced a career crisis that put an end to his misplaced hope that if he put his best talents to use, fame and fortune would follow.

For some years I had been trying to break into show business. On this particular day, I was in Las Vegas, walking from hotel to hotel, sometimes getting directions mixed up and walking two miles out of my way. I was carrying folders that had gotten dirty during the week of toting them up and down the strip. It must have been a hundred degrees every day. I was near exhaustion.

I felt alone, maybe for the first time in my life. My parents were dead, and my wife, who was not in touch with me, didn't support my quest—particularly the idea of going to Vegas. She had a point, of course, but her disapproval left me with no ally.

My feet hurt from walking on the hot concrete, so I stopped to rest. I glanced into a window at the back of the Desert Inn Casino and noticed the room was full of people in formal attire. The men all wore tuxedos; the women all seemed to be gorgeous, with long blond hair.

My eyes fell on one man who looked vaguely familiar, and with a start I realized that he was none other than Frank, by God, Sinatra. I suppose he was getting ready to go onstage. Here I was, staring through a window at the King, the man who could make your career with one phone call. I must have sat there a full minute, in shock, before I burst into tears. I felt so stupid. Just awful. So small. So alone. And so ashamed of being a loser.

I stood there for a while longer, on the outside looking in, crying and feeling totally defeated. I must have walked away, though, because I suddenly found myself standing under a very beautiful tree on the nearby golf course. Strange as it sounds, as I stood there, my whole life passed before me. My mother, one of the few people who ever believed in me, and my father, who was very precious to me once I finally got to know him, had both been dead about four years at that point, and when I thought about them, I started to bawl. How disappointed they would be to think their son was in Las Vegas, an outsider wanting in.

I thought about how sad it was to be walking up and down that dirty old strip begging people to let me show them what I could do.

I felt sure that I could no longer believe in God. And I couldn't quit crying. Finally, I lay down on a bench near the tree and tossed the folders, which contained routines I had spent months writing, into the trash can behind my head. I sobbed so hard I gagged. Occasionally I would break out laughing, like a crazy person, and had to stop and look around to make sure nobody heard me.

As day flowed into evening and evening into night, I found myself looking at the desert sky. It filled with ten million stars, and I thought how utterly stupid I must have been to spend my last few hundred dollars on this venture.

Eventually I went home and got on with my life, but when I look back on the experience I realize that it was a turning point for me. It forced me to realize that I had never been protected by some kind of friendly, grandfatherlike God up in the clouds, that I was, as we all are, truly alone. No one was going to take care of me; all bets were off. My fate was in my own hands. It was that night that helped me decide, deep in my heart, to follow a different path from the one I thought I wanted. I stopped chasing fame and fortune and began to search for other ways to apply my talents.

Fortunately, the deeper the pain, the greater the potential for growth. Grady made good use of his heartache, allowing it to dispel a debilitating belief system that said he had to be famous to be worthwhile. He went on to a career in journalism and keynote speaking, which he finds more fulfilling than he ever dreamed, as it makes excellent use of his skills and helps other people. Ironically, he has achieved a good deal of fame in his field, fame he enjoys but does not trust. He tells me that to this day, he recalls the lessons he learned on that golf course whenever he begins to fall into the trap of confusing fame with self-worth.

Changing the way you view suffering and learning to put its lessons to good use are two of the best ways to get the most out of your midlife adventure. The Self-Renewal Practice below will help you prepare for your next disappointment by teaching you how to put past suffering into a positive perspective.

SELF-RENEWAL PRACTICE

Dispelling Dangerous Illusions

1. Recall an episode of great disappointment, despair, loss, or sadness. Let the darkness, emptiness, or turmoil of that moment engulf your spirit, just as it did when you experienced it. You need not fear being destroyed by this moment; you have already proved you can survive it. Allow yourself to feel the full depth of your fear, anger, and frustration.

2. In your journal, note as specifically as you can the illusions you clung to as you tried to come to terms with your personal trauma. Were you striving to maintain your view of the world as a fair place? Trusting in the goodness of life? Hoping against hope that your elaborate plans would finally pay off?

3. Ask yourself what truth about life the episode held for you. Don't berate yourself if you did not take its message to heart at the time; you are doing so now. Ask and answer questions such as: What lessons about myself did that suffering teach me? What misplaced dreams and hopes did my suffering destroy? How can I improve my understanding of life as the result of having endured that suffering?

   As you begin to formulate answers to these tough questions, note them in your journal under the headings "Truths About Me" and "Truths About Life."

4. For the next month or so, reflect on these truths at the end of each day. Add to or shorten your list as you see fit.

   Try to live each day with your "truths" in mind. Whenever a similar situation comes your way, recall the lessons you learned from that episode of despair. Remind yourself that once you weather an unusually devastating storm, all other storms are easier to bear. You will most likely recover more quickly from each of the squalls that follow.

One of my clients used this Self-Renewal Practice to come to terms with the overall disillusionment common in midlifers. He described his personal "dark night of the soul" for me, explaining what led up to his feelings of despair.

1. As a boy, I believed in God, heaven and hell, and the power of the Devil. In fact, I was positive that if I followed the Ten Commandments, I would go to heaven. After all, good boys get Christmas presents, don't they?

   By the time I was a teenager, my life grew more complicated and confusing. I had these wild urges to run away and elope with Barbara Hanks, my high school sweetheart. No kidding, I could barely restrain myself from kidnapping her at the end of every Saturday night. It was only lack of money and my lousy car that stopped me—my religious upbringing did not deter me one bit!

   At about this time, I abandoned my allegiance to God as the sole provider of happiness and added college to my lists of prerequisites for a happy life. The way I had it figured, heaven was a long way away and I'd better count on something a little more worldly to bring me satisfaction and success.

   I studied hard and made it into Princeton, thanks to a couple of teachers who had some pull and thought I was terrific. My college years flew by, and I found myself in law school at Georgetown before I knew what hit me. Those were the greatest days.

   After graduation, I joined the firm I'm now with as one of the most promising young attorneys they'd ever seen come down the pipeline. I spent fifteen years trying to prove they were right about me.

   When I was thirty-eight I started feeling restless. The court cases weren't as challenging anymore; two of my three kids were going through the terrible teens; and my wife, Stacy, was starting to show signs of battle fatigue.

   One morning while shaving, I stared into the mirror, thought I had discovered a new level of regression in my hairline, and yelled, "I've been led on, cheated! What a bitch! I'm not done yet!" My wife came running.

   Ever since that morning shave, I've been on a kind of spiritual quest. I am looking under every conceivable rock I can find for guidance. It is as if I have no answers, no answers that really matter, anyway. This time in my life is very disconcerting. I wake up each day wondering "Is this all there is?" "Who am I?" "What do I really want?" "What does it all mean?"

2. My disillusionments:

- Success is sweet, but my life still lacks meaning.
- My marriage is good, yet I'm still lonely.
- I'm forty years old and I'm still not sure what I want to be when I grow up.
- No matter how much I exercise, how well I eat, how healthy I am, my hair still falls out!

3. **Truths About Me**

I am continuously growing and changing, and so are my needs, wants, and desires.

Fulfilling my responsibilities (to my wife, my company) is important, but my inner life with myself is important, too.

I am in control.

I am getting older.

Truths About Life

New opportunities and new limitations keep revealing themselves.

Life is meaningless and meaningful at the same time.

Outer life suffers without inner life.

Silence teaches better than words.

4. [Written sometime later] The other day I felt that familiar sense of despair when I realized that my oldest child will be leaving soon for college. I panicked. How could my time with him be almost at an end? Had I passed on the right values? I began to question everything all over again, just as I had when shaving that morning.

   I reminded myself of the truths I had learned, and they really helped calm me down. Obviously, if I am getting older, so are my children. I cannot hang on to them forever. My relative "neglect" of them had enabled my wife to teach them some terrific values, and as far as what I personally have given them, I am discussing with them now the very questions I go over in my journal. Maybe they won't have to agonize like this when they turn forty!

I'm certain I will continue to have a meaningful relationship with my son—it will just be different. I think I must be investing this whole "college" thing with too much meaning, and not giving enough weight to the strong ties I already have with my son.

Thinking about the truths I learned also helped me learn another truth, which is that my expectation for a "family life" is still stuck in *Leave It to Beaver* land. I'll have to remember that in the future.

By reminding yourself of the truths your suffering has revealed, you can empty yourself of the disillusionment that weighs you down and fill yourself instead with the wonderful experiences and insights life has to offer. Although suffering is always painful, it really is easier to take if you think of it as the key to emptiness, and emptiness as the key to spiritual growth.

Stop struggling with life. Go, as they used to say, with the flow. Be willing to be surprised, and you'll be closer to the peace and happiness you once thought your illusions would bring.

Gifts of Mortality

On a sunny Tuesday morning in the spring of 1994, Michael left home at 6:00 a.m. for a workout at the YMCA. For more than ten years, Michael had followed this same ritual three times a week. Laps in the pool until 7:15, a quick shower before 7:45 Bible-study group, and work at 9:00. On this particular morning, however, Michael did not make it to work. He didn't even get in his swim. As he stepped out of his Jeep Cherokee in the parking lot of the Y, he was shot in the face and killed. The two gunmen, who were apprehended by police later that same day, confessed to the murder, claiming all they intended to do was to steal the Cherokee.

News of Michael's death traveled fast, consuming the minds, hearts, and conversations of the entire community for days. Dinner-party guests at the home of one of Michael's neighbors talked of nothing else. Michael's contemporaries, adults in midlife, could not get over their horror at such a tragic, untimely, and unjust death.

As I listened to one of Michael's colleagues struggling to comprehend the loss of his good friend, it struck me how difficult it is for most of us to conceive of death, much less to put our thoughts and feelings about it into words. We all know, intellectually, that we will die at some point. Yet when someone we know, or, worse, someone we love, dies, we are jolted out of our complacency, forced to face the inevitability of death, not just for others, but for ourselves. Death rudely interrupts our otherwise steadfast preoccupation with living.

On the surface, living life without dwelling on death seems healthy and rational. A morose preoccupation with death can be quite harmful and may, under certain conditions, provoke suicide. Yet denying death can be dangerous, too, particularly during the midlife years, when most of us naturally encounter the loss of grandparents, parents, and the occasional friend. At the most extreme, being unprepared for the inevitable can mean that each time we encounter death we are devastated, unable to function.

Now imagine what it must be like to *die* unprepared, with important words unsaid, deeds undone, lessons unlearned. Though the actuarial tables may predict you will live to be eighty-five, we all know that death can come at "inconvenient" times, as it did for Michael, when we still have a lot of living to do. Although it is unlikely, today or tomorrow could be your last day on earth. Knowing that, do you feel you are spending today wisely?

Midlifers who hide from the reality of death often become obsessed with youth. These are the fifty-year-olds who dress like twenty-year-olds, or date them. They are the forty-, fifty-, and sixty-year-olds who construct fast-forward, death-denying days and nights, filled to the brim with urgent responsibilities. Even their leisure is designed to be so thrilling and all-consuming that any thought of death is obliterated. Silence and solitude are the archenemies of those who cling desperately to life because they are so afraid to die.

Because death represents the ultimate uncertainty (no one has proved what happens after death), it is bound to trigger anxiety.

Research into normal, age-related death anxiety, however, reveals that what we fear about death changes as we mature through adulthood. Death concerns among young adults revolve primarily around losing someone they care for. During middle adulthood, death anxiety is focused on the physical pain of dying and dying before one is ready. The elderly worry about being helpless, and about taking a long time to die. Interestingly, studies also demonstrate that people are most anxious about dying during periods of inner turmoil that revolutionize their attitudes, values, personality, or behavior—a classic definition of the midlife crisis.

All the reading I have done on the topic of death suggests that there are two ways to come to terms with it. The first is to come to terms with *life*. Researchers have found that those of any age who believe that life as a whole is meaningful, and who are purposeful and highly satisfied with their lives, tend to be less frightened of dying than those who doubt the intrinsic meaning of existence and lack a personal sense of purpose and satisfaction. In other words, the inevitability of death is less devastating if you feel you have made the most of your life.

The second method that appears successful in battling death anxiety is giving in to your curiosity about death. Reading and conversing about death can help you to arrive at a "truth" about death you can live with. Crystallizing your feelings about death can also lead to a clearer sense of life purpose and a greater degree of life satisfaction, which, as noted above, are two of the best ways to diminish death fear.

For many midlifers, traditional religious and spiritual teachings about life after death do not provide us with comfort and understanding as they once did. This can create a deep need for a new belief system regarding life and death, a new cosmology.

Creating a personal cosmology is hard work. Fortunately, there is more information available to help the spiritually "unattached"—in books, audiotapes, and lectures, and with counselors of all types—than at any time in human history.

Those of us who are parents, stepparents, or godparents usually get some sense of the viability of our own personal cosmology when the children we love ask questions like "What will happen to me when I die?" or "Who is God?" I once heard developmental psychologist Bruno Bettelheim quoted as saying, "Children will not be afraid to live whose parents are not afraid to die." Children need to know that we do not fear death, because children (or adults, for that matter) who themselves fear death always hold something back. Like the little boy who will not cross the street because he fears the neighbor's dog, humans need a hand to hold when crossing the street to death. And that hand is the certainty that death is not more than we can handle.

Even if you are comfortable with your view of the cosmos, consider updating or affirming it. The Self-Renewal Practice that follows should be a help in outlining your beliefs. It is best undertaken when you have a chunk of uninterrupted time.

SELF-RENEWAL PRACTICE

Of Death Styles and Lifestyles

1. Insofar as you are able to say it, draw it, sing it, read it, dance it, or dream it, conjure up your current images of death and what, if anything, happens after death. Most people find it helpful to start out with the poetry, music, or art of others; many end up creating their own artistic images, such as self-made collages (which might include photographs or other pictures) or poems, to portray their imaginings about what it is to die and be dead. Try not to do a straight "I believe . . ." statement. Instead, free yourself to express your feelings, questions, and images of death artistically.

    If you find it difficult to begin this process, it might help to do a Life Map, as outlined in Chapter 2, for your beliefs about death. Some people also find it useful to discuss the topic with a trusted friend.

    Make your artistic statement as complete as you can. Do not worry if your work includes contradictory elements—a gory skeleton drawn next to a beautiful flower, for example, or a dance that conveys images of great pain and great pleasure. Be open to all your impressions of death. Record or express everything you can.

2. In your journal or using a tape recorder, explain what these death images mean to you. Do not censor any thought or idea; simply record everything you feel like saying about your views of the mystery of death. If anything in your expression makes you scared or sad, joyful or curious, be sure to include it. Here is the place to make "I believe" or "I wonder" or "I doubt" statements if they are appropriate.

3. Compare your artistic rendering of "death" with your explanation of it. Notice how they are related, but different. Which is easier for you to use when describing your views on the subject?

4. Create in your journal (or on tape) a scenario that describes in detail your "ideal" death. What will be the cause of your death? When will you die? Who will be present? What will you be feeling? Ask and answer these questions freely, without judgment. Forecast your own *death style* in as positive a way as you can.

5. Now reflect on your current *lifestyle*. Evaluate the ways in which your lifestyle today supports your death style, and the ways your life is at odds with the way you would prefer to die. You may decide to change the way you treat your body, your friends, or yourself. Remember that the choices you make today create your future. Ask yourself if you need to make any alterations in your lifestyle so that your living becomes more consistent with your dying.

Think, too, about how your moral, ethical, or spiritual choices fit with what you believe happens *after* you die. You might want to change the way you live—a little or completely. If you believe in reincarnation, you may want to be more vigilant about figuring out what lessons you need to learn in this lifetime. If you think death is the end, period, you'll probably want to get a whole lot of living in. No matter what you believe death to mean, it may hold a message for the way you live now.

6. Take a few minutes and mentally put yourself into the death scenario in Step 4, imagining that you did indeed make all the lifestyle changes you could to create the death you wanted. Look back over your life, and anticipate death calmly. Feel the fullness of your life and the promise of your death.

When you reach a point where you feel you have bridged the gap between being and dying—understood it, come to terms with it, felt its mystery and wonder—discover or create a "reminder" of this experience, one that can bring back the feeling. You might use the lighting of a candle, the holding of a special piece of jewelry, the viewing of a certain image, or the making of a meaningful physical gesture as a key to your positive death feeling. Perform the ritual, hold the object, "see" the image. Repeat the gesture many times until you are certain you can reconnect with ease with that peaceful feeling.

7. Use your symbol or ritual whenever you feel the familiar anxiety descending upon you. The more you practice using it, the more helpful it will be. Use it when you are tempted not to make the lifestyle changes you feel you should. Know it will be there for you when your time comes.

The notes that follow are excerpted from my own journal.

1. Recently I heard this short poem by Oscar Wilde quoted during an interview on National Public Radio: "Death plucked me on the ear and said, 'Live, for I am coming!' "

2. This poem revels death in the darkness just over the horizon where it has been all along, silently waiting for me to acknowledge it as my partner in life. I can grasp death better in the darkness. Darkness eliminates my visual distractions, but I can still hear words and voices speaking their minds. For me, death is a journey into energy fields bulging full of consciousness. It is space empty of material fictions yet full of potential. Personal conscious language dances within cosmic awareness.

3. Somehow that poem brings with it darkness and a powerful sense of urgency. The poem scares me to death and dares me to live all at once.

4. My death will be a calm, welcomed escape from a life lived long (age ninety-five-plus) and with great energy. I will be physically weak but mentally alert and happy for the chances life gave me to be engaged. My loved ones (my family and friends) will be in

and out, enjoying my last days and our conversations. The spirits of my parents and brothers and all those I have loved who died before me will be with me in that death-space.

5. My lifestyle supports my death style in its "go for it" fashion, but I am too busy and too driven these days to earn the calm, reflective, hopeful death I desire. I need more silence and solitude.

6. I choose silence as my totem. I will find five minutes of silence every day to contemplate dying, darkness, silence, the abyss, emptiness, and how it fits in with the great merging of energy I believe to be out there for me. By closing my eyes, breathing deeply and holding my body still, I will pay tribute to the death that plucks me on the ear and whispers, "Live, for I am coming."

7. Since I have been performing my ritual, I feel less anxious, not just about death, but about my life. I also find myself with many more instances of spontaneous joy.

According to religious scholars, meditations on death permeate almost every kind of worship known to humankind. Make use of the Self-Renewal Practice above, or any other inner search that works for you, whenever you feel anxiety over death weighing you down.

No matter how prepared you are for death, it is, unless you are a mystic, occasion for some sadness. Even if you have come to terms with the cessation of life (yours or someone else's), you will still need to mourn what is, or will have been, lost. We know from psychological studies of those who survive the death of a loved one that grieving is necessary in order to recover from the loss and engage in life again. My description in Chapter 1 of the pain I faced when I lost my pregnancy echoes those findings.

To focus only on moving on without looking back means missing out on the opportunity to honor the finality of death. In truth, we cannot move forward unless we do.

In order to comprehend death fully, especially our own, it is helpful to acknowledge that life itself is full of little deaths, rehearsals, if you will, for the big one. We must honor the nevermores and never-will-bes of our own existence. Many adults, for example, have not fully mourned their lost childhoods, the childhoods they did not get because they felt compelled to grow up fast. Others have not grieved adequately over lost dreams of a specific career, lover, or goal. Mourning must also extend to the selves we are becoming now. You have probably experienced many of these small deaths if you have done the Self-Renewal Practices in this book, because self-renewal of any kind encourages deep, sometimes sweeping change, which by its nature kills the outmoded, if once self-defining, parts of you. Old ways of being in control die, antiquated concepts of who you are die, ineffectual ways of relating die.

Reflect on the previous pathways in this book and determine what aspects of yourself "died" in order to make room for new, more mature aspects. For example, many people who travel the pathway of Physical Vigor put to rest their strenuous, youthful approach to exercise, their twenty-two-year-old appearance, and their disregard for the rest and nutrition their bodies need. Along the pathway of Emotional Vitality, many adults say goodbye to decades-old resentments and outdated emotional self-protections that used to help them avoid the pain and confusion of life.

Until we bid farewell to these former parts of ourselves, we will not be fully prepared to step into the void and grasp the new sense of identity that awaits us on our journey. Allow yourself to feel the depth of your sadness, your anger, your pain over any of the losses that hurt you. If you need to, go back to the chapter on Emotional Vitality for help in coping with these sometimes overwhelming feelings.

Human beings resist change, even in a positive direction, when we cannot be sure of what lies ahead. To confront this void takes great courage. The next Self-Renewal Practice is designed to give you the confidence you need to face death head on. Please do not attempt this exercise unless you have already completed the previous one, on death styles and lifestyles; success with this exercise depends on your having made a kind of peace with death.

SELF-RENEWAL PRACTICE

Stepping into the Void

1. List three of the most important changes in your life, changes that required you to give something up in order to gain something else. It doesn't matter whether you initiated the changes. A few examples follow:

   - Moving to the country
   - Marrying my spouse
   - My father's death
   - Having a baby
   - Losing my job
   - Giving up an unhealthy friendship
   - Getting a degree
   - Starting to smoke
   - Finding out that others think I'm boring
   - Finding a God I could live with

2. For each of the incidents you chose, list all the things you gave up, and all the things you gained. For "Moving to the country," the list might read like this:

WHAT I GAVE UP
A familiar place
Good shopping
Day-to-day contact with close friends
Contact with what's "in" and "happening"
My support system for getting on with my life
Prestige

WHAT I GAINED
Nature, fresh air, beauty
More room for the things I value, such as books and our art
A more relaxed lifestyle

More down-to-earth people
Better schools for my children
New friends
A place to entertain old friends
New adventures

For "My father's death," your list might look like this:

WHAT I GAVE UP
The idea that Dad would live forever
Being with a man I love
The chance to ask and tell him things I wish I had
Belief in my ability to control life

WHAT I GAINED
Determination not to leave things unsaid
A new perspective on the importance of what I do each day
Curiosity about what happens after we die
The realization that life's mysteries won't be clear to me until I, too, die
A vague sense that I will see Dad again

3. Go over your lists, one by one, and take a moment to feel the full impact of anything you lost. Allow yourself to experience conflicting waves of relief and regret that are likely to come.

    Next, celebrate the new aspects of your experience that were born as a result of your willingness to let old habits, behaviors, and attitudes die.

4. *This is the most important step in this practice.* Recall how you felt as you let go of your "old" ways of being and dived into the new. Remember what it felt like to release the familiar and face the unknown. What particular blend of excitement, anxiety, hope, determination, fear, loneliness, or faith made you willing to make the leap between the old ways you clung to and the new ways you had no knowledge of? What were the sources of inner strength that helped you? What did it feel like to use your courage?

5. Now imagine yourself facing death square in the eye, with the same strength and courage you recalled in Step 4. Remind yourself that *every time you have ever let go of something good, you have gotten something else you could appreciate.* In your mind's eye, allow yourself to let go of your body, of earth, and step into death with confidence and hope, calm and grace.

Repeat this Self-Renewal Practice whenever you feel too attached to the world to let go with the dignity and wisdom you desire. Reverence for who you once were and what you once had is one of the best ways to instill in yourself the unshakable sense that you are ever-changing, ever-growing. In making the most of your small deaths, you can build confidence that one day you will have what it takes to greet your physical death with courage and honor. In your final hour, if you are able to say goodbye to what has been your life and welcome whatever transformation the universe has in store for you, you will have triumphed in the most crucial, self-defining moment of all.

VICTORIES OF SPIRITUAL SERENITY

Albert Einstein once said, "There are only two ways to live your life. One is as though nothing is a miracle, the other is as though everything is a miracle." The difference between the two may be not only the key to happiness, but the key to sanity; research from the National Social Survey reports a high correlation between spirituality and mental health.

Lawrence Kohlberg, a psychologist and scholar who has devoted his career to the study of moral development, believes that advances in midlife spirituality are what allow a person to be the author of his or her own moral life. In my own practice, I have observed that middle-aged adults who have done the demanding work of figuring out their own spiritual beliefs are more able than others to make moral decisions and stand by them, even if the decision causes them some pain. In short, these people make the best leaders.

Muhammad was nearly forty when he received his challenge from

Gabriel to enter the cave and decipher the words that are the cornerstone of Islam. In his book *Forty: The Age and the Symbol*, anthropologist Stanley Brandes notes:

A number of well-known Islamic saints experienced turning points at age forty; this is the age, for example, when Abu Baqr was converted. It is also the time when, according to the Koran, a man is said to achieve full strength. That is, according to official Islamic doctrine, as well as in the life of its major prophet, forty is defined as the beginning of a new era of life, an era characterized above all by maturity, be it physical or spiritual.

Brandes considers the symbolism of age forty in the Jewish tradition as well. His research shows that for many key figures in Hebrew history, spiritual awakening occurred at age forty or beyond. According to one popular version of his story, Abraham recognized God at age forty. Cain and Abel were forty when they offered their sacrifice. Moses was forty when he left Egypt. Brandes explains that countless other personages of religious and historical significance—Isaac, Esau, Ishbosheth, and others—entered advanced stages of spiritual renewal only at age forty.

Regardless of whether we subscribe to the particular faiths from which they come, these stories of spiritual rebirth and leadership at midlife reflect deep psychological truths. Many scholars believe that midlife offers the best opportunity for a deep conversion of the spirit because it is during this period that a person experiences a convergence of life skills, confidence, pain over the harsh realities and compelling necessities of life, and a desire to rethink inconsistencies or untenable spiritual beliefs. Pastoral psychologist Walter Conn of Villanova University offers the example of the famous Christian mystic Thomas Merton (1915–1968), who experienced a critical conversion of the spirit during midlife as the result of a a severe conflict with his abbot and the new responsibility of overseeing the spiritual development of novices. Conn feels that Merton's unexpected struggle and newly acquired leadership role encouraged him to take full possession of his moral life. Only after Merton had completely integrated and owned his personal spiritual beliefs could he embrace the social and political problems of the world.

Even if you grew up with a strong faith, you faith needs to be reaffirmed or replenished at middle age. For midlife presents you with a wonderful chance to transcend the boundaries of your own identity and participate in the greater reality of nature, the cosmos, and the God-source.

CHAPTER 9

Pathway #7
Personal Integrity

When we die, and go to meet our Maker, we're not going to be asked why we didn't become a Messiah or find a cure for cancer. Instead, we will be asked, "Why didn't you become you?"

—ELIE WIESEL

The idea of "becoming oneself" may strike you as a bit odd. Clearly, you are already yourself. Others recognize you as you. Who else could you be?

At the core of each of us, however, is an essential self, one we have been trying to uncover in this book. As you traveled down the pathways of Mental Mastery, Physical Vigor, Emotional Vitality, Interpersonal Effectiveness, Exceptional Competence, and Spiritual Serenity, you undoubtedly noticed that the key to "becoming" your true self in each of these areas is accepting who you are, making the most of it, and living with it honorably, rather than becoming something or someone else. Coming to terms with oneself *as a whole being* requires the same kind of attitude, and the same kind of work.

Think of the "real you" as Sleeping Beauty—beautiful, though untouched and untried—lying behind an overgrowth of brier bushes so tangled that anyone who tries to get in from the outside must ultimately fail. True happiness can only be found once the spell is broken. *Your* spell, which includes the limitations of circumstance, societal expectations, and your own fears, has, with any luck, begun to break as you performed the Self-Renewal Practices in the preceding chapters and gave yourself some much-needed time and attention.

If you are like most of my clients, you have experienced glimmers of knowing the "real you" throughout life. You know in your heart when you are operating out of this *best self*, because you are able to think clearly, act decisively, and stand your ground with courage.

Being your best self requires a quality I call *Personal Integrity*. Contrary to the way most of us perceive it, integrity is not some personality trait to be cultivated. Nor is it a gift bestowed upon that one person in a crowd who is able to behave honorably while others around him are confused or consumed with greed. Integrity is, in fact, the one grace we can all aspire to. In a very literal sense, Personal Integrity is a true integration of all the many parts of ourselves working together as one cohesive whole so we don't act one way at work and another way at home . . . we don't say one thing and feel another . . . we don't experience the miserable dissonance we feel when the person we are on the inside has nothing to do with the person we are in the world. Being "disintegrated" in this way is as uncomfortable as trying to turn left with our feet and right with our body. It is a fragmentation of who we are.

At another level, Personal Integrity is the ability to act out of our most basic, personal sense of what is right for us and the world. The Messiah, the doctor who cures cancer, the people who saved Jews from the Nazis, were not *given* more integrity than anyone else; they found it within themselves, by knowing themselves. You can, too.

THE CALL TO PERSONAL INTEGRITY

Many of my clients mention experiencing moments of deep self-knowledge as they progress through the exercises in this book. These marvelous "aha" discoveries, the result of breaking down the barriers to ourselves, allow us to feel important connections between the many facets of our personalities. If you have been fortunate enough to get a glimpse of your best self and your ability to operate out of Personal Integrity, you know how wonderful it feels. You are ready for more. But even if you have no conscious sense of that self, there are other signs you may be ready to travel this pathway.

Midlife Readiness Signals for Personal Integrity
You may find yourself:

- more willing to take risks in order to do what you believe to be right, or to earn what you believe is right for you
- viewing your strengths and weaknesses more as a consequence of your own choices than as immutable traits
- refusing to compromise your morals and ethics, no matter what the short-term gains for doing so may be
- accepting your successes and failures at face value, as markers for new directions rather than as ends in themselves
- appreciating the complex course your life has taken, is taking, and will continue to take
- developing a personal philosophy that acknowledges the profound interconnectedness between your inner and outer worlds
- curious about ways you can reconcile all the things you want to be

The inevitable changes of midlife almost always cause us to cultivate a deep interest in issues of Personal Integrity, but it is a pathway that presents us with more demanding and frightening challenges the farther we travel down its terrain. Knowing oneself takes a lot of courage. What if you turn out to be less of a person than you'd hoped? What if you cannot live up to the values you espouse? What if you die before you have a chance to live with that magical best self as a guiding force?

As with many of life's important endeavors, in our struggle to gain Personal Integrity we often are too hard on ourselves, failing to recognize our successes. Fortunately, each time you locate your best self and act on it, you have made a huge leap in your personal development. And it gets easier the next time.

I would caution you not to look at integrity as a state you can "achieve." Like other pathways, the pathway of Personal Integrity is one you have been on your whole life, and will continue on until you die. If you attempt to approach your daily routines with honesty and goodwill, you may notice that sometimes you experience a sense of "rightness" you have never before displayed or felt. These times will keep you going when you do the "wrong" thing, or face confusion over what to think or do. Recognize that no one on earth experiences his or her best self all the time. Simply strive to find that state as often as you can. Personal Integrity is not perfection; it is the ability to pull yourself back onto the path when you find yourself straying.

ADVENTURES IN PERSONAL INTEGRITY

One of the hallmarks of integrity is solitude. By definition, people who operate out of true integrity go their own way much of the time. The more you follow what Thoreau calls your "different drummer," the more comfortable you become with that solitary self. In this way, self-knowledge begets integrity begets self-knowledge.

Yet, paradoxically, one of the gifts of integrity is the *loss of loneliness*. The more you go your own way, the less lonely you are. First, you find you are fine company for yourself. The search for inner knowledge becomes more and more fascinating as you proceed down this pathway. Moreover, as you integrate your many facets you will find that others are drawn to you. Not all others—just the ones whose values approximate yours. (Don't expect that jerk of a girlfriend you dated six years ago to suddenly figure out how great you are.) People will enjoy you and learn from you, just as you enjoy and learn from them.

For many people who take the journey toward Personal Integrity, the very idea of "community" changes. They are surprised to note a profound concern for people they do not know, for animals, and for humanity in general. Though not always sure how to make the world a better place, they treat it with the same love with which they now treat themselves.

Work in the area of Personal Integrity also has tremendous pay-offs along each of the six pathways discussed in previous chapters. Mental and physical needs, often ignored, get equal time in an integrated self. Emotional Vitality and Spiritual Serenity deepen when we have the strength to face the truths we perceive. And we grow by leaps and bounds in the areas of Interpersonal Effectiveness and

Exceptional Competence when we affirm our beliefs by acting on them.

Finally, as you gain a new perspective on yourself as an intricate being made up of distinct yet overlapping dimensions, you are in store for a boost in self-esteem. You can't view the mystery and majesty of your inner world and not marvel at how far you have come in the process of maturing.

Putting It All Together

If you are a workaholic perfectionist, as I am, you may feel compelled to perform every Self-Renewal Practice in this book on a regular basis. You also need to go to work, spend time with family and friends, and floss your teeth at night. Most likely, you finished Chapter 3 all set to work on your mental skills, only to be derailed by the demands of Chapter 4. You'd like to revive all of the important areas of your life, but cannot imagine how it can be done. The truth is, it can't. That's where Personal Integrity comes in.

Personal Integrity enables us to balance the ever-changing needs of our bodies, minds, and spirits. It is the ability to take the many dimensions of ourselves and make the best use of them *as they are now*, all the while keeping in mind what you *hope they will be*.

The integrated self is constantly looking. Visually, it might resemble the sigmoid learning/performance curve described in Chapter 7, only compounded. The integrated self incorporates each aspect of the personality, and grows just as the other "selves" grow.

Seeing yourself as a whole person, if you have not done so before, will create changes in three areas of your life. The first is *awareness*. Conscious awareness of the different demands of your various "sides" (your funny and sad sides, your mental and physical sides), as well as the interplay between them, means no longer being able to ignore your own needs and values.

Out of this awareness comes *choice*, the way you prioritize the many demands you make on your body and soul. Choice means making a commitment to living out of your best self as often as you can. Of course, deciding to operate out of one's best self does not make daily choices easy. Sometimes you'll need to choose between

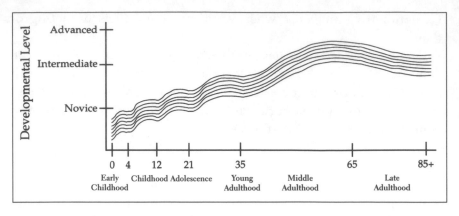

Model of healthy development for seven pathways of personal growth across the life span

two things you want (to sit with a sick friend or go to an important environmental meeting), or two you do not (to fire an employee or put up with her bad work). Choice also extends to the manner in which you approach these issues—with kindness or callousness, with creativity or passivity.

Choosing is something you must do every day. Even an "established" choice, such as the choice to be married, must be constantly reaffirmed. Failure to think and rethink choices leads to decisions that do not serve your total self.

The third and most difficult aspect of Personal Integrity is *action*. It is not enough to decide, or even verbalize, your priorities. You must act upon them. If your boss wants you to work late (again!) and you've determined that nothing will get in the way of family dinners, you must act according to your choice. You must have the courage to do what you believe is right. In short, you must take risks. *When you put action with awareness and choice, you experience a moment of Personal Integrity.*

Far too many midlife adults make an uneasy peace with themselves when it comes to integrating their many facets and desires. Unwilling to examine, choose, or act on their inner wisdom, they go through life compartmentalized—perhaps hardworking and aggressive at the office, passive at home, and funny at parties.

The imbalance that occurs when we deny one or more aspects of ourselves parallels physical illness. If you have a hurt foot and do not give it the time and attention it needs to heal, you will favor the other foot. The healthy foot will get stronger and stronger—and you more dependent on it—as the sick foot continues to weaken. The longer this deterioration continues, the more difficult it is to address the imbalance. Eventually, overreliance on the strong foot leads to weakness there, too.

Typically, those who compartmentalize their lives feel as if they are many people, instead of one integrated whole. Though not mentally ill in the clinical sense, they make use of multiple mini-personalities, switching from one to the other as the situation dictates. The physical self (the "jock," for instance) bears no relation to the social self (the "party animal") and often acts in direct opposition to it. For a person with a minimally developed sense of personal identity, the eight-, ten-, or twelve-hour workday might fall to the "business self," which thinks, acts, and feels one way, with the "whole" self existing primarily to prevent the business self from subsuming the rest. To a more fully integrated person, the business self, family self, and spiritual self (and any other selves) would be one and the same. In general, the easier time you have "switching gears" as you move from task to task, the better integrated you are.

Like many of the positive human characteristics discussed in this book, Personal Integrity is something we are born with and lose. As children, we had no trouble being firefighter, dancer, doctor, pirate, and dog; happy, sad, and angry; energetic, quiet, and intensely focused—all on the same day. We saw all these roles, all these ways of being, as *us*, because children have an innate sense that all these roles come together in the person who makes those roles possible. They understand instinctively that, in the words of artist Wassily Kandinsky, "the trunk of the tree does not become superfluous because of a new branch; it makes the branch possible."

You can encourage yourself to form a central, deep, integrated sense of who you are; what you feel, value, believe, and cherish; how you relate; and what you contribute by engaging in the next Self-Renewal Practice.

SELF-RENEWAL PRACTICE

Savoring Your Best Self

1. Think about the last time you enjoyed a delicious meal. Imagine yourself back at that table for a few moments. Reexperience the exciting aromas, the attractive presentation, the variety of pleasant textures, the delicious flavors of the food. Was music playing? Was there good conversation? Flowers on the table? Allow these sensations to reemerge in your mind. Notice their impact on your total experience of the meal, how each separate dimension of the experience contributes to the overall dining pleasure.

2. Now recall when your mind, heart, body, and spirit were acting in concert to accomplish a task or communicate with another person.

    Frequently mentioned "best self" moments include especially intense lovemaking sessions, taking part in political protests, giving a speech on a topic about which you feel strongly, attending a concert by a favorite artist or group, and cavorting with one's children. No instance is too grand or too mundane to bring out one's best self.

3. Just as you did with your mealtime reverie, focus on the specific, disparate aspects of who you are that made your "best self" memory so vivid. For example, you might zero in on the quality and clarity of your thinking, the intensity and expression of your emotions, or the physical high you felt as your heart beat faster (or slower). Notice the values that guided your actions. Identify the overall purpose of your participation in the event, the skill you displayed, and how you treated other people. Savor each of these contributions.

4. Now allow yourself to reexperience the "best self" moment you just dissected. Step back into the coherent system of mental, physical, emotional, and spiritual convergence and feel the flow, the joy of knowing that every move you make is the right one, that every word and gesture comes from the heart. Let the instruments of your many selves create the music that is your best self.

Once you feel you are again in that moment, dwell on the inner harmony. Ask yourself: Who am I? What do I believe in? Whom do I love? What talents and skills do I possess? How do I feel?

5. Take whatever strengths you identified at the end of Step 3 and use them to create affirmations to remind yourself of feelings you had in Step 4. The following format generally works well: *Because I am* _____ (fill in the blank), *I am* _____ . (Do not create affirmations for which you have no backup; I believe affirmations only work when they are based in truth, because the human mind is too smart to accept being lied to.) After a recent "peak self" experience, I came up with the following affirmations:

- Because I am principled, I am honest.
- Because I am loving, I am lovable.
- Because I am interested in the welfare of others, I am respected.
- Because my ideas work, I am worth listening to.
- Because I am determined, I am able to get things done.

Repeat these affirmations to yourself whenever you are unsure of your ability to operate out of your best, most integrated self. An identity anchored in the essentials of who you really are is your best tool for meeting the challenges of your life head on with grace.

There is no better way to promote progress along all your personal pathways than to advance down the pathway of Personal Integrity. As Personal Integrity becomes a more permanent frame of reference from which you operate, you are far less likely to violate one set of needs by satisfying another set. Just as the riverbed guides the river, your best self will guide the way you live your life.

Robert Bly, poet and teacher, helps us grasp the omnipresence of our deepest, truest selves in his translation of a poem by Juan Ramón Jiménez:

I am not I.
        I am this one
walking beside me whom I do not see,
whom at times I manage to visit,
and whom at other times I forget;
who remains calm and silent while I talk,
and forgives, gently, what I hate,
who walks where I am not,
who will remain standing when I die.

In my work with executives (and other overly cerebral types), I have noted that poems, such as the Jiménez work just cited, simultaneously engage and circumvent the intellect in order to convey deceptively simple but profound concepts. These artistic expressions speak to the universal truths that lie buried just under the detritus of the day. They speak directly to the inner voice we all hear, but few of us attend.

To achieve Personal Integrity, we have to create a kind of internal poem: we must find a way back to the inborn knowledge we had as children—that voice within that is the key to happiness—without losing the selfless "world concern" we internalized in adulthood.

One of my clients, whom I will call Nora, has done a terrific job reintegrating the many parts of herself into a coherent, focused whole that is much more than the sum of its parts, and one that has a voice of its own:

> I had a boringly normal life until age thirty-five. Educated, married young, two kids, bang bang. Then, just as the gray hair was starting to come in, I found out that my husband had run our fifteen-year-old business into the ground while I was busy raising the children.
>
> I have a lot of energy, so I threw myself back into the business with gusto. I took over the operations, and within six months had turned the company around. In the wake of my success, my marriage died, and I found myself with a completely different life from what I'd had just a half year before.
>
> As I plugged away at my exciting new career, my kids, who were

approaching their teens, needed me less and less. Finally I was able to get into some of the civic activities that had long interested me. I was really pretty happy, but went to see Kathy because I was too prone to overwork. "Driven" would be more like it.

My attempt to integrate myself involved more than just juggling my new roles. I had to learn to do something I'd never taken time to learn in almost four decades of living. I had to listen to what was in my heart. And not just the part I wanted to hear (like "Go to work"). I had to listen to the little voice that said, "Slow down," and the one that said, "Why did you take on another responsibility?" In short, I had to put my "whole self in" (in the words of the famous "Hokey Pokey") and "turn myself around." An arm here and a leg there were not enough.

All of this boiled down, for me anyway, into one very concrete life change. I had to somehow find ten or fifteen minutes every day to spend in reverie. Bear in mind that I have a tendency to fill every moment so I have no time at all. Five years ago, even two years ago, I could not have foreseen squeezing in one more chore that, like eating well, provided no excitement other than the promise of long-term benefits. Now I could not live without my late-night reverie.

Just the other day I told Kathy how the specific details of these quiet moments change my perspective. Even the coolness of my bed linens when I climb into bed can flood me with peace now. I look out my window and look for the North Star as a focal point. Then I slow my breathing. No matter how tired I am, or how early I have to get up, I make it a point to relish just being alive. I enjoy the silence of my otherwise bustling household. Sometimes I think about the next day. How will I run the Chamber of Commerce meeting so that every agenda item is covered? Be sure to check your phone messages after the United Way board meeting! The budget is due at work, and so are the financial forecasts. But I never think very long about these worldly matters.

Most of the time I focus on internal things. How does my body feel? What are my emotions? Who am I? What do I believe? What gifts do I possess? Which memories are pulling themselves into the edge of my mind? What skills will I groom? Which will I count on tomorrow, this month, this year? What do I appreciate the most about myself?

I know it sounds weird, but I always get surprising answers to these questions. There is this other self inside me that has a voice that has the answers. No matter how hard I try, I cannot hear that voice during the day, but at night, when I do my bedtime thing, it's loud and clear.

This extra voice has given me so much peace. I now find it easier to go from role to role. I have very little inner conflict over how to act or how to spend my time. It's like I have a kind of cosmic glue holding me together now. I used to be all fragments, pieces of me darting about in different orbits. Now I'm one planet in one great orbit, unsure of my destiny but not my goal.

Not that this is the perfect panacea. I still need to get more exercise (though better eating habits have already helped eliminate excess poundage and increase energy). If truth be told, I should probably do some "internal" stuff during the day, too. But all in all, I find that listening to all of me has helped me more than I ever thought possible. What is most remarkable is that the work I do on the nonbusiness aspects of myself have such a great payoff at work. My creativity grew as soon as I started these practices, and suddenly I found myself wanting more on-the-job stimulation. Once I got more into my emotions, I felt as if I wanted to be closer to my coworkers (and kids). I feel as if every part of me is blossoming. Suddenly I can stand up to my enemies, feel compassion for them, even. I am not riddled by worry and doubt. I think I may finally be becoming an adult. Imagine that!

The reunion of Nora's surface self with her subterranean self brought her a genuine, compassionate sense of who she *is* at her very core. Psychologists Dennis O'Connor of Le Moyne College and Donald Wolfe of Case Western Reserve, both researchers studying the effects of major transitions (job loss, career change, divorce, and marriage, for example) on adults, discovered that the subjects who came through the experiences more internally focused, autonomous, and self-directed were those with an integrated sense of self-identity. Instead of basing their identities in career or family roles, the hardier, more self-sufficient, and more inner-directed survivors based their identity in their true selves.

When you learn to trust enough in the wisdom of your own soul to accept how all the various aspects of your personality come together, you discover the miraculous truth that the whole that is you *transcends* your individual personality traits. Viewed as a composite, your life has an almost magical coherence and continuity.

One of the best ways to appreciate the wonder of your essential self is to look at your life as a story—a fairy tale, fable, or epic. Most of my clients confess that the last vestiges of meaninglessness or futility in their lives are shattered when they crystallize their sense of their best self in this manner.

The Self-Renewal Practice that follows is intended to help any of you for whom the pattern of your successes and failures is not obvious. Scour your life for shape and texture. Take the time to reconceptualize who you are, and commit yourself to making choices that harmonize with your development to date. Your reward will be a renewed sense of contentment, purpose, and hope.

SELF-RENEWAL PRACTICE

Telling Your Story

In this practice, I am going to ask you to narrate a short autobiography. In preparation, you might want to look over your journal at the notes you made as you performed various Self-Renewal Practices. *The Ageless Me* practice on page 103 and any Life Maps you have drawn are particularly helpful.

Set side at least forty-five minutes for this practice.

1. Close your eyes and envision your life to date as a time line. Mentally note the "big" events (graduations, weddings, deaths) as well as personal epiphanies, successes, or failures. Pay special attention to events that, though they seem unimportant, keep popping into your mind.

   When you feel ready, record some of the highlights of your time line in your journal. Then go back to remembering, eyes closed, until you come up with something else worthy of notation. Keep going until you feel you have highlighted most of the interesting and meaningful experiences in your life.

2. Examine your notes with an eye toward patterns in your thoughts and behavior. Look especially at the ways in which you typically approach challenge or conflict, and whether these methods brought success or failure.

Some of my clients note crossroads that are negotiated successfully only if they follow certain inner directives. Other common patterns are:

- The need to face fears (refusing to deal with them can engender failure, while facing them generally brings success of some kind)
- The need to learn from disappointment
- The need to stand up for what we believe in
- The need to connect with others (or with nature, or God, or beauty)

The more patterns you detect, the more interesting and helpful your story will be. Make special note of the times, over the years, when you have been successful in conquering the challenges presented to you.

3. In the third person (in which you write about yourself as a character, saying "he" did this or "she" said that), and with you as the hero, relate the story of your life thus far. Imagine you were born a prince or princess (i.e., someone special), and have had to face certain challenges before you can "live happily ever after." Posit these challenges literally (qualifying for a mortgage) or metaphorically (satisfying the whims of a gnome).

Shape your narrative a bit. Imagine your story being read by schoolchildren who can learn from your mistakes and triumphs. Can you relate the overcoming of a great demon—smoking? anger?—Can you describe a few failures that were followed by great successes on the same battleground (two failed relationships followed by a happy marriage?)?

Follow the path of your inner terrain, as well. What beliefs and attitudes have prevented your complete happiness? How have you conquered any negative thought patterns? Which ones are you still battling?

Do not try to end your story yet. After all, your life is not over. Leave the hero of the story in midstream, wherever you are now in your life, hopeful for a happy ending.

Note: If you are not a confident writer, feel free to write separate vignettes for each of your travails. At the very minimum, make note of the issues in your life and how well you have dealt with and are dealing with them.

4. Read your story, and root for the hero. Have compassion for him or her. Have faith in the hero's ability to attain the much-desired "happiness ever after."

   Honor the valor and persistence of your hero. Look at the amazing feats he or she has accomplished, at the nobility of the goals. Revel in how far this marvelous person has come, from a tiny infant to a fully grown adult, with many skills and accomplishments.

   Now look at your hero dispassionately and see if you can instruct him or her in the ways that happiness can best be achieved. Perhaps your character is taking the wrong path too often. Have your hero's heroic acts been misplaced? Maybe his or her standards are too high.

   Write yourself a happy ending.

5. The next time you face a personal challenge, think of yourself as the hero of your own story. Realize that each day gives you the opportunity to make the tale a richer, more rewarding one.

Look for opportunities to display your best self wherever you can. Your best self is the aspect of you that brings out the best in others and the world, that graces ordinary experience with extraordinary clarity, and that, if the believers are correct, goes with you into the next world.

VICTORIES OF PERSONAL INTEGRITY

When Abraham Maslow attempted to describe the pinnacle of human development, which he called *self-actualization,* he looked to much-admired historical figures, such as Thomas Jefferson, Abraham Lincoln, Albert Schweitzer, and Eleanor Roosevelt, for inspiration. He found that self-actualized individuals operated on a kind of "meta-need" level, in which they strove to satisfy their personal, higher-order yearnings for truth, beauty, justice, emotional self-sufficiency, and altruism. Similarly, in my practice I have noticed that once a person earns the rewards of Personal Integrity in midlife, his or her inner desire to benefit others grows stronger. Integrated adults do not merely believe they should help others; they desire to help others in much the same way a thirsty person desires water. Once all personal needs are met, altruism becomes a basic human trait. When you become more yourself, you have more of yourself to give away.

When you have ready (if not constant) access to your best self, amazing things can happen. If the experiences of the people listed above are any indication, you are eligible for a kind of genius. You become open to new ideas, more able to weigh tough options, more creative in the way you approach the problems in your life. You may also begin to get a dose of the cosmic truths whose promise makes every moment an adventure.

Recently I was operating at full throttle, challenged simultaneously at work, at home, and in my civic life. I did everything I could think of to operate out of my best self—by letting go, staying integrated, listening to my inner voice—and found that, as a reward, I was rising to every one of the many strenuous occasions of the day. At one juncture, however, I got stuck. I was writing an important speech and needed backup for an especially tough-to-convey point. At 6:00 on a Monday night, with just a day to finalize the presentation, I decided to head for the A-frame to clear my mind. Maybe I could find another way around the problem tomorrow. On the way out the door, almost without thinking, I grabbed two books off my bookshelf at random—I find that undirected "research" of this kind sometimes gets my creative juices flowing.

That night, somewhere between waking and sleeping (though it could have been either), I had a very clear vision of a name on the page of a book. It was the name of a prominent social scientist whose work covers any number of important topics. Frankly I didn't think much about my "vision" until the next morning when, on a whim, I opened up one of the books I had brought and saw *the same name I'd seen in my vision.* Had it not been for the dream of the night before, I would have passed right by the passage. Oddly enough, the researcher in question was not the author of this book, nor the topic of it. His findings were, in fact, a very small part of the volume. Even more strangely, the particular essay I had flipped to *provided exactly the information I needed to complete my talk.*

Some people believe that coincidences are fate; others believe that they are evidence of God's hand reaching out to us. Even if you believe that serendipitous experiences have no meaning at all, why not accept these little gifts as they come your way, and create a welcoming place for them if there appears to be a pattern to their coming? As for me, I think I earned that cosmic present through hard work and perseverance. It is not the first time the universe has rewarded me for my efforts, and, since I have a lot of say in the matter, it will not be the last.

PART III

The Return Home

CHAPTER 10

Reunion with a World in Waiting

No man is a Iland, intire of it selfe;
every man is a peece of the Continent,
a part of the maine; if a Clod bee washed
away by the Sea, Europe is the lesse,
as well as if a Promontorie were, as well as
if a Mannor of thy friends or of thine own were;
any man's death diminishes me, because I am
involved in Mankinde.

—JOHN DONNE

In Homer's epic tale the *Odyssey*, Odysseus sets out for Ithaca, only to find himself on an adventure of monumental proportions. His ship is blown off course countless times, and he is forced to land on islands whose inhabitants torture him with temptations of the flesh and trials of strength, character, and spirit. Buried in each challenge, of course, is a gem of self-understanding.

As Odysseus meets each foe and overcomes each obstacle, he grows stronger and wiser, but before long he begins to despair of ever making it back home again. Nevertheless, he holds the memory and promise of Ithaca, his island homeland, in his heart.

In a verse of his poem *Ithaka*, modern Greek poet Constantine Cavafy reminds us of the psychological and spiritual importance of an anticipated homecoming:

Keep Ithaka always in your mind.
Arriving there is what you're destined for.

But don't hurry the journey at all.
Better if it lasts for years, so you're
old by the time you reach the island,
wealthy with all you've gained on the way,
not expecting Ithaka to make you rich.
Ithaka gave you the marvelous journey.

Without her you wouldn't have set out.
She has nothing left to give you now.

And if you find her poor, Ithaka won't have fooled you.
Wise as you will have become, so full of experience,
you'll have understood by then what these Ithakas mean.

It was to Ithaca that Odysseus did finally, happily return, an Ithaca quite different from the island he had left so many years before. Odysseus's new perspective, born of both success and suffering, enabled him not only to cope with the changes he found in his homeland, but to be a better leader to his fellow islanders as well.

In her efforts to teach our generation how to use the wisdom in ancient myths to change our lives for the better, author Jean Houston suggests that all epic heroes experience trauma so that they themselves can be reborn and so that they can serve as midwives in the larger society "for the continuum necessary to redeem" the society and bring it to a higher level of functioning.

In *The Hero and the Goddess*, Houston reminds us that we can rekindle a spirit of adventure in ourselves by visiting the homelands of heroes past. For example, if you sail today to the small Greek island of Odysseus's birth, you can see the sign that reads: EVERY TRAVELER IS A CITIZEN OF ITHACA.

All famous travelers who undertake perilous and rewarding adventures are eager to return to familiar shores. From Beowulf to Hiawatha, Sir Gawain to Penelope, Joan of Arc to E.T., once heroes have been transformed by their ordeals they head for home. Now is the time for you to do the same.

The larger world that awaits your return is the same one you left behind. It spews out pollution and nuclear waste. Materialism suffocates its spirit. The feminine wars with the masculine, institutions fail to fulfill their purpose, and the public trust is violated. Few of us find comfort in the knowledge that the world has always held out similar problems to returning travelers.

The return home is the final challenge of maturity at midlife. Already, thanks to your diligent journey down each of the seven pathways, you have won the power to see with newfound wisdom, to listen with newfound compassion, and to act with newfound purpose and integrity. As you begin your homeward journey, realize that you reenter the world as a more powerful and more effective person than you were when you left. Your renewed self, no longer lacking courage and confidence, finally has the strength and vision to tackle all worthwhile goals that plagued you so long ago, back before you were able to do anything about them. Your journey is not complete until your new self steps back into the world with the intent of learning to answer the earth's needs, just as you have learned to answer your own.

Forgetting Yourself to Remember the World

At the turn of the century, adults sought psychological help for concrete symptoms, such as paralysis medical doctors could not explain, or obsessional thoughts that would not go away. Erich Fromm, eminent psychologist of our day, says of those seeking treatment that "they were sick in the sense the word 'sickness' is used in medicine; something prevented them from functioning socially as the so-called normal person functions. . . . Their concept of 'wellness' was—not to be sick."

Today, however, people with "presenting" symptoms such as those mentioned above are in the minority of psychologists' clientele; most people coming to a psychologist at the end of the twentieth century are not certain what they suffer from. They come in complaining of "anxiety" or "depression" or "low self-esteem," because their "marriages are in trouble," or their "productivity is falling off." Yet, as Fromm suggests in his essay "Zen Buddhism & Psychoanalysis," the most common sources of psychological suffering today stem from three levels of alienation:

Alienation from oneself
Alienation from other human beings
Alienation from nature

Most people experience some degree of separation on each level. If our alienation on any one level becomes too great, symptoms of emotional distress appear. Fromm believes that symptoms of alienation breed a profound sense of helplessness and hopelessness expressed in "the awareness that life runs out of one's hand like sand, and that one will die without having lived; that one lives in the midst of plenty and yet is joyless."

By traveling down the seven pathways described in this book, you have, I hope, begun to cure the alienation from the self that is often so pronounced in middle age. I have confidence that you have also begun or continued to make mutually satisfying connections with others. These lessons prepare you for the biggest step of all, which is the union with what Fromm calls nature. To me, nature means not only the "great outdoors," but the wider world in which we live.

As you present your new self to the world, you will probably notice a great paradox. While you really do not care much about the *judgments* of others, you care more than ever about the quality of the *lives* of others and everything around you. You are therefore likely to find yourself *forgetting yourself* more often, because you are so engaged in the world.

In his essay "Where Is the Self?" Jashu Sasaki Roshi states that "human life is basically the endlessly repetitious cycle of forgetting the self and affirming the self."

Now when you embrace your lover or when you hold your pet dog, where does the self go? To where does the belly button disappear? When I rub this table, feeling how smooth it is, how fine it is, where does my self go? There is no need to explain this, because clearly my center of gravity and the table's center of gravity have become one. My individual self is given up completely to the individual self of this table and I no longer need to affirm a separate self. When two people embrace, it is not that the self is lost. There is simply no need to assert the self. There is no need to argue the self. And this is what is meant by absolute self in Buddhism. I call this *absolute center of gravity*. . . .

I have been working with Americans for sixteen years, but somehow it seems that the reality behind such words as *absolute self* and *absolute center of gravity* is very difficult for them to grasp. You have been educated and trained to affirm the self as "I am," to see and think about life and the world from that assertion of self without even questioning its validity. Probably you have never been trained in the activity of absolute self. This is why, even though all of you are constantly manifesting absolute self, you lack the recognition of the function and the ability to revive it when it is appropriate in your life.

Put yourself in the scenario Roshi describes. What do you feel when you embrace someone you love? Whether you put your arms around a parent, child, friend, or lover, in the most intimate moment of that embrace you suspend any thoughts of yourself. You have no awareness of an "I" separate from the moment or from the person you are embracing. At that instant, you know you are all that you need to be. You know that this union is enough.

When you lose your self inside a greater self, you affirm your oneness with all of life. Daring to let go of your hard-won sense of identity is the ultimate coming home.

Merge into selflessness whenever you can. Enjoy an experience free of thought, self-consciousness, striving, or judgment. Only *after* the moment is over should you ask yourself what the merging meant, what it taught you that can now be amplified, replicated, shared, acted on.

I have designed one last Self-Renewal Practice to help you deepen the wonderful, cosmic connections you find upon coming home.

SELF-RENEWAL PRACTICE

From Oneness to Action

1. The next time you experience a oneness with another—be it a person, an animal, or a sense of the greater power that connects us all—fully enjoy the experience in the now. Fall into an embrace, stroke soft fur, bask in the sunlight, float on the surface of a body of water. Allow yourself to be selfless.

2. When the experience is over, ask yourself how your essential self resonated with the essence of the person, object, or energy with which you were merging. For example, how is your essence similar to:

   • A person you embraced (full of desire? talented? awake?)
   • Fur you stroked (protective? attractive? sensual?)
   • The sunlight you absorbed (energetic? warm? reliable?)
   • The water that carried you (flexible? strong? always moving?)

   The more similarities you notice, the closer you will be to the essence of your connection.

3. Note the *manner* in which you merged with the other. For example:

   • Person (gracefully? passionately?)
   • Fur (joyfully? playfully?)
   • Sunlight (instantaneously? languorously?)
   • Water (slowly? calmly?)

4. Now ask yourself what you admire about that with which you merged.

   • The person (his sense of humor? her truthfulness?)
   • The fur (its beauty? its texture?)
   • The sunlight (its contribution to life? its ability to bring cheer?)
   • The water (its ability to quench thirst, its ability to soothe?)

5. Finally, ask yourself what the "other" you merged with might need from you to sustain itself.

- The person (encouragement? understanding? affection?)
- The fur (cleaning? conditioning? untangling?)
- The sunlight (replenishment of the ozone? appreciation of its power?)
- The water (protection from pollution? a new well?)

Make a habit of thinking of the needs of everyone and everything with which you come into contact.

Keeping the needs of others and nature in mind is at the heart of a successful homecoming. Once you stop looking at the world from what is called a *subject-object* perspective (in which you are the subject and the world exists only as it relates to you) and begin to see it from a *subject-subject* viewpoint (wherein the world, and everything in it, is a living entity worthy of respect), you will begin to see how your own personal growth can contribute to the betterment of the world.

The diagrams on page 322 show how our deeply personal natures and our social natures evolve changing us profoundly and influencing how we relate to the world.

Diagram A shows that we start out (in infancy) as a singular self, relating to the world as though it existed strictly for our own individual purposes. We feel and believe that we should always be warm, well-fed, secure, amused, and treated as the special person we long to be.

The world and other people inevitably fail to satisfy our boundless needs. We learn very quickly that we can get *some* of our needs met if we separate ourselves from our own desires, delay the gratification of our needs, deny some potentials and capitalize on others. In some cases we split off our needs and potentials from our awareness completely. The world tames us, dictating how we ask, when we ask, and, to some degree, what we ask for.

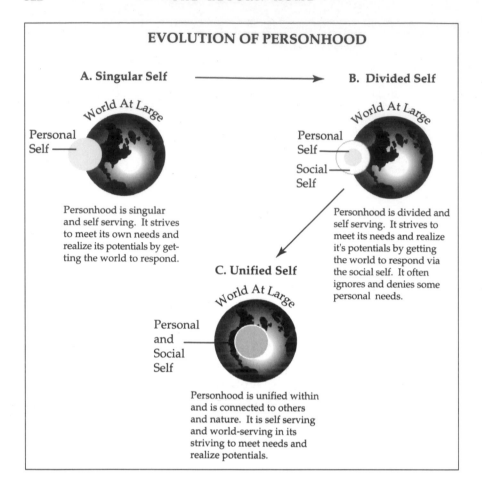

EVOLUTION OF PERSONHOOD

A. Singular Self ——————————→ B. Divided Self

Personal Self

Personhood is singular and self serving. It strives to meet its own needs and realize its potentials by getting the world to respond.

C. Unified Self

Personal Self
Social Self

Personhood is divided and self serving. It strives to meet its needs and realize it's potentials by getting the world to respond via the social self. It often ignores and denies some personal needs.

Personal and Social Self

Personhood is unified within and is connected to others and nature. It is self serving and world-serving in its striving to meet needs and realize potentials.

Through these processes of selective satisfaction, delayed gratification, denial, and repression, we give birth to our Divided Self (Diagram B). Not only do we separate our social self from our personal self, we also maintain our sense of separateness from the world at large. We still operate in what some call a *subject-object dynamic*, in which the person (subject) interacts with the world and others in it (objects) for the self-serving purposes of getting needs met and realizing potentials.

If midlife growth occurs and we continue to mature, we soon become aware of the potential of the Unified Self (Diagram C). In this phase we attempt to merge the personal and social self into one congruent, unified source of personhood. Once we operate as a largely Unified Self, we finally become capable of forming deep ties with others, nature, and the world at large. This connection is the ultimate cure for our sense of alienation that Fromm suggests creates such profound discontent.

The Power of Leadership

As we return home triumphant, those who know us best will rejoice with us. Our fellow travelers can benefit from the wisdom of our experience. The world itself will surely be better for having gained a responsible citizen who listens to its needs and responds with compassion. Yet, to make the most of your homecoming, you need to take on the mantle of leadership.

Our Ithaca is troubled, but it welcomes us home in an era of great opportunity. The same technology that has highlighted many of the problems in our world also allows us to be the first generation in history to be able to share our newfound bounties of mind, heart, and spirit with the entire planet. In what Marshall McLuhan terms our "global village," the midlife journeyer returns home to a territory much larger than that which houses family, friends, and matters of local concern. Our potential to do good is limitless.

You are not Odysseus, with a ready-made kingdom to rule, but there are nevertheless many ways in which you can make a difference. Leadership does not necessarily mean vanquishing an enemy single-handedly or coming up with brilliant new ideas, although it can be both of these things. At its heart, leadership is simply doing *what you can* to improve the world. However you choose to lead —by spearheading a legal suit to stop nuclear waste production, by teaching the Bible to youngsters, by taking a stand at a board meeting, by remaining positive when those around you are steeped in grief—be assured that by taking action based in belief, feeling, and a strong sense of self, you are enabling others to do so as well.

In my work with companies, hospitals, school systems, volunteer organizations, and the military, I have seen revolutionary improvements take place when a nucleus of mature adults comes together to make life better. Using their midlife wisdom, confidence, and commitment, several adults can transform the culture of an entire system by convincing other people to become accountable for quality, morale, and profits. Relying on their wit, courage, seasoned communication skills, and solid belief that even one person can make a difference, adults who have lost their jobs after twenty years of service can band together to reinvent their own careers and to rectify an unhealthy economy. In the midst of chaotic, impersonal institutions, one master sergeant, one clinical nurse supervisor, one school principal can become a refuge for those less secure in themselves and less convinced of the incredible opportunities that emerge in times of rapid change.

Imagine what our world would be like if every midlifer decided to travel down the seven pathways described in this book. What kind of a world would it be if all of us over forty felt good about ourselves, cared about others, and approached life with self-knowledge and integrity? How much more pleasant daily existence would be. How nice it would be for teenagers, and twenty- and thirty-year-olds, to be able to look forward to the second half of life, instead of dreading it.

What would happen if all these voyagers worked together to make the world a better place? Out of these self-suspending momentary mergers, mature compassion for all of life would be born in our whole generation. By becoming this type of leader, you could celebrate all that is good and hear more clearly what others, nature, and the world cry out for from you.

Whenever you feel the pangs of loneliness in the world, shadows of despair, or a longing for purpose, find ways to connect with whoever or whatever is suffering and begging for your help. Love it. Listen to it. Give it what it needs and you will satisfy more deeply than ever before the yearnings within.

> *All things and all men so speak, call on us*
> *with small or loud voices. They want us to listen,*
> *they want us to understand their intrinsic claims,*
> *their justice of being . . . but we can give it to them*
> *only through the love that listens. . . .*
>
> —PAUL TILLICH

Bibliography

Abra, Jock. "Changes in Creativity with Age: Data, Explanations and Further Predictions." *International Journal of Aging and Human Development* 28:105–26 (1989).

Amoss, P., and S. Harrell, eds. *Other Ways of Growing Old: Anthropological Perspectives.* Stanford: Stanford University Press, 1981.

Arrien, Angeles. *The Four-fold Way: Walking the Paths of the Warrior, Teacher, Healer, and Visionary.* San Francisco: Harper, 1993.

Atchley, R. C. "A Continuity Theory of Normal Aging." *The Gerontological Society of America* 29:183–90 (1989).

Bailey, J. "Built to Last." *Health* 21:60–88 (1989).

Bandura, Albert. "The Psychology of Chance Encounters and Life Paths." *American Psychologist* 87:747–55 (1982).

Baruch, G. K., and R. Barnett. "Role Quality, Multiple Role Involvement, and Psychological Well-Being in Midlife Women." *Journal of Personality and Social Psychology* 51:578–585 (1986).

Bateson, G. *Mind and Nature.* New York: Bantam Books, 1979.

Bateson, M. C. *Composing a Life.* New York: Atlantic Monthly Press, 1989.

Beardsley, T. "Aging Comes of Age." *Scientific American* 260:17–21 (1989).

Belloc, Nadia, and Lester Breslow as cited in Chopra, Deepak. *Ageless Body, Timeless Mind. The Quantum Alternative to Growing Old.* New York: Harmony Books, 1993.

Belsky, J. K. *Here Tomorrow.* New York: Ballantine Books, 1988.

Benson, H. B. *Relaxation Response.* New York: William Morrow, 1975.

Birchmore, S. "The Thermodynamics of Learning." *New Scientist* 199:60–61 (1988).

Birren, James, and Vern Bengston, eds. *Emergent Theories of Aging.* New York: Springer, 1988.

Black, S. M., and C. E. Hill. "The Psychological Well-Being of Women in Their Middle Years." *Psychology of Women Quarterly* 8:282–92 (1984).

Blai, B. "Emotional Maturity at Work: Tips for the HR Executive." *Personnel* 64:56–58 (1987).

Block, Marilyn, Janice Davidson, and Jean Grambs. *Women over Forty: Visions and Realities.* New York: Springer, 1982.

Bly, Robert. *Lorca and Jimenez: Selected Poems.* Boston: Beacon Press, 1973.

Bolen, J. S. *Goddesses in Everywoman.* New York: Harper & Row, 1984.

Boswell, D. A. *Gods in Everyman.* New York: Harper & Row, 1989.

———. "Metaphoric Processing in the Mature Years." *Human Development* 22:373–84 (1979).

Brandes, Stanley. *Forty: The Age and the Symbol.* Knoxville: University of Tennessee Press, 1985.

Brewi, J., and A. Brennan. *Celebrate Mid-Life.* New York: Crossroad, 1988.

Bridges, W. *Transitions.* Reading, Mass.: Addison-Wesley, 1980.

Brinkley, Donnion. *Saved by the Light: The True Story of a Man Who Died Twice and the Profound Revelations He Had.* New York: Random House, 1994.

Brown, J. K., and V. Kernes, eds. *In Her Prime: A New View of Middle-Aged Women.* South Hadley, Mass.: Bergin & Garvey, 1985.

Broyles, W. "Pushing the Mid-life Envelope." *Esquire* 107:73–91 (1987).

Bruner, Jerome. *Acts of Meaning.* Washington, D.C.: Howard University Press, 1990.

———. *Actual Minds, Possible World.* Washington, D.C.: Howard University Press, 1986.

Buechner, Frederick. *The Hungering Dark.* San Francisco: Harper, 1985.

———. *The Sacred Journey.* San Francisco: Harper, 1982.

Buela, C. G., V. E. Caballo, and C. E. Garcia. "Differences Between Morning and Evening Types in Performance." *Personality and Individual Differences* 11:447–50 (1990).

Capra, Fritjof. *The Tao of Physics: An Exploration of the Parallels Between Modern Physics and Eastern Mysticism.* Boston: Shambhala Pub., 1991.

Carlson, B. E., and L. Videka-Sherman. "An Empirical Test of Androgyny in the Middle Years: Evidence from a National Survey." *Sex Roles* 23: 305–24 (1990).

Castaneda, Carlos. *The Teachings of Don Juan: A Yaqui Way of Knowledge.* Berkeley: University of California Press, 1968.

Cavafy, I.C.P. Ithaka. *Collected Poems.* Trans. Edmund Keeley and Philip Sherrad. Princeton: Princeton University Press, 1980.

Charness, N. *Age and Expertise: Responding to Talland's Challenge.* In L. W. Poon, D. C. Rubin, and B. A. Wilson, eds., *Everyday Cognition in*

Adulthood and Late Life. Cambridge: Cambridge University Press, 1989.

Chinen, A. B. *Once Upon a Midlife*. Los Angeles: Jeremy P. Tarcher, 1992.

Chopra, D. *Ageless Body, Timeless Mind*. New York: Crown, 1993.

Ciernia, J. R. "Death Concern and Businessmen's Midlife Crisis." *Psychological Reports* 56:83–87 (1985).

Cobb, Noel. *Now Could Be the Time*. In Noel Cobb and Eva Loewe, eds., *Sphinx 4*. London: London Convivium for Archtypal Studies, 1990.

Colen, B. D. "The Generation Blur." *Health* 21:30–31 (1989).

Commons, M. L., J. D. Sinnott, F. A. Richards, and C. Armon, eds. *Adult Development*. Vol. 3, *Models and Methodologies in the Study of Adult Thought*. In press.

Conn, W. E. "Adult Conversions." *Pastoral Psychology* 34:225–36 (1986).

Cook, Roger. *The Tree of Life: Image for the Cosmos*. New York: Thames & Hudson, 1974.

Cornelius, S. W., and A. Caspi. "Self-Perceptions of Intellectual Control and Aging." *Educational Gerontology* 12:345–57 (1986).

Cosby, W. *Time Flies*. New York: Bantam Books, 1988.

Costa, P. T., and R. R. McCrae. "Personality in Adulthood: A Six-Year Longitudinal Study of Self-Reports and Spouse Ratings on the NEO Personality Inventory." *Journal of Personality and Social Psychology* 54: 853–63 (1988).

Craig G. J. *Human Development*. Engelwood Cliffs, N. J.: Prentice-Hall, 1989.

Cramer, K. D. *Staying on Top When Your World Turns Upside Down*. New York: Viking Penguin, 1990.

Csikszentmihalyi, M. *Flow*. New York: Harper & Row, 1990.

cummings, e. e. *Complete Poems: 1904–1962*. New York: Liveright Publishing Corp., 1985.

Davidson, A. Commentary. In David Cohen, ed., *The Circle of Life: Rituals from the Human Family Album*. San Francisco: Harper, 1991.

De Brabander, B., C. Boone, and P. Gerits. "Locus of Control, Fatalism, Arousal, and Activation." *Perceptual and Motor Skills* 69:701–2 (1989).

DeLuccie, M. F., R. J. Scheidt, and A. J. Davis. "The Men's Adult Life Experiences Inventory: An Instrument for Assessing Developmental Concerns of Middle Age." *Psychological Reports* 64:479–85 (1989).

Dent, C. "The Development of Metaphoric Competence: A Symposium." *Human Development* 29:223–44 (1986).

Diaz, Adriana. *Freeing the Creative Spirit, Drawing on the Power of Art to Tap the Magic and Wisdom Within*. New York: HarperCollins, 1992.

Donahue, E. M., R. W. Robins, B. W. Roberts, and O. P. John. "The Divided Self: Concurrent and Longitudinal Effects of Psychological Adjustment and Social Roles on Self Concept Differentiation." *Journal of Personality and Social Psychology* 64:834–46 (1993).

Doubiago, Sharon. *The Book of Seeing with One's Own Eyes*. St. Paul: Graywolf Press, 1988.

Dunne, M. P., F. Roche, and L. R. Hartley. "Effects of Time of Day on Immediate Recall and Sustained Retrieval from Semantic Memory." *Journal of General Psychology* 117:403–10 (1990).

Dychtwald, K. *Age Wave*. New York: Bantam Books, 1990.

Dychtwald, K., and J. Flower. "Meeting the Challenges of an Aging Nation." *Utne Reader* 37:82–86 (1990).

Eadie, B. J., and C. Taylor. *Embraced by the Light*. Placerville, CA.: Gold Leaf Press, 1992.

Edelman, G. M. *Neural Darwinism: The Theory of Neuronal Group Selection*. New York: Basic Books, 1987.

Eliade, Mircea. *Yoga, Immortality and Freedom*. New York: Viking Penguin, 1989.

Eliot, Robert S. *A Change of Heart: Converting Your Stresses to Strengths*. New York: Bantam, 1994.

Employee Burnout: America's Newest Epidemic. Northwestern National Life Insurance Company, Minneapolis, 1990.

Erikson, Erik H. *Identity and the Life Cycle*. New York: Norton, 1980.

Erikson, E., J. M. Erikson, and H. Q. Kivnick. *Vital Involvement in Old Age*. New York: Norton, 1986.

Evans, W., and I. H. Rosenberg. *Biomarkers*. New York: Simon & Schuster, 1991.

F.A.C.T.: First Aid for Children Today. Washington, D.C.: American Red Cross, 1992. Reprinted with permission by The American Red Cross.

Falletta, N. *The Paradoxicon: A Collection of Contradictory Challenges, Problematical Puzzles, and Impossible Illustrations*. New York: John Wiley, 1990.

Farrell, C. "The Age Wave—and How to Ride It." *Business Week* 3128: 112–16 (1989).

Fiebert, M. S., and K. S. Wright. "Midlife Friendships in an American Faculty Sample." *Psychological Reports* 64:1127–30 (1989).

Fields, R., P. Taylor, R. Weyler, and R. Ingrasci. *Chop Wood, Carry Water*. Los Angeles: Jeremy P. Tarcher, 1984.

Fischer, K. W., P. R. Shaver, and P. Carnochan. "How Emotions Develop and How They Organize Development." *Cognition and Emotion* 4:81–127 (1990).

Fisher, Roger, and William Ury. *Getting to Yes: Negotiating Agreement Without Giving In*. New York: Penguin Group, 1981.

Ford, M. *Life Journey*. Grand Rapids: Triumph Publications, 1987.

Fowler, J. W. *Stages of Faith: The Psychology of Human Development and the Quest for Meaning*. San Francisco: Harper & Row, 1981.

Fox, Matthew. *The Coming of the Cosmic Christ*. San Francisco: Harper & Row, 1988.

————. *Meditations with Meister Eckhart*. Sante Fe: Bear, 1983.

Frank, J. "One Woman's View from 40." *Utne Reader* 37:84–85 (1990).

Frankl, Viktor E. *The Unheard Cry for Meaning: Psychotherapy and Humanism*. New York: Touchstone, 1978.

Fritz, Robert. *Creating*. New York: Fawcett, 1991.

Fromm, Erich, D. T. Suzuki, and Richard De Martino. *Zen Buddhism and Psychoanalysis*. New York: Harper and Row, 1960.

Gerzon, M. "Starting Over at Midlife: Why There's More Satisfaction to Life After 40." *Utne Reader* 37:70–77 (1990).

Gilligan, C. *In a Different Voice*. Cambridge: Harvard University Press, 1982.

Glasser, William, M. D. *Stations of the Mind: New Directions for Reality Therapy*. New York: Harper & Row, 1981.

Goldberg, N. *Writing Down the Bones*. Boston: Shambhala Publications, 1986.

Goldstein, R., and D. Landau. *Fortysomething*. Los Angeles: Jeremy P. Tarcher, 1990.

Goleman, Daniel, Paul Kaufman, and Michael Ray. *The Creative Spirit*. New York: Dutton, 1992.

Gould, R. L. *Transformations*. New York: Simon & Schuster, 1978.

Gove, W. R., S. T. Ortega, and C. B. Style. "The Maturational and Role Perspectives on Aging and Self through the Adult Years: An Empirical Evaluation." *AJS* 94:1117–45 (1989).

Greene, R. "Growing Up Is Hard to Do." *Esquire*. 108:31–32 (1987).

Groeschel, Benedict J. *Spiritual Passages: The Psychology of Spiritual Development*. New York: Crossroad, 1984.

Grote, N. K. "Love Relationships at Midlife." *Smith Alumnae Quarterly* 82:21–25 (1991).

Gutmann, David. *Reclaimed Powers: Toward a New Psychology of Men and Women in Later Life*. New York: Basic Books, 1987.

Halligan, F. R., and J. J. Shea. "Sacred Images in Dreamwork: The Journey into Self as Journey into God." *Pastoral Psychology* 40:29–38 (1991).

Hamachek, D. "Evaluating Self-Concept and Ego Status in Erikson's Last Three Psychosocial Stages." *Journal of Counseling and Development* 68:677–83 (1990).

Harris, J. *The Prime of Ms. America: The American Woman at Forty*. New York: Putnam, 1975.

Heath, Douglas H. and Harriet E. Heath. *Fulfilling Lives: Paths to Maturity and Success.* San Francisco: Jossey-Bass, 1991.

Helson, R., T. Elliott, and J. Leigh. "Number and Quality of Roles: A Longitudinal Personality View." *Psychology of Women Quarterly* 14:83–101 (1990).

Helson, R., and P. Wink. "Two Conceptions of Maturity Examined in the Findings of a Longitudinal Study." *Journal of Personality and Social Psychology* 53:531–41 (1987).

Hesse, H. *Siddhartha.* Trans. Hilda Rosner. New York: Bantam, 1951.

Hollister Inc. *Hollister Presents . . . Why Didn't I Think of That?* New York: Dover, 1970.

Homer. *The Odyssey.* Trans. Robert Fitzgerald. Garden City, N.Y.: Doubleday, 1963.

Horn, J. "Peaking After 65: Here's How." *Psychology Today* 23:33–34 (1989).

Houston, J. *The Hero and the Goddess.* New York: Ballantine Books, 1992.

———. *The Possible Human.* Los Angeles: Jeremy P. Tarcher, 1982.

Hunter, Ski, and Martin Sundel, eds. *Midlife Myths: Issues, Findings and Practice Implications.* Newbury Park, Calif.: Sage Publications, 1989.

Hyman, R. B. "Four Stages of Adulthood: An Exploratory Study of Growth Patterns of Inner Direction and Time-Competence in Women." *Journal of Research in Personality* 22:117–27 (1988).

Jackowski, Karol A. *Ten Fun Things to Do Before You Die.* Notre Dame: Ave Maria Press, 1989.

Johnson, Robert A. *Inner Work.* San Francisco: Harper & Row, 1986.

———. *Transformation: Understanding the Three Levels of Masculine Consciousness.* San Francisco: Harper & Row, 1991.

———. *We.* San Francisco: Harper & Row, 1983.

Jonas, D. *Young Till We Die.* New York: Coward, McCann & Geoghegan, 1973.

Jones, L. Y. *Great Expectations.* New York: Coward, McCann & Geoghegan, 1980.

Julian, T. W., P. C. McKenry, and K. Arnold. "Psychosocial Predictors of Stress Associated with the Male Midlife Transition." *Sex Roles* 22:707–22 (1990).

Jung, C. G. *Memories, Dreams, Reflections.* New York: Vintage Books, 1965.

———. *The Portable Jung.* Ed. J. Campbell. New York: Viking, 1971.

———. *The Undiscovered Self.* Canada: Mentor, 1958.

———. Stages of Life. In *Collected Works.* Vol. 8. Princeton: Princeton University Press, 1960.

Kahana, R. J. "Discussion: Frontiers of Adult Development in Theory and Practice." *Journal of Geriatric Psychology* 21:29–35 (1988).

Kandinsky, Wassily. *Reminiscences. Modern Artists on Art*, ed. Robert L. Herbert. New Jersey: Prentice-Hall, 1964.

Keen, S. *The Passionate Life*. San Francisco: Harper & Row, 1983.

———. *To a Dancing God*. New York: Harper & Row, 1970.

Keen, S., and A. Valley-Fox. *Your Mythic Journey*. Los Angeles: Jeremy P. Tarcher, 1989.

Kohlberg, Lawrence. *The Philosophy of Moral Development: Essays in Moral Development*. San Francisco: Harper, 1981.

Krosnick, J. A., and D. F. Alwin. "Aging and Susceptibility to Attitude Change." *Journal of Personality and Social Psychology* 57:416–25 (1989).

Labouvie-Vief, G., J. Hakim-Larson, M. DeVoe, and S. Schoeberlein. "Emotions and Self-Regulation: A Life Span View." *Human Development* 32:279–99 (1989).

Langer, E. J. *Mindfulness*. Reading, Mass.: Addison-Wesley, 1989.

Lash, J. *The Seekers Handbook*. New York: Harmony Books, 1990.

Leerhsen, C., and E. A. Leonard. "Silver-Haired Athletes Reaching for the Gold." *Newsweek* 115:62–63 (1990).

Levenson, M. R., C. M. Aldwin, R. Bossé, and A. Spiro. "Emotionality and Mental Health: Longitudinal Findings from the Normative Aging Study." *Journal of Abnormal Psychology* 97:94–96 (1988).

Levinson, D. J. "A Conception of Adult Development." *American Psychologist* 41:3–12 (1986).

Levinson, D. J., C. N. Darrow, E. B. Klein, M. H. Levinson, and B. McKee. *The Seasons of a Man's Life*. New York: Ballantine Books, 1978.

Levinthal, C. F. *Messengers of Paradise*. New York: Doubleday, 1988.

Lévi-Strauss, Claude. *Myth and Meaning*. New York: Schocken Books, 1979.

Lieblich, A. "Successful Career Women at Midlife: Crises and Transitions." *International Journal of Aging and Human Development* 23:301–12 (1986).

Luce, G. G. *Your Second Life*. New York: Delacorte Press, 1979.

Lynch, James J. *The Language of the Heart: The Body's Response to Human Dialogue*. New York: Basic Books, 1985.

Marburg, G. S. Loving: "A Developmental Challenge of Middle Age." *Journal of Religion and Health* 25:122–36 (1986).

Mark, V., and J. P. Mark. "Why We Forget." *Modern Maturity* 33:70–75 (1990).

Marquardt, K. "*What* Mid-Life Crisis?" *Health* 19:16 (1987).

Maslow, Abraham. *The Farther Reaches of Human Nature*. Magnolia, MA: Peter Smith, 1983.

———. *Toward a Psychology of Being*. New York: Van Nostrand Reinhold, 1968.

Mather, K., and S. K. Bhattacharya. "Time of Day Dependent Performance Efficiency in Student Nurses." *Journal of Human Ergology* 20:67–75 (1991).

May, R. *The Cry for Myth*. New York: W. W. Norton, 1991.

McAdams, D. P. *The Stories We Live By*. New York: William Morrow, 1993.

McAdams, D. P., K. Ruetzel, and J. M. Foley. "Complexity and Generativity at Mid-Life: Relations Among Social Motives, Ego Development, and Adults' Plans for the Future." *Journal of Personality and Social Psychology* 50:800–7 (1986).

McGill, M. E. *The 40 to 60 Year Old Male*. New York: Simon & Schuster, 1980.

McLeish, J. *The Ulyssean Adult: Creativity in the Middle and Later Years*. New York: McGraw-Hill Ryerson, 1976.

McLuhan, Marshall. *The Global Village: Transformations in World Life and Media in the 21st Century*. North Hollywood: Outcomes Unlimited Press, 1992.

McNichol, A., and J. A. Nelson. *Handwriting Analysis: Putting It to Work for You*. Chicago: Contemporary Books, 1994.

Mehdevi, A. S. *Persian Folk and Fairy Tales*. New York: Knopf, 1965.

Merowitz, M. "Development in Midlife: Some Preliminary Notes." *Journal of Geriatric Psychology* 21:3–5 (1988).

Miller, A. *Breaking Down the Wall of Silence*. New York: Dutton, 1991.

Miller, William A. *Your Golden Shadow: Discovering and Fulfilling Your Undeveloped Self*. San Francisco: Harper & Row, 1989.

Montville, L. "One for the Middle Ages," *Sports Illustrated* 72:98 (1990).

Morris, D. C. "Church Attendance, Religious Activities, and the Life Satisfaction of Older Adults in Middletown, U.S.A." *Journal of Religious Gerontology* 8:83–96 (1991).

Moyers, B. *Healing and the Mind*. New York: Doubleday, 1993.

Myers, J. E. "The Mid/Late Life Generation Gap: Adult Children with Aging Parents." *Journal of Counseling and Development* 66:331–35 (1988).

Nahemow, Lucille, Kathleen McCluskey-Fawcett, and Paul McGhee, eds. *Humor and Aging*. New York: Academic Press, 1986.

Neff, D. "Have I Done Well?" *Christianity Today* 33:22–25 (1989).

Nemiroff, R. A., and C. A. Colarusso. "Frontiers of Adult Development in Theory and Practice." *Journal of Geriatric Psychology* 21:7–27 (1988).

Netz, Y., G. Tenenbaum, and M. Sagiv. "Pattern of Psychological Fitness as Related to Pattern of Physical Fitness Among Older Adults." *Perceptual and Motor Skills* 67:647–55 (1988).

Neugarten, B. L., and D. A. Neugarten. "The Changing Meanings of Age." *Psychology Today* 21:29–33 (1987).

Nhat Hanh, T. *Being Peace.* Berkeley: Parallax Press, 1987.

Norman, William, and Thomas Scaramella. *Mid-Life: Developmental and Clinical Issues.* New York: Brunner/Mazel, 1980.

O'Connor, D. J., and D. M. Wolfe. "On Managing Midlife Transitions in Career and Family." *Human Relations* 40:799–816 (1987).

Oldham, John, and Robert Liebert, eds. *The Middle Years: New Psychoanalytic Perspectives.* New Haven: Yale University Press. (1989).

Olivastro, D. *Ancient Puzzles.* New York: Bantam Books, 1993.

O'Neil, J. R. *The Paradox of Success: When Winning at Work Means Losing at Life: A Book of Renewal for Leaders.* New York: Putnam, 1994.

Pagels, E. *Adam, Eve, and the Serpent.* New York: Random House, 1988.

Panksepp, J. "The Nuerochemistry of Behavior." *Annual Review of Psychology* 37:77–107 (1986).

Peck, M. S. *People of the Lie.* New York: Simon & Schuster, 1983.

―――. *A World Waiting to Be Born.* New York: Bantam Books, 1993.

Perera, S. B. *Descent to the Goddess: A Way of Initiation for Women.* Toronto: Inner City Books, 1981.

Pratt, M. W., M. Prancer, and B. Hunsberger. "Reasoning About the Self and Relationships in Maturity: An Integrative Complexity Analysis of Individual Differences." *Journal of Personality and Social Psychology* 59:575–81 (1990).

Progoff, Ira. *The Symbolic and the Real.* New York: McGraw-Hill, 1963.

Raup, J. L., and J. E. Myers. "The Empty Nest Syndrome: Myth or Reality?" *Journal of Counseling and Development* 68:180–83 (1989).

Rebok, G. W., L. R. Offermann, P. W. Wirtz, and C. J. Montaglione. "Work and Intellectual Aging: The Psychological Concomitants of Social-Organizational Conditions." *Educational Gerontology* 12:359–74 (1986).

Reisman, J. M. "An Indirect Measure of the Value of Friendship for Aging Men." *Journal of Gerontology* 43:109–10 (1988).

Richardson, V., and R. Sands. "Death Attitudes Among Mid-Life Women." *Omega* 17:327–41 (1987).

Rimland, Bernard. The Altruism Paradox. *Psychological Reports* 51:521–22 (1982).

Rogers, Carl. *Carl Rogers on Personal Power.* New York: Delacorte Press, 1977.

Rosenberg, Stanley D., and Michael P. Farrell. "Identity and Crisis in

Middle-Aged Men." *International Journal of Aging and Human Development* 7:153–70 (1976).

Rosenfeld, A., and E. Stark. "The Prime of Our Lives." *Psychology Today* 21:63–72 (1987).

Rowe, J. W., and R. L. Kahn. "Human Aging: Usual and Successful." *Science* 237:143–49 (1987).

Rozak, M. "The Mid-Life Fitness Peak." *Psychology Today* 23:32–33 (1989).

Ryff, C. D. "In the Eye of the Beholder: Views of Psychological Well-Being Among Middle-Aged and Older Adults." *Psychology and Aging* 4:195–210 (1989).

Salney, A. F. *The Mensa Genius Quiz-A-Day Book*. Reading, Mass.: Addison-Wesley, 1989.

Sanford, J. A. *Invisible Partners*. Mahwah, N.J.: Paulist Press, 1980.

Sargent, A. G., and N. K. Schlossberg. "Managing Adult Transitions." *Training and Development Journal* 42:58–61 (1988).

Sasaki, Roshi J. Where Is the Self? In John Welwood, ed., *Awakening the Heart: East/West Approaches to Psychotherapy and the Healing Relationship*. Boulder: Shambhala Publications, 1983.

Satir, Virginia. *New Peoplemaking*. Palo Alto: Science and Behavior, 1988.

Schlossberg, N. K. "A Model for Analyzing Human Adaptation to Transition." *The Counseling Psychologist* 9:2–18 (1981).

———. "Taking the Mystery Out of Change." *Psychology Today* 21:74–75 (1987).

Seligmann, J. "For Longer Life, Take a Wife." *Newsweek* 116:73 (1990).

Selye, H. *The Stress of Life*. Rev. ed. New York: McGraw-Hill, 1976.

Shames, L. "Has the Thirty- and Fortysomething Generation Passed Its Peak?" *Utne Reader* 37:78–82 (1990).

Shane, M., and E. Shane. "The Struggle for Otherhood: Implications for Development in Adulthood of the Capacity to Be a Good-Enough Object for Another." In R. A. Nemiroff and C. A. Colarusso, eds., *New Dimensions in Adult Development*. New York: Basic Books, 1990.

Sheehy, G. *Passages*. New York: Dutton, 1974.

———. *Pathfinders*. New York: Bantam Books, 1982.

Sinnott, Jan D. *Sex Roles and Aging: Theory and Research from a Systems Perspective*. Basel: Karger, 1986.

Smelser, Neil J., and Erik H. Erikson, eds. *Themes of Work and Love in Adulthood*. Cambridge: Harvard University Press, 1980.

Sobel, D. "Sex Grows Up." *Health* 21:76 (1989).

Sommers, Shula. "Emotionality Reconsidered: The Role of Cognition in Emotional Responsiveness." *Journal of Personality and Social Psychology* 41:553–61 (1981).

Stafford, T. "The Graying of the Church." *Christianity Today* 31:17–22 (1987).

"Stages of the Family Life Cycle." *Journal of Marriage and the Family* 49:751–60 (1987).

Staudinger, U. M., S. W. Cornelius, and P. B. Bates. "The Aging of Intelligence: Potential and Limits." *Annals of the American Academy* 503: 43–59 (1989).

Stein, M. *In MidLife*. Dallas: Spring Publications, 1983.

Steinberg, L., and S. B. Silverberg. "Influences on Marital Satisfaction During the Middle Stages of the Family Life Cycle." *Journal of Marriage and the Family* 49:751–60 (1987).

Steinem, Gloria. *Revolution from Within*. Boston: Little, Brown, 1992.

Stevens-Long, J. "Adult Development: Theories Past and Future." In R. A. Nemiroff and C. A. Colarusso, eds., *New Dimensions in Adult Development*. New York: Basic Books, 1990.

Stockton, W. "The Trick of Growing Older." *New York Times Magazine* 139:55–76 (1990).

Super, D. E. "A Life-Span, Life-Space, Approach to Career Development." *Journal of Vocational Behavior* 16:282–98 (1980).

Thayer, R. E. *The Biopsychology of Mood and Arousal*. North Hollywood: Outcomes Unlimited Press, 1990.

Topper, M. D., and G. M. Schoepfle. "Becoming a Medicine Man: A Means to Successful Midlife Transition Among Traditional Navajo Men." In R. A. Nemiroff and C. A. Colarusso, eds., *New Dimensions in Adult Development*. New York: Basic Books, 1990.

Viorst, J. *Necessary Losses*. New York: Ballantine Books, 1986.

Waley, Arthur. *Three Ways of Thought in Ancient China*. Stanford: Stanford University Press, 1939.

Wallace, R. Keith, et al. "Systolic Blood Pressure and Long Term Practice of the Transcendental Meditation and TM-Sidhi Programs: Effects of TM on Systolic Blood Pressure." *Psychosomatic Medicine* 45:41–46 (1983).

Walton, S. "A Ride on the Age Wave." *Health* 21:40–88 (1989).

Welwood, John. *Awakening the Heart: East/West Approaches to Psychotherapy and the Healing Relationship*. Boulder: Shambhala Publications, 1983.

Witkin-Lanoil, G. "Beat the Clock." *Health* 19:8 (1987).

Wolfe, D., D. O'Connor, and M. Crary. "Transformations of Life Structure and Personal Paradigm During the Midlife Transition." *Human Relations* 43:957–73 (1990).

Woodman, M. *The Pregnant Virgin*. Toronto: Inner City Books, 1985.

Permissions

Index

J